Victorian Fantasy

Victorian Fantasy

Second Revised and Expanded Edition

Stephen Prickett

Baylor University Press
Waco, Texas USA

Book Design: Diane Smith
Cover Design: Cynthia Dunne
Cover Art: Arthur Hughes (1832–1915), "The Eve of Saint Agnes," 1856. Used by permission from the Tate Gallery, London / Art Resource, NY
Interior art: All interior artwork is public domain except Figure 1.3: William Blake (1757–1827). Beatrice Addressing Dante from the Car, 1824–1827. Illustration to *Purgatory*, Cantos 29–30 of Dante's *Divine Comedy*. Watercolor, 37.2 x 52.7 cm. Used by permission from the Tate Gallery, London/Art Resource, NY.

First published in 1979 by
THE HARVESTER PRESS LIMITED
Publisher: John Spiers
2 Stanford Terrace, Hassocks, Sussex

Library of Congress Cataloging-in-Publication Data

Prickett, Stephen.
  Victorian fantasy / Stephen Prickett.– 2nd rev. and expanded ed.
      p. cm.
  Includes bibliographical references and index.
  ISBN 1-932792-30-9 (pbk. : acid-free paper)
  1. English literature–19th century–History and criticism. 2. Fantasy literature, English–History and criticism. 3. Fantasy in literature. I. Title.

  PR468.F35P7 2005
  820.9'15–dc22
                        2005015940

For Patsy with love

Contents

List of Illustrations

Preface

Twenty five years have passed since this book first appeared with Harvester Press in the U.K. and Indiana University Press in the U.S.A. During that period there has been a huge revival in fantasy writing, and enormous commercial and screen successes for some of its finest twentieth-century practitioners—most notably J. K. Rowling, with the Harry Potter series; Philip Pullman with *Northern Lights* and its successors; and, of course, posthumous mass popularity for C. S. Lewis and J. R. R. Tolkien. Perhaps partly as a result of that contemporary upsurge of the genre, and the critical interest it has generated, by comparison studies of these writers' Victorian ancestors have been relatively modest.

Of these, the greatest number have probably been spin-offs from the popular "fantasy" conferences, pioneered by Howard Pierce and Robert Collins in the U.S.A.; by Kath Filmer-Davies in Australia; and by Adelheid Kegler and the German "Inklings" Society, all of which have produced substantial collections of essays on aspects of fantasy of all periods.[1] Good work has also appeared in *Seven*, a journal specifically devoted to the study of George MacDonald and six other Christian fantasy writers.[2]

In addition, there has, of course, been a steady trickle of books giving a broad introduction to the period. As befits a biographer and editor of

---

[1] See, for instance, Robert A. Collins and Howard D. Pierce, eds. *The Scope of the Fantastic—Theory, Technique, Major Authors* (Westport, Conn.: Greenwood Press, 1985) or Kath Filmer, ed. *The Victorian Fantasists: Essays on Culture, Society, and Belief in the Mythopoeic Fiction of the Victorians* (New York: St. Martin's Press, 1991).

[2] *Seven: An Anglo-American Literary Review*, published by the Marion E. Wade Center of Wheaton College, Illinois. The other six are Barfield, Chesterton, Lewis, Sayers, Tolkien, and Williams.

Tolkien (1977; 1981), the *Oxford Companion to Children's Literature* (1984), and a book on the Inklings (1978), Humphrey Carpenter's *Secret Gardens: A Study of the Golden Age of Children's Literature* (1985) is more concerned with background to the twentieth-century efflorescence of fantasy and the nature of Victorian children's literature than with radically new ideas on the subject. Others, such as Susan Ang's *The Widening World of Children's Literature* (2000), and U. C. Knoepflmacher's *Ventures into Childhood* (1998) are unashamedly the products of substantial periods of academic research on childhood, politics, and society in the period.

Others still, such as Roderick McGillis's *The Nimble Reader: Literary Theory and Children's Literature*, follow the lead of Eric Rabkin's 1976 classic, *The Fantastic in Literature*, and have been more specifically concerned with theory and fantasy as a genre. Robert Dingley, Anne Cranny Francis, Ken Goodwin, Alice Mills, and John Strugnell also have made significant contributions to the history of the genre—a need highlighted by weaker attempts, such as Karen Michalson's historicizing of the genre in *Victorian Fantasy Literature: Literary Battles with Church and Empire* (1990). Very different has been a tradition exemplified by Rosemary Jackson's *Fantasy: the Literature of Subversion* (1981) and Alison Lurie's *Don't Tell the Grown-Ups: Subversive Children's Literature* (1990), which portrays fantasy literature as part of the counterculture of childhood, resisting rather than accepting the normal socialization processes of conventional books written for children.

George MacDonald, I have been glad to notice, has come under increasing discussion since the early 1980s. David Robb's biography of 1987, was matched by no less than two from Rolland Hein, *The Harmony Within: the Spiritual Vision of George MacDonald* (1982) and *George MacDonald: Victorian Mythmaker* (1993), both of which attempted, not always convincingly, to see in MacDonald a reflection of the author's own evangelical leanings. More balanced, perhaps, was Roderick McGillis's ably edited collection of essays *For the Childlike: George MacDonald's Fantasies for Children* (1992). Undoubtedly the greatest loss to scholarship in the field was the untimely death of William Raeper, a young scholar of great promise, who was killed in an airplane crash in Nepal in the early 1990s after pushing a handicapped friend round the Himalayas in a wheelchair. His 1987 biography of MacDonald was followed in 1990 by *The Gold Thread*, a collection of essays including work by Robb, McGillis, Manlove, and myself.

Radically different in approach is a tradition going back to Robert Lee Wolff's *The Golden Key* (1961), a ruthlessly Freudian interpretation of George MacDonald which appeared to be inspired chiefly by intense personal dislike of him and all his works. Much of this dislike was apparently shared by Colin Manlove in his *Modern Fantasy* (1975) from which, indeed, it is hard to resist the conclusion that he disliked the whole genre. In both cases, however, this initial hostility was followed by recantation. Wolff's *Gains and Losses: Novels of Faith and Doubt in Victorian England* (1977) together with various journal articles, makes it clear that in the sixteen-year interval between the two books he had come to see MacDonald as a towering figure of nineteenth-century mythopoeic literature. Manlove's trajectory has been later, but much the same. By the time of *The Impulse of Fantasy Literature* (1983) and his 1990 essay on MacDonald and Kingsley for Raeper, we find a much more positive attitude to MacDonald, a view amplified and on a larger canvas by *Christian Fantasy: from 1200 to the Present* (1992).

More radical still, though much more appreciative, is John Docherty, the deceptively prosaic title of whose book, *The Literary Products of the Lewis Carroll–George MacDonald Friendship* (1997) concealed a boldly original thesis of literary cooperation between the two writers far beyond that envisaged by any other critic. Following a trend noticeable in both Wolff and Manlove, Docherty makes little pretence of treating either Carroll's or MacDonald's works as specifically "children's literature" at all. For him both are serious creators in their own right, whose works must simply be judged as "literature" without any condescending suggestions of the age or limitations of the readership. Some of his conclusions, especially the degree to which the two writers' books may be read as a dialogue between friends, may not carry his more skeptical readers with him, but the degree of close reading that goes into his interpretations represents a welcome trend.

My own interpretations of these, and the other works covered by the first edition of this book were, similarly, always intended to be "audience blind"—except in so far as technical questions of illustration, printing, and sales intruded. It has always seemed to me that the romantic concept of "literature," as writing of a certain intrinsic aesthetic value, does not and should not require such qualifiers as "children's" or "adult"—the latter a word that nowadays more often suggests pornography than maturity. Most of my own researches in the field over the past quarter-century have been not so much in the subsequent development and astonishing efflorescence

of the genre, as in its origins, and, in particular, in its origins in German
Romantic literature, criticism, and theology. While I now understand much
more clearly something of the impact of Goethe, Hoffmann, Novalis, the
Schlegels, Schleiermacher, and Tieck over the whole development of nineteenth-century English fantasy, I am also clearer about the pivotal role of the
central conduits of that influence: the two Scottish Germanophiles, Carlyle
and MacDonald—the former as translator, the latter as the most prolific
adaptor.

To this second edition I therefore have made some changes to the section of chapter five dealing with MacDonald, and added an entirely new
chapter six to deal specifically with *Phantastes* and *Lilith*, MacDonald's
two great "adult" fantasies, and the way in which he has adapted German
Romantic writers and the idea of the *Bildungsroman* to create what is, in
effect, a whole new genre. Given the way in which it was to be taken up by
such figures as Lewis and Tolkien in the twentieth century, it was to prove
not so much a dead end—as it must have appeared to many a hundred
years ago at the time of his death—as the main stream of its subsequent
development.

The first edition of this book owed much to John Spiers, then of
Harvester Press, who originally commissioned it. I am also grateful to
Norman Vance for allowing me to read his (then) unpublished doctoral
thesis on Kingsley, and for the help he has given me over some points of
nineteenth-century theology; also Sheila Haines and Dorothy Harrison for
permission to read their M.A. theses, and for information about Mrs.
Trimmer and Kipling respectively. From Norman Mackenzie I learned
much about Hubert Bland. I also owe thanks to Stephen Medcalf and
Morwenna and Nicholas Bielby for reading the manuscript and making
many helpful comments and suggestions. Adrian Peasgood and the staff of
Sussex University Library excelled themselves in their helpfulness in finding material and tracing obscure sources, and the staff of Brighton Public
Library were also of great assistance. The illustrations owed an enormous
debt to the patience and skill of Ronald Bielby, who performed miracles
with sepia lines and foxed pages to produce prints sometimes clearer than
the originals. It would be impossible to mention the multitude of friends,
colleagues, and correspondents who have helped to shape the development
of my ideas in this field since the publication of the first edition—especially
since such influences are, by their nature, often subliminal. It is a pleasure,
however, to thank a number of former students whose ideas and discoveries, because presented more formally, have influenced my own thinking at
a more conscious level—most notably Maria Zentai, of Szeged University,

Hungary, with whom I worked at Sussex University; Jeanette Sky, now of the University of Trondheim, whom I worked with at Glasgow, whose book now appears in the bibliography; and Benjamin Morris, of Duke University, North Carolina. I must also thank Carey C. Newman, of Baylor University Press, without whom this edition would never have happened; Brenda Welch, who has been invaluable in correcting and checking the bibliography and footnotes; and my research assistant, Dana White, who has done similar feats with the illustrations. For all errors, inaccuracies, and, doubtless, patches of ignorance that remain, I have no one to thank but myself.

When the first edition of this book appeared, critics were quick to note (with differing degrees of friendliness) that my main interests were always historical rather than theoretical. Though no work of criticism, especially on such a topic as this, is devoid of theoretical underpinning, this is indeed correct. By and large, the reader will look in vain for up-to-the-minute discussions of current theories of imperialism, colonialism, and feminism. This reflects not merely my own interests, then and now, but also a great wariness of critical and theoretical fashions. Dean Inge once commented that "He who marries the spirit of his age is likely to find himself a widower in the next." I suspect that if I had attempted to enter into the field of contemporary literary theory in 1979, no one today would be interested in a second edition of my book.

Stephen Prickett
Armstrong Browning Library
Baylor University, September 2004

Introduction

> He could not feel that they were an island of life journeying through an abyss of death. He felt almost the opposite—that life was waiting outside the little iron eggshell in which they rode, ready at any moment to break in, and that, if it killed them, it would kill them by an excess of its vitality.[1]

Anyone who begins a discussion of Victorian fantasy with Horace Walpole and ends with Edith Nesbit and Rudyard Kipling may plausibly be accused of being overambitious. Yet, as I hope to show, such a time span is necessary if we are to see that astonishing phenomenon in any kind of perspective.

The classic ideal of nineteenth-century realism was ostensibly one of order, coherence, and limitation. George Eliot, for instance, offers us the image of a pier glass or piece of polished steel covered with minute random scratches that, when a candle is held to it, seem to arrange themselves in a fine series of concentric circles. "It is demonstrable," she wrote, "that the scratches are going everywhere impartially, and it is only your candle which produces the flattering illusion of a concentric arrangement, its light falling with an exclusive optical selection."[2] Like the candle flame of the individual's egotism, the novelist too tried to create "an exclusive selection" from the apparent chaos of events and impressions that make up human life. It is a measure of George Eliot's greatness that we have come to take such a model so much for granted that it often escapes our notice how reductionist this convention is—and how circumscribed the "reality" it portrays. This book is about a counter tradition. It attempts to describe a variety of writers who came, more or less accidentally, to adopt a quite different approach, not in opposition to the prevailing realism, but in addition to it. This tradition was not a new one. Some years after he had first published *The Ancient Mariner*, Samuel Taylor Coleridge added as a kind of preface a

1

Latin quotation from the seventeenth-century theologian, Thomas Burnet. In English it runs:

> I can easily believe that there are more invisible than visible beings in the universe. But of their families, degrees, connections, distinctions, and functions, who shall tell us? How do they act? Where are they to be found? About such matters the human mind has always circled without attaining knowledge. Yet I do not doubt that sometimes it is well for the soul to contemplate as in a picture the image of a larger and better world, lest the mind, habituated to the small concerns of daily life, limit itself too much and sink entirely into trivial thinking.

As so often, Coleridge's desire for "the image of a larger and better world" was to prove prophetic. Towards the end of the century Arthur Machen, himself a confessed Coleridgean, tried to create a fiction that would adequately convey his own "overpowering impression of 'strangeness,' of remoteness, of withdrawal from the common ways of life"[3] that accompanied the most ordinary events of lower middle-class London.

> To Darnell the true life would have seemed madness, and when, now and again, the shadows and vague images reflected from its splendour fell across his path, he was afraid, and took refuge in what he would have called the sane "reality" of common and usual incidents and interests. [. . .] He was sincerely of the opinion that he was a City clerk, living in Shepherd's Bush—having forgotten the mysteries and the far shining glories of the kingdom which was his by legitimate inheritance.[4]

What was at stake, ultimately, was a quite different view of man.

> Darnell had received what is called a sound commercial education, and would therefore have found very great difficulty in putting into articulate speech any thought that was worth thinking; but he grew certain on these mornings that the "common sense" which he had always heard exalted as man's supremest faculty was, in all probability, the smallest and least considered item in the equipment of an ant of average intelligence. And with this, as an almost necessary corollary, came a firm belief that the whole fabric of life in which he moved was sunken, past all thinking, in the grossest absurdity; that he and all his friends and acquaintances and fellow workers were interested in matters in which men were never meant to be interested, were pursuing aims which they were never meant to pursue, were, indeed, much like fair stones of an altar serving as a pigsty wall.[5]

Machen's conclusion, that "man is made a mystery for mysteries and visions" is one that would have found an echo in almost every one of the minority tradition of writers in this book. Deliberately, they tried to extend and enrich ways of perceiving "reality" by a variety of nonrealistic techniques that included nonsense, dreams, visions, and the creation of other worlds. Against the mainstream of realistic fiction there developed a much stranger undercurrent that included works by Thomas Hood, Charles Dickens, Edward Lear, Lewis Carroll, Charles Kingsley, George MacDonald, Nesbit, and Kipling. In place of limitation and exclusion, each in his or her own way was in search of a wider vision, seeking the complexity and ambiguity that reflected their own experiences, even at the expense of form.

The difference is sometimes more of emphasis than of kind. All fiction is an artefact. "Realism" is always an illusion. William Makepeace Thackeray is primarily a "realist" who only occasionally lowers his guard, in such "fireside pantomimes," as *The Rose and the Ring*. Dickens and Kipling were both supreme masters of conventional realism: but, increasingly, it was not their natural medium. As they struggle to do justice to the richness and complexity of their worlds they shade off imperceptibly into fantasy. But as their greater forerunners, Plato and Dante, knew well, fantasy is ultimately the most philosophic form of fiction, giving scope to man's deepest dreams and most potent ideas. If it is also true that many of the fantasies of the Victorian period were children's books, that is not because they were simplistic, but because children, until they are educated out of it, are interested in everything. The tales of *Rewards and Fairies* "had to be read by children," Kipling explained, "before people realized that they were meant for grownups." Moreover, as we shall see, the boundary between children's fairy story and adult sexual fantasy is a very thin one indeed. Over the last two hundred years fantasy has helped us to evolve new languages for new kinds of human experience; it has pointed the way towards new kinds of thinking and feeling. In seeking to preserve and recreate a world we were in danger of losing, it has also created far other worlds and other seas. By them we have been able to hold a mirror to the shadowy and more mysterious sides of our own, and see reflected in a glass darkly mysteries not otherwise to be seen at all.

Chapter 1

The Evolution of a Word

At the beginning of the nineteenth century the word *fantasy* changed its meaning radically in the course of a single generation. The word had been used in the English language since the Middle Ages, and its roots go back even further to the Greek word *phantasia*—which meant, literally, "a making visible." Longinus, in his highly influential treatise *On the Sublime*, tells us that *phantasia* "has in our time come to be applied specially to those cases where, moved by enthusiasm and passion, you seem to see the things of which you speak, and place them under the eyes of your hearers."[1] From its earliest usages in English the word has been associated with two other related ones, *imagination* and *fancy*—which share the same Greek root as *fantasy*. Chaucer uses both imagination and fantasy to mean "a mental image"; in particular, "an image of something that does not exist." The tone of these early uses of the word is often semi-contemptuous, implying delusion, hallucination, or simply wishful thinking. Fantasy might be horrible, it might be delightful, but it was definitely unreal, and therefore of little more than clinical interest to sane and practical citizens. Mercutio in *Romeo and Juliet* sums up his stories of Queen Mab by saying:

> I talk of dreams
> Which are the children of an idle brain,
> Begot of nothing but vain fantasy;
> Which is as thin of substance as the air,
> And more inconstant than the wind.
> (Act I, sc. iv 102–6)

In the opening scene of *Hamlet*, Marcellus is indignant with the sceptical Horatio for daring to suggest that the ghost of Hamlet's father is "but fantasy"[2] his point being that a real, genuine ghost was a much more solid and serious proposition than a mere mental aberration.

5

Except that the late eighteenth century might have been a little less inclined to believe in ghosts, a person living in, say, 1775 would, by and large, have had very similar feelings about the word. It signified a kind of imagination one might expect to find in madmen—or in children. But by 1825 something very extraordinary had happened. From being terms of derision, or descriptions of daydreaming, words like *fantasy* and *imagination* suddenly began to take on new status as hurrah words. People began to feel that the very unreality of fantasy gave its creations a kind of separate existence, an autonomy, even a "real life" of their own. They even began to feel differently about madmen and children, who now became objects of interest. The word *Romanticism* is a loose enough term to describe this shift in sensibility, yet it must be used if we are to try and see how the nineteenth-century use of words like *fantasy* differs so sharply from its predecessors.

One barometer in this change of emotional climates was Samuel Taylor Coleridge. He was in many ways an archetype of what the Victorian period imagined a "Romantic poet" to be. The author of *The Rhyme of the Ancient Mariner*, *Kubla Khan*, and *Christabel* was a creator of dreamworlds, both beautiful and sinister, an opium addict, and a ruined man. In fact, in the course of his life he was a multitude of things: poet, critic, political journalist, philosopher, metaphysician, and theologian. He was the most original thinker of his generation, and probably the most shameless plagiarist—a saint and a sponger. In his voluminous and disorganized writings, and even more in his letters and notebooks, he has left us with a succession of autobiographical sketches through which we can trace his own development—and also, more generally, the development of this shift in sensibility in the age in which he was growing up. As a boy he was a dreamer.

> My father's Sister kept an *every-thing* Shop at Crediton—and there I read thro' all the gilt cover little books that could be had at that time, & likewise all the uncovered tales of Tom Hickathrift, Jack the Giant killer, &c &c &c &c -/- and I used to lie by the wall, and *mope*—and my spirits used to come upon me suddenly, & in a flood—& then I was accustomed to run up and down the churchyard, and act over all I had been reading on the docks, the nettles, and the rankgrass.[3]

At six years old he had read *Robinson Crusoe* and turned to the *The Arabian Nights*, which so frightened him that he was, he tells us, "haunted by spectres" whenever he was alone in the dark. His father was so alarmed by the effects of this precocious reading that he confiscated all his son's books of fairy stories and burned them. With typical half-humorous self-contempt Coleridge describes his character at the age of eight as compounded of "sensibility, imagination, vanity, and sloth." The last two characteristics are common enough to boys of all ages, but in his choice of the first two words, Coleridge is using the key words of an age to describe his own development. This early reading, he argues in another letter, was vital to his own mental growth.

> For from my early reading of Faery Tales, & Genii &c &c—my mind had been habituated to the Vast—& I never regarded my *senses* in any way as the criteria of my belief. I regulated all my creeds by my conceptions not by my *sight*—even at that age. Should children be permitted to read Romances, & Relations of Giants & Magicians, & Genii?—I know all that has been said against it; but I have formed my faith in the affirmative.—I know no other way of giving the mind a love of "the Great," & "the Whole."—Those who have been led to the same truths step by step thro' the constant testimony of their senses, seem to me to want a sense which I possess—They contemplate nothing but *parts*—and all *parts* are necessarily little—and the Universe to them is but a mass of *little things*. [. . .] I have known some who have been *rationally* educated, as it is styled. They were marked by a microscopic acuteness; but when they looked at great things, all became a blank & they saw nothing—and denied (very illogically) that any thing could be seen.[4]

Coleridge was writing to a friend in 1797, and probably very few then would have agreed with him on the value of fairy stories. That there might be important areas of human knowledge and experience not available to the senses would have seemed to many an even more extraordinary idea. The following year the Edgeworths, father and daughter, in their two volume tome on *Practical Education*, commented, "We do not allude to fairy tales for we apprehend these are not now much read."[5]

Nevertheless, there was clearly a sufficient number of such stories still in circulation for Mrs. Trimmer, a stalwart of the S.P.C.K. Tract Committee and indefatigable do-gooder, to find it worth her while attacking them again only a few years later in 1803. In her review of *A Collection of Entertaining Stories* for *The Guardian of Education* she acknowledges that fairytales are old-fashioned, but still clearly suspects that they might have an insidious appeal to the unwary or unenlightened. "This collection consists of the histories of Little Jack Horner, Cinderella or the Glass Slipper, Fortunatus and other tales, which were in fashion half a century ago, full of romantic nonsense." She goes on: "We cannot approve of those (books) which are only fit to fill the heads of children with confused notions of wonderful and supernatural events, brought about by the agency of imaginary beings."[6] There were plenty of others to agree with her. With nice historical irony, E. Nesbit's grandfather, Anthony Nesbit, urged readers of the *Introduction to his English Parsing* (1817) to "Beware of reading tales and novels, for they generally exhibit pictures that never had any existence, except in the airy imaginations of the brain."[7] He recommended instead the works of Hannah Moore, the prominent Evangelical.

Yet Coleridge's delight in tales of the marvelous and supernatural was prophetic. In 1823 a selection of the Grimm brothers' fairytales, *German Popular Stories*, was published for the first time in England. The new translation was beautifully illustrated by George Cruikshank, probably the best illustrator of the day, and was an overnight success. The boy John Ruskin was entranced by it, and later described the illustrations with pardonable exaggeration as "the finest things next to Rembrandt that have been done since etching was invented." "Beauty, fun, and fancy were united in these admirable designs," wrote Thackeray in 1840. "They have been copied all over Europe." They had indeed. In Germany the *Tales* were reissued with Cruikshank's pictures, while in France, one Ambrose Tardieu copied and published them as his own work. Suddenly fairy stories had become respectable—for antiquarians, for poets, and even for children. The skill of new illustrators, such as Cruikshank, drawing on a popular tradition of caricature and cartoon, gave new images to the old stories. In 1828 we find the poet John Clare describing to his wife how he had bought *Puss in Boots*, *Cinderella*, *Little Rhymes*, and *The Old Woman and the Pig*, all with colored pictures, for their own children.[8] The Rossettis—Dante Gabriel, William, and Christina—growing up in the 1830s rejected with disgust an official diet of edifying literature, such as Maria Edgeworth's *Moral Tales*, or Day's *Sandford and Merton*, and turned instead to *The Arabian Nights*, Keightley's fairy stories, and Gothic novels.[9] When, in 1846, Hans Andersen's tales were translated in no less than five volumes, they took England by storm. The following year Andersen himself visited England, making a triumphant tour as a celebrity and finally being seen off from Ramsgate pier by Charles Dickens. 1846 was also the year of publication of Edward Lear's first *Book of Nonsense*. The worlds of children and adults which had seemed in the eighteenth century to be growing farther and farther apart had suddenly begun to come together again. The 1823 preface to Grimms' *German Popular Stories* had compared them with "Christmas Pantomimes, ostensibly brought forth to tickle the palate of the young, but often received with as keen an appetite by those of graver years." Magical and marvelous stories which had been attacked by such diverse authorities as Rousseau, Mrs. Trimmer, and Mr. Gradgrind,[10] were now being rediscovered as a source of spiritual "dynamism" in what Thomas Carlyle attacked as a "mechanical" and "prudential" age. They tapped "he primary unmodified forces and energies of man, the mysterious springs of Love, and Fear, and Wonder, or Enthusiasm, Poetry, Religion, all of which have a truly vital and indefinite character."[11] The imagination had been freed.

In the process, the word *imagination* had itself been freed from its siblings and rivals, *fantasy* and *fancy*. It was Coleridge again who, once and for all, separated imagination and fancy. For him the imagination was a "living power" that transformed the elements with which it dealt, shaping them into a new unity. Fancy, on the other hand, was "a mere dead arrangement" of "fixities and definites": a scissors and paste job of the mind.[12] *Fantasy*, as the word now came to be used, was at the opposite pole from this meaning of fancy. In contrast with the aesthetic and creative power attributed to the imagination, it came to be seen as the quality of dreams and reverie. James Russell Lowell, the American critic, spoke for his age when he attacked the misunderstanding by which people confused imagination with "mere fantasy, the image making power common to all who have the gift of dreams."[13] That was in 1870, but he is expressing a point of view common enough for at least half a century. He could have been writing any time after 1830, for even by then the words had established a kind of curious polarity, constantly being used as opposites as people tried to account for the workings of their minds in quite a new way. Imagination and fantasy had come to stand for two sides of the Victorian psyche: its sacred and profane loves. Following Coleridge, the imagination was elevated onto a pedestal: it was the supreme gift of the poet, the creative power of the artist, "a repetition in the finite mind of the eternal act of creation in the infinite I AM"[14]—in short, a reflection in man of the divine and life giving spirit of God the Creator. Fantasy, by contrast, was the gift of dreams; the haunting magic of John Keats's *La Belle Dame Sans Merci*; it was delightful, alluring, compulsive, disturbing, nightmare and hag ridden. It was akin to madness. Matthew Arnold, in the second preface to his *Poems* of 1854, attacked what he saw as "the great vice of our intellect, manifesting itself in our incredible vagaries in literature, in art, in religion, in morals; namely that it is *fantastic* and wants sanity." Clearly the *vice* was becoming interesting—for some, perhaps, too interesting.

Carlyle gives us some startling examples of what could happen. "Fantasy," he casually announces in *Sartor Resartus* (1831), is "the organ of the Godlike [. . .] Man thereby, though based to all seeming, on the small Visible, does nevertheless extend down into the infinite deeps of the Invisible, of which Invisible, indeed, his Life is properly the bodying forth."[15] It seems at first sight here as if he is simply using the word *fantasy* where Coleridge would have said *imagination*, thus compounding confusion, but his use of the word actually reveals a fundamentally different way of thinking. The key word is *symbol.* Coleridge in *The Statesman's Manual,* had defined a symbol in terms of "the translucence of the Eternal through and in the Temporal," partaking of "the Reality which it renders intelligible."[16] For him, the power of creating poetic symbols was connected with the imagination. The symbol belonged to a Platonic world, showing us in this imperfect state the eternal and changeless forms of things. Now Carlyle's description of a symbol is so similar that it sounds, once again, as if he is merely substituting fantasy for imagination:

> In a Symbol there is concealment and yet revelation. [. . .] For it is here that Fantasy with her mystic wonderland plays into the small prose domain of Sense, and becomes incorporated therewith. In the Symbol proper, what we can call a Symbol, there is ever, more or less distinctly and directly, some embodiment and revelation of the Infinite; the Infinite is made to blend itself with the Finite, to stand visible, and as it were, attainable there [. . .] even for the basest Sensualist, what is Sense but the implement of Fantasy; the vessel it drinks out of? Ever in the dullest existence there is a sheen either of Inspiration or of Madness (thou partly hast it in thy choice, which of the two), that gleams in from the circumambient Eternity, and colours with its own hues our little islet of Time. The Understanding is indeed thy window, too clear thou canst not make it; but Fantasy is thy eye, with its colour giving retina, healthy or diseased.[17]

It is the *tone* of these passages that is crucial. Coleridge believed that in the poetic symbol there was a real revelation: it embodied an *epiphany* or a "showing" of eternal truths in finite form. Carlyle was a Calvinist who had lost his faith and taken to reading German philosophy instead. As a result he is lost in subjectivism. Though there is much play with Eternity and the Infinite (always with capital letters to show respect for such weighty matters) the fact remains that the things made by this "Godlike" organ, Fantasy, are essentially arbitrary and subjective. The terms used are invariably so exaggerated and overblown as to imply ironic belittlement. Fantasy opens a "mystic wonderland" with a "sheen either of Inspiration or Madness"–take your pick, all is subjective. There is (and can be) no point of objective reference. Eternal truths are what we make of them; man is the measure of all things. Hence Carlyle's wild and whirling style, as if the epiphany must be achieved by force of rhetoric alone. Teufelsdrockh's "conversion" in *Sartor Resartus* is to the Will, not to any extra human and transcendent truth. In such a context, as Carlyle was doubtless very well aware, the word *fantasy*, so far from being used to suggest the shaping and unifying qualities of Coleridge's imagination is employed in a remarkably *traditional* sense, as the power by which the unseen is made visible. But whereas for Longinus, Chaucer, or Shakespeare, such a power was either a trick of rhetoric or a sign of madness, for Carlyle it is the vehicle by which the new subjectivist religion of the heart is to be brought about. Fantasy has been internalized as a kind of devil's parody of Kantian *Reason* and Coleridge's *imagination*. Both Coleridge and Carlyle interpreted Immanuel Kant's idea of Reason to mean that man could grasp instinctively deep spiritual truths denied to the calculations of the "Understanding," but however much Carlyle may have been attracted by such a notion,[18] it seems to have remained for him a sublime confidence trick, a brilliant projection of wishful-thinking—a piece of marvelous, even necessary, Fantasy.

Significantly, Coleridge himself is not free of this ambiguity of attitude we find in Carlyle. Indeed, to many contemporaries he seemed to sum up in his own life the very contrast suggested by the two words. If, on the one hand, he was the great theorizer of the imagination, always seeking to demonstrate how it could point towards the divine vision, on the other, he was lost in a haze of opium dreams identified forever in the Victorian mind as the author of such haunting fragments as *Kubla Khan* and *Christabel*, or the purgatorial and irrational world of *The Ancient Mariner*. If we are to understand Victorian fantasy, we must see it as the underside, or obverse, of the Victorian imagination. In the compelling image of one of the greatest of the period's mythmakers George MacDonald, it was its "shadow." Imagination and fantasy forever turn about each other in the Victorian mind, light and dark. Beneath the studied wholesomeness of the pre-Raphaelites lurked drugs and madness. Ruskin strangled his cat, believing it to be the devil. Dante Gabriel Rossetti became addicted to laudanum and died insane. Their works reflect the strange mixture of art and dream in which they lived. Similarly Lear, the self-styled "Lord High Bosh and Nonsense Producer," was also a serious and conventional landscape artist. Lewis Carroll in his *alter ego* was a clergyman, mathematician, and Oxford don. Both were lonely, inadequate, frustrated men. Richard Dadd, painter of fairies and biblical scenes, killed his father with a knife and spent most of his life in lunatic asylums. Jonathan Martin, obsessed by the same grandiose visions as his brother John, the artist, became disillusioned with his attempts to reform the Church of England along Methodist lines, and set fire to York Minster.[19] Only with such late-Victorian fantasists as Swinburne, Dowson, or Beardsley, sometimes called *decadents*, does the ambiguity that haunted so much of nineteenth-century art become open and explicit, if not resolved.

Yet it is easy to generalize over a broad enough canvas. Any age as artistically rich as the Victorian will furnish examples of aesthetic ambiguity. As we shall see, the eighteenth century contained many such figures—Horace Walpole, perhaps, or William Beckford, who lived in a society more tolerant and permissive to those who wished to act out their fantasies in real life. If the Victorians did evolve forms of fantasy that were genuinely different from those of earlier and later periods, we must look for evidence not merely at a number of specific examples in detail, but also for the development of an artistic theory that would show the significance of those examples. That, in essence, is the aim of this book. In it we shall trace how the idea of fantasy as an art form developed during the nineteenth century. Thus, if Edward Lear often seems to be unconscious of what he is doing in his nonsense writings, the same cannot be said a few years later of Lewis Carroll, whose writings, while they may have effectively concealed sexual fantasies, certainly rested upon very complex and consciously worked out mathematical structures—often much more speculatively daring than his rather conventional and unadventurous academic work. In Kingsley, the fantasy has a moral, and allegorical basis, sometimes subtle and well integrated, at other times crude and obtrusive. It is only with the works of George MacDonald, possibly the greatest fantasy-writer of that (or any other) period, that something like a fully balanced artistic theory emerges. Before him we are always aware of the ambiguity as an *unconscious* creative force—the product of an unresolved tension in the writer. With MacDonald, and those who follow him, the tension is not removed, but sublimated into a framework of rich and complicated symbolism—at once literary and theological. As we shall see, the much more "modern" literary fantasies of Kipling and Edith Nesbit depend on this critical development, and also to a surprising degree on its metaphysical foundations.

But to see what is distinctively new about nineteenth-century fantasy we must look back at the period immediately preceding it. Out of a confluence of intermingled currents and eddies of thought we can, perhaps, select a number of streams which were to feed the reservoirs of Romanticism at the turn of the century. One is the idea of the *Gothick*; another is a revival of religious mysticism and a renewed feeling for the numinous—the irrational and mysterious elements in religious experience; a third is the purely human revulsion against the squalid and degrading conditions of the early industrial revolution. In all three we can trace that curious ambivalence between imagination and fantasy that was to so haunt the Victorian consciousness, and turn it inwards towards the creation of dreamworlds. Coming to terms with this ambivalence in art, in literature, and in religion was the greatest self-critical act of the age. From it was to grow a new kind of study of consciousness: the "psychology" of therapists like Freud and Jung, whose attempts to come to terms with it was to transform the twentieth-century view of man.

1.1 Horace Walpole's Strawberry Hill. From a contemporary print.

Horace Walpole (1717–1797) is sometimes credited with having begun the Gothic revival with his extraordinary architectural fantasia at Strawberry Hill, near Twickenham, but in fact the fashion predates him. Indeed, it is doubtful if it can be argued that it had ever died out in England.[20] All the great classical architects, including Sir Christopher Wren, Sir John

Vanbrugh, Nicholas Hawksmoor, and James Gibbs had also tried their hands at Gothic designs. In 1753, at a time when Walpole had only just completed his first very modest alterations to Strawberry Hill, *The World*, a magazine dealing with taste and fashion, declared that as a style the Gothic was altogether passé; chinoiserie was now the "in" thing.

> A few years ago everything was Gothic; our houses, our beds, our book cases, and our couches were all copied from some parts or other of our old cathedrals. [. . .] This, however, odd it might seem, and however unworthy of the name of TASTE, was cultivated, was admired, and still has its professors in different parts of England. There is something, they say, in it congenial to our old Gothic constitution; I should rather think to our modern idea of liberty, which allows every one the privilege of playing the fool, and making himself ridiculous in whatever way he pleases. According to the present prevailing whim everything is Chinese, or in the Chinese taste. [. . .] Chairs, tables, chimney pieces, frames for looking glasses, and even our most vulgar utensils are all reduced to this new fangled standard: and without doors so universally has it spread, that every gate to a cow yard is in T's and Z's, and every hovel for the cows has bells hanging at its corners. The good people in the city are, I perceive, struck with this novelty; and though some of them still retain the last fashion, the Gothic, yet others have begun to ornament the doors and windows of their shops with the more modern improvements.[21]

Walpole certainly helped to revive a taste for the Gothic among the upper classes, and free it from what was held to be middle-class vulgarity, but his real significance, for our purposes, is much more far reaching than as a modish reviver and trendsetter. It was he, more than any other single person, who turned the Gothic from fashion into fantasy. In his hands, the Gothic became the *Gothick*. Walpole brought to a particular architectural style a quite new kind of emotional and aesthetic sensibility. "I almost think," he wrote to his friend Montague, "there is no wisdom comparable to that of exchanging what is called the realities of life for dreams. Old castles, old pictures, old histories, and the babble of old people make one live back into centuries, that cannot disappoint one. One holds fast and surely to what is past. The dead have exhausted their power of deceiving—one can trust Catherine of Medicis now."[22]

It is typical of him to describe his house to a friend resident in Italy by an imaginary guided tour. Strawberry Hill, though cozy and domestic, was a building designed to take people round. All was make believe: an elaborate charade, at once antiquarian and unashamedly escapist.

Now you shall walk into the house. The bow window below leads into a little parlour, hung with a stone colour Gothic paper, and Jackson's Venetian prints. . . . From hence, under two gloomy arches, you come to the hall and staircase, which it is impossible to describe to you, as it is the most particular and chief beauty of the castle. . . . Imagine the wall covered with (I call it paper, but it is really paper printed in perspective, to represent) Gothic fretwork: the lightest Gothic balustrade to the staircase, adorned with antelopes . . . bearing shields; lean windows fattened with rich saints in painted glass, and a vestibule open with three arches on the landing place, and niches full of trophies of old coats of mail, Indian shields made of rhinoceros's hide, broadswords, quivers, longbows, arrows and spears—all *supposed* to be taken by Sir Terry Robsart, in the holy wars.[23]

Further plans were in hand continually over the next forty years. "I must tell you, by the way, that the castle, when finished, will have two and thirty windows enriched with painted glass." Later, Walpole was to add the famous Long Gallery leading at the far end to a Round Tower. The grandiose and the domestic were artfully combined. The Long Gallery was, in reality, only fifty-six feet long and fifteen feet wide—no bigger than a small hotel lounge—but it was resplendent with gilt mirrors in Gothic niches and with a ceiling of massive fan vaulting, transposed and appropriately miniaturized from the Henry VII Chapel, Westminster. At the far end it led through a small lobby into the round Drawing Room in the Great Tower (each room had its proper name). Here even the sofas were curved to fit the arc of the walls. The fireplace was a copy of the tomb of Edward the Confessor, "improved by Mr. Adam, and beautifully executed in white marble inlaid with scagliuola, by Richter."[24] Even the plaster moldings on the ceiling were faithfully copied from the design of the rose window at Chartres.

In this "little rural bijou," Walpole acted out a fantasy life with his amazing collection of art treasures and historical bric-a-brac. He used to wear a pair of gloves that had belonged to James I (sold at the auction after Walpole's death for £2 10s 0d.) and sleep with Charles I's death warrant on one side of his bed, and the Magna Carta on the other. It was in this bed in June 1764 that he dreamed "that on the uppermost banister of a great staircase" he "saw a gigantic hand in armour."[25] The staircase was, of course, his own, but appropriately magnified. From it grew the mysterious giant haunting the doomed Castle of Otranto. "In the evening," he tells us, "I sat down and began to write, without knowing in the least what I intended to say or relate." It was, as he said, "a very natural dream for a head filled like mine with Gothic story" and it is wholly fitting that Strawberry Hill should have provided the inspiration for the first Gothic novel, since it is itself such an essentially literary creation.

The *Castle of Otranto* is a story of memorable images and a brooding atmosphere which, nearly (but not quite) compensates for a plot of cardboard passion and intrigue that usually seems both boring and preposterous to a modern reader. In fact, the plot did not matter: the book had two elements that were to become staples of nineteenth-century fantasy: a dream-like atmosphere and a monster. It was an instant success, and in its train came a host of imitations, mostly superior in construction, if not in probability. M. G. Lewis's *The Monk*—which earned him the name of "Monk Lewis"—hinges on a case of mistaken identity when the hero inadvertently elopes with the (veiled) ghost of a bleeding nun. . . . Beckford's *Vathek* concerns a Caliph of that name whose aspect when enraged was so terrible that he was obliged to control himself in order not to depopulate his dominions. Bestseller of all was Mrs. Radcliffe's *The Mysteries of Udolpho*, only nowadays overshadowed by Jane Austen's satire of it, *Northanger Abbey*. It is, in fact, one of the most rational of all its far-fetched genre, since it dispenses with the supernatural altogether, and is in many ways one of the best. Most lasting of all the Gothic novels, however, has been Mary Shelley's *Frankenstein*, with its terrifying and yet sympathetic monster.

What distinguishes the Gothick of Walpole or Beckford from its early eighteenth-century manifestations, or from the spirit of the true Gothic Revival of the nineteenth century, and what makes it so essentially *literary* in character, is precisely this quality of fantasy which pervaded it. The atmosphere of dream and even hallucination is ever present. As a boy, Beckford, like Coleridge, had been obsessed by stories from the *The Arabian Nights*, and his description of a party he organized at the age of twenty-one in his family house (a vast mansion called Fonthill Splendens) is in the language of his most extravagant Eastern daydreams.

> The glowing haze investing every object, the mystic look, the vastness, the intricacy of this vaulted labyrinth occasioned so bewildering an effect that it became impossible for anyone to define—at that moment—where he stood, or where he had been, or to whither he was wandering—such was the confusion—the perplexity so many stories of infinitely varied apartments gave rise to. It was, in short, the realization of romance in the most extravagant intensity.[26]

It was in the attempt to realize romance in even more extravagant intensity that led Beckford, with his architect James Wyatt, to create Fonthill Abbey on his estate in Wiltshire. It was a Gothic Cathedral of a palace with vast vaulted rooms and poky bedchambers, visually dwarfed by a slender octagonal tower two hundred and sixty feet high—as unstable in reality as it was in appearance. It was truly the stuff of dreams. For its greatest ceremonial occasion, the reception of Horatio Nelson as a national hero in December 1800, it was only partially finished, and had to be seen by night for fear of spoiling the effect. Though even the coal in the scuttles was gilded, no amount of coal of whatever color could ever have heated the great banqueting hall which was eighty feet high with a hammer beam roof. The actual dinner had to be held in a smaller chamber. In effect, the whole Abbey was a stage set. It had cost Beckford a fortune—he had been known as "England's wealthiest son"—but it was jerry built on hastily dug and inadequate foundations. Lath and plaster, timber and cement rendering were used too often in place of stone and brick. The tower's proportions were visually spectacular but architecturally unsound. In 1823 it collapsed. Within a few years most of the building had gone as well. Fonthill had been a theatrical set in which speed of construction had been part of the drama: a building not designed to live in, but to arouse the emotions of the

1.2 William Beckford's House: Fonthill Abbey

beholder. "Fonthill," says Nikolaus Pevsner, "was the first neo-Gothic building to create sentiments of amazement, of shock, even of awe. The effects of Strawberry Hill are playful, those of Fonthill sensational."[27]

The contrasts between the two architectural fantasies of Walpole and Beckford are as instructive as their similarities. Though both were creators of dreams, Beckford's were essentially backward looking towards youthful memories of a happier past.[28] He was not a medievalist and had none of the scholarly interests of Walpole. He was not interested in communicating his ideas, nor, indeed, was he apparently conscious of any wider implications of his activities. Both in the writing of *Vathek* and in the construction of Fonthill Abbey he is like a man acting under compulsions he does not fully understand. He seems to have shared with many of the early Victorian creators of literary fantasies a strange unselfconsciousness about his own desires and their forms of expression—strange, that is, for a later and more self-analytic age. By contrast, Walpole was more ironic and detached; his "playfulness" is also a quality of greater self-awareness. *Otranto* had nothing to do with his personal relationships, in the sense in which Beckford was to pour out the complications of his private life in *Vathek*.[29]

If we take them as expressing between them the psychology of an age, it is tempting to see in Walpole the restraint and irony of its consciousness, and in Beckford the more instinctive but no less complex expression of its unconscious. But such a view would miss the essential difference between the sensibilities of the late eighteenth century and the Victorians. Walpole still sees "dreaming" as an essentially *outward* process leading to a recapture of the past—in spirit if not in authentic accuracy of detail (neither he nor Wyatt understood, or were interested in understanding the engineering and constructional principles on which real Gothic architecture depended). This is, in one sense, symbolized by the shift from architecture to literature as a vehicle of fantasy with the coming of the true Romantics. Architecture effectively ceased to be a satisfactory expression of dreamworlds once the Gothic Revival proper was underway. Its character was inevitably altered once the *literary* taste for the Gothic had led to a genuine study of the past.

With the coming of Walter Scott's novels we find the first serious attempt at historical research in literature.[30] The true Gothic Revival of the 1830s was not merely painstaking and academic in its attention to detail, but it was part of a much wider movement of religious sensibility and social awareness. "It was not until the advent of Pugin," writes Brockman in his architectural approach to Beckford's work, "that the use of Gothic architecture became the passport to salvation."[31] A. W. Pugin's *Contrasts* was first published in 1836, and greatly expanded in a second edition of 1841. His portraits of contrasting towns, or of houses for the poor in the fourteenth century and his own time, are not merely assertions of new aesthetic values, but of moral judgment on a soulless and greedy society. Pugin himself, in fierce reaction against the spirit of his age, had become a Roman Catholic in 1833, and in that same year there began in Oxford the last great religious upsurge of Romanticism that was to be known to the world as the Oxford Movement. Though it eventually brought such men as F. W. Faber, John Henry Newman, Henry Manning, and the poet Gerard Manley Hopkins to the Church of Rome, it was no less effective in transforming the Church of England. It was a period when it was impossible to separate aesthetics from theology and social thought: the Gothick of the previous century was now a part of all three. William Morris's passionate delight in Gothic literature was to lead him directly to socialism. In the Victorian religious conscious-ness we find retained and enlarged the ambivalence between imagination and fantasy we noted earlier. Charles Kingsley, a public, though unwilling, exponent of "muscular Christianity" and for a time an ardent Christian Socialist, was also the author of *The Water Babies*. The religious and emo-tional tensions latent in the children's books are made much more fully explicit in the eroticism of many of his private drawings—in particular in his *Life of St. Elizabeth of Hungary* which he wrote as a wedding present for his wife.[32] Few works skate more ambiguously along the borders of imag-ination and fantasy than that great poem of Kingsley's arch-opponent, John Henry Newman's "Dream of Gerontius." George MacDonald's "adult fairy stories" *Phantastes* and *Lilith*, are at once imaginative and fantastic. Both more spiritual and more erotic than Kingsley's work, they are nevertheless charged with a vision of social justice so condemnatory of Victorian busi-ness ethics that perhaps it needed the creation of a complete "other world" in which to express itself. It was to the MacDonald children that Lewis Carroll sent the manuscript of *Alice in Wonderland*, and it was their enthusiastic approval that finally decided him on publication.

The *Castle of Otranto* has been described as *surrealist*, yet in fact that overworked word is less than appropriate if we compare that novel with Walpole's final flowering of fantasy—his children's stories, the *Hieroglyphic Tales*, written between 1766 and 1772 to amuse the little niece of a friend.[33] Here in these stories, we find the literary climax of the spirit with which Walpole had so successfully transformed the sensibility of his day. The Gothick was still, however tenuously, rooted in history, but in these tales written for a child Walpole was able to cut loose from the last restraints of fact, and create a totally imaginary and nonsensical world. One of his sto-ries, for instance, is about a Princess who forgot to be born:

There was formerly a King who had three daughters—that is, he would
have had three, if he had had one more, but somehow or other the eldest
was never born. She was extremely handsome, had a great deal of wit, and
spoke French in perfection, as all the authors of that age affirm, and yet
none of them pretend that she ever existed. It is very certain that the
other two princesses were far from beauties; the second had a strong
Yorkshire dialect, and the youngest had bad teeth and but one leg, which
occasioned her dancing very ill.[34]

They reveal to us a side of Walpole that while not quite unique in his age,[35]
seems to take us straightforward to the nonsense of the following century—
Lear, Carroll, or even the MacDonald of *The Light Princess*. Walpole's
greatest admirer, W. S. Lewis, has confessed himself slightly nonplussed by
their extravagance.[36] Certainly, even Walpole's own comments on the
Hieroglyphic Tales are difficult to place in a purely eighteenth-century context without resort to more modern comparisons. He, himself, was at pains
to stress their irrationality. The merits of such "an Hieroglyphic Tale," he
noted in one of the seven copies printed at his Strawberry Hill press, "consists in its being written *extempore* and without any plan."[37] In his introduction he comments how strange it was that "there should have been so
little fancy, so little variety, and so little novelty in writings in which the
imagination is fettered by no rules, and by no obligation of speaking
truth."[38] His own *Hieroglyphic Tales* "deserve at most to be considered as
an attempt to vary the stale and beaten class of stories and novels which,
though works of invention, are almost always devoid of imagination."[39]

Yet such disclaimers raise almost as many questions as they settle about
Walpole's intentions. Is he emphasizing their irrationality as an excuse to
forestall criticism, or as an artistic theory? Though Walpole had made use of
disingenuous covers when he first published the *Castle of Otranto*, by
employing an assumed name and claiming the authority of old documents
recently come to light, there was no need of such devices here. The
Hieroglyphic Tales were written for a known audience, and only seven
copies were printed at Strawberry Hill.[40] They only reached a wider audience
when they were reprinted in the collected edition of Walpole's works in
1798, the year after his death.[41] Prefaces, postscripts, and annotations were
also unnecessary for the immediate situation. We are left with the impression that Walpole, if he was writing for a wider audience at all, was writing,
as so often, for the future. "I have everything in the world to tell posterity,"
he once declared.[42] Certainly, his annotations suggest that he himself was
very interested in the writing and construction of the stories. The title
Hieroglyphic Tales is in keeping with Walpole's interests in the exotic and

antiquarian, but it carries as well the half-humorous suggestion of a hidden symbolism beneath the playfulness. Seven copies is itself crazily emblematic. The immediate source for the princess who had every accomplishment to her credit except that of being born is, of course the "ontological argument" in philosophy. The fundamental problem behind St. Anselm's elegant "proof" for the existence of God is whether *existence* is an attribute like, say, *wisdom* or *love*, that can be assigned to a Supreme Being. Is it possible to imagine a God with every conceivable virtue but who does not exist? For a traditional Platonist it would be impossible. Though it is doubtful if many of Walpole's contemporaries would have been so convinced, the Enlightenment joke at the expense of metaphysics still had force. But there is another structure to these jokes that looks forward rather than backwards. Walpole had read in Bayle that the Greeks had "a controversy about things that never were nor shall be, whether some are not possible."[43] and clearly the idea fascinated him. In many of his *Hieroglyphic Tales* the nonsense is created simply by suspending time. The preface tells us that these tales were written "a little before the creation of the world, and have ever since been preserved, by oral tradition, in the mountains of Crampcraggiri, an unhabited island not yet discovered," by a clergyman not yet born.[44] Compared with those of Lewis Carroll, the joke is a bit thin, but there is, in embryo at least here, a foreshadowing of the time jokes of the Mad Hatter's tea party.

Moreover, this impression of modernity is reinforced by the curiously un-eighteenth-century language that Walpole seems to be using to describe his "hieroglyphs." Twice, in the passages just quoted the word *imagination* occurs in a sense that strikes the modern reader as ambiguous. Is it being used purely in its eighteenth-century sense, or are there much more Romantic and nineteenth-century overtones? He refers to it, for instance, as a power over and beyond those of *fancy, variety, novelty,* and *invention.* Is this merely a description of the Lockean process of recalling and creating images by association, or is there implied here a unifying power of aesthetic organization in a *romantic* sense?[45] A comparison with another book written at almost the same time by the greatest contemporary humorist and fantasist, Lawrence Sterne, serves to illustrate how striking is Walpole's use of imagination. *A Sentimental Journey* was published in 1768, while Walpole was at work on his *Hieroglyphic Tales*, and in the second volume, describing the plight of the caged starling, Sterne tells us how he "gave full scope" to his imagination.[46] Thereafter follows a lurid and truly Gothick fantasy of the horrors of imprisonment. But all this, Sterne twice tells us, is a *picture* or *portrait* in his mind.[47] Though it is in the form of a dream or reverie, it has an utterly different psychological classification from

Walpole's; it is, in the most literal and deliberate sense, a mental picture composed by a sequence of Lockean "trains of association."[48] Walpole's imagination may well have been *associative*, just as one might also argue that Sterne's method relies on writing, like Walpole, "without plan or forethought," but it is clear that Walpole finds in the imagination a much more active and organizing power than Sterne allows.[49] In short, it seems to me that by the 1770s—and possibly much earlier—Walpole has, in embryo at least, a theory of the unconscious.

However nineteenth-century Walpole's use of imagination may sometimes appear, there is still lacking one quality to the word that is so often present to the Romantics: a religious and metaphysical dimension. The word *mystic* was still unfashionable with the first generation of Romantics, partly because of the behavior of small extremist sects such as the followers of Joanna Southcott; and many poets (such as William Wordsworth), whom we might today describe as *mystical* in some of their moods, were quick to deny that there was anything in their states of consciousness not immediately open or communicable to the general reader.[50] Yet Wordsworth, Coleridge, and William Blake were all in touch with a living tradition of European mystical writing, which extended back for more than five hundred years, but which (with a few exceptions) is scarcely known in the twentieth century. Boehme, Giordano Bruno, Jeremy Taylor, and Swedenborg, if not widely read at large, were all known to the circles in which the early Romantics moved. For Blake, an apprenticeship which included drawing the Gothic tombs of the kings and queens of England in Westminster Abbey for Richard Gough's *Sepulchral Monuments in Great Britain*, early reinforced a natural love of the symbolic and the mysterious.[51] Above all, like many of his fellow Romantics, he shared in a rediscovery of Dante. Blake began his magnificent series of illustrations to the *The Divine Comedy* in 1825 and worked on them during the final and crowning years of his life.

For Dante, as he tells us in his *Convivio*, *fantasia* is the power by which the intellect represents what it sees. That this can be more a visionary than a rational process becomes clear from his own use of the word at the end and climax of the *Paradiso*. At the final mystical vision of the Trinity, Dante is overcome and forced at last to break off his narration:

> All'alta fantasia qui manco possa;
> ma gia volgeva il mio disio e 'l velle,
> si come rota ch' igualmente e mossa,
> l'amor che move il sole e l'altre stelle.

> Here power failed the high phantasy; but now my desire and will, like a
> wheel that spins with even motion, were revolved by the Love that moves
> the sun and the other stars.[52]

It is one of the few occasions when Dante actually uses the word *fantasia* in
The Divine Comedy, but its place at the very climax suggests that it can be
taken in some sense to describe the whole action of the poem. It encom-
passes the very quality of highly structured visionary mysticism that became
so increasingly important to Blake. One example will do.

Dante's first meeting with Beatrice at the end of the *Purgatorio* is one
of the great foci of the poem. His meeting involves him in both exaltation
and humiliation. Under Virgil's guidance he has come through both Hell
and Purgatory: now, here in the Earthly Paradise, Dante is told that for the
first time his will and intellect are now free. He may literally do what he
likes. But in the meeting with Beatrice that follows hard on the heels of this
new "adulthood," all his sense of achievement is undermined and finally
destroyed by a series of bewildering misunderstandings and humiliations
which culminate in an apparently undeserved public rebuke by his beloved
for faithlessness. So devastating and unexpected is this attack that even her
own entourage are moved to protest. Still in a state of shock from this hum-
bling of *reason* by *revelation*, Dante is led forward to be rewarded by a
curious vision. Beatrice is mounted in a "triumph car" (a vehicle the equivalent of a modern carnival float, and nearly as incongruous in this context)
which is drawn by a griffin. Until this point in the poem the griffin has
been but one wonder among many: as relatively ordinary a mythical beast
as one with the head of an eagle and the body of a lion can hope to pass for.
Now, from his new position, Dante can see it reflected in the emerald eyes
of Beatrice herself.

> A thousand desires hotter than flame held my eyes on the shining eyes,
> which remained still fixed on the Griffin, and even like the sun in a mir-
> ror the two fold beast shone within them, now with the one, now with
> the other nature. Think, reader, if I marvelled when I saw the thing still
> in itself and in its image changing. (XXXI:118–26)

He sees reflected something very odd indeed: the griffin is not a composite
creature at all, it seems, but "twofold." Seen through Beatrice's eyes it has
two totally different and incompatible forms: wholly lion and wholly eagle.
At an allegorical level Beatrice's eyes are the mirror of revelation, showing
Dante what he cannot yet see directly: the double nature of Christ as incar-
nate love, both wholly human and wholly divine.

1.3 Beatrice Addressing Dante from the Car, 1824–1827.
Illustration to Purgatory, Cantos 29-30.

It is this moment that Blake has chosen to illustrate. At the extreme right of the picture stands Dante, his head bowed in humility while his eyes are fixed still on Beatrice's face. Beatrice herself stands newly unveiled on the car whose platform decorations suggest an altar. By the wheel are the three virgins who are mentioned in canto XXIX. Hope, in green, raises her hands to heaven; Charity, in red, is surrounded by tiny children apparently in her golden hair; and Faith is running forward, pointing to the open book and to Dante apparently in intercession against the charge of faithlessness. Around Beatrice are grouped "four living creatures," each crowned with green leaves, and plumed with six wings full of eyes—a Dantesque conflation of Ezekiel and Revelation to represent the four Evangelists. In all this, even down to the colors of the griffin, Blake has been visually faithful to Dante—far more so than Flaxman, who had illustrated this same scene shortly before, and whose work had influenced Blake. Blake's alterations of Dante are the more significant. In Dante, the actual moment of Beatrice's unveiling and Dante's vision of the griffin's ambiguous nature does not in fact occur until canto XXXI. Blake has compressed certain elements of the earlier masque in cantos XXIX, and XXX, into the moment of meeting for symbolic purposes of his own. The wheel of the car, a swirling vortex of reflections of the eyes in the wings and the three virgin's faces, though it is taken from Ezekiel, is not to be found at all in Dante. Beatrice (here, perhaps, the sacrament) is upheld by revelation and virtue. We can perhaps see something of Blake's overall intention in this tableau if we compare it with something he had written more than thirty years earlier in a very peculiar work called *The Marriage of Heaven and Hell*:

> Without Contraries is no progression. Attraction and Repulsion,
>   Reason and Energy,
> Love and Hate, are necessary to Human Existence.
> From these contraries spring what the religious call Good and Evil.
>   Good is the passive
> that obeys Reason. Evil is the active springing from Energy.
> Good is Heaven. Evil is Hell.[53]

What interests Blake in Dante, I suspect, is the same as interested him here: a vision of *dialectic*. The ambiguous twofold form of the griffin is a union of contraries as basic as that of Reason and Energy, Love and Hate. Unlike Hegel's or Marx's, Blake's dialectic is a continual tension or polarity between incompatible opposites. The metaphor of marriage is important. A marriage is neither a fusion or a synthesis; it is a tension of varying degrees between incompatible differences. If one pole becomes lost or submerged the polarity ceases to be creative. The creativity of opposites is obvious in the most immediate sexual sense, and in the sometimes equally obvious spiritual sense. Blake, in his *Marriage of Heaven and Hell*, uses Milton's *Paradise Lost* to satirize the rigid spiritual geography of the eighteenth century. Heaven was a reflection of the Augustan order. Its virtues were reason, decorum, and elegance; desire, energy, enthusiasm, and strong emotions of all kinds were banished to Hell, along with most of the qualities we have come to associate with the intuitive and noncognitive sides of our being. In short, the division between Heaven and Hell had become a division between the conscious and unconscious. It is hardly surprising that so many of those we think of as most typical of Augustan writers—Swift, Pope, or Johnson—were deeply neurotic figures, torn between irreconcilable aspects of their own natures. By this divine cosmology of the Miltonic Augustan metaphysics the creativity of the artist, which is both rational *and* intuitive, had been disastrously separated into a false antithesis. *The Marriage of Heaven and Hell* was a reassertion of the *moral* bases of human creativity. Blake turns to the men he sees as the great poetic geniuses of the Church. How was Milton, a man who was apparently bound by this crippling and blasphemous dichotomy, able to write a great spiritual epic such as *Paradise Lost*? Blake's answer is that he was, like all artists, "of the Devil's party without knowing it." Milton's Satan, uniting in himself perpetual contraries, is really, did his creator but know it, the image of the "true Christ," everlastingly at war with "Old Nobodaddy up aloft"—who "farted and belched and cough'd"—God the Nobody's Father, the cruel vengeful tyrant of the Old Testament. Blake's final turning to Dante stems from precisely the same quest, but this time positive rather than negative. Here is a great Christian poet—an orthodox Trinitarian as Milton was not—who sees in Christ's dual nature the very dialectical union without which imagination in prophecy and poetry alike cannot exist. Unlike Coleridge and Wordsworth, to whom he is so closely parallel in many respects, Blake uses the word *imagination* to mean the power of perceiving things that lie beyond the reach of the senses—whereas *phantasy* is a mere use of the mind's eye. Ostensibly Blake is no more interested in this latter power of mere image making than his fellow Romantic poets, but just as *The Ancient Mariner* provides one of the great archetypes to the world of Victorian fantasy, so too Blake's interpretations of Milton and Dante are also sources of images that recur in the nineteenth-century dreamworld.

Very often, as in the cases of John Martin and Gustave Doré, we find that the same artists who attempt Milton are also fascinated by Dante.

1.4 John Martin: Satan and the Rebel Angels Bridging Chaos (Milton, Paradise Lost *X:312–47).*

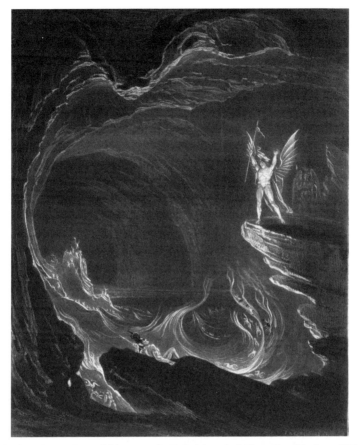

1.5 John Martin: Satan Addressing the Rebel Angels (Milton, Paradise Lost *I:314).*

Blake did not, of course, begin the tradition of illustrating epic fantasy worlds—there is a long tradition of eighteenth-century classical engraving—but he transformed it.[54] One only has to compare the world of Martin with the continental classical training of Doré to see the difference. Martin, like Turner, has none of the technical skill in figure drawing that Doré seems effortlessly to achieve, yet he has a sense of the sublime—a feeling for the Miltonic "darkness visible" that takes him into a different world. Doré rarely seems to show either the sense of symbolism or of sheer space that Martin does. Paradoxically, his views of London are far more mysterious and haunting than his conceptions of heaven and hell.

Blake had to invent his own methods of color printing, and many of his plates were hand-colored. By the middle of the nineteenth century the lithograph (introduced in 1818) and the mezzotint steel engraving (greatly

improved by Thomas Lupton's innovations which earned him the Isis
Medal from the Society of Arts in 1822) had made possible a much higher
quality of detail in mass production. Significantly, John Martin was the
first person to apply the new process to a book, with his illustrations to
Paradise Lost in 1827. The mezzotint was to open up a whole new class of
viewers and to make his name a household world in a way that no artist's
had hitherto been. The Victorian era is the great age of the illustrated
book. Doré's output for British publishers alone is enormous—and often
suffers in consequence. Coleridge's *The Ancient Mariner*, which was one
of the first books he illustrated, in addition to reissues and combinations,
went through no less than ten different illustrated editions between 1850

1.6 Gustave Doré: "Warehousing in the City."
Illustration to Blanchard Jerrold's London *(1872).*

and 1900–the rate of publication climbing steeply toward the end of the century.

F. D. Klingender in *Art and the Industrial Revolution* has shown us how the new technology not merely changed the nature of the arts in the nineteenth century by making books and prints more widely available, it also suggested new forms and perspectives in design. Nor was the sense of exuberance in the new power of steam and steel confined to the visual arts. A school of industrial poets sprang up to welcome the new dawn and hymn in epic lines the might of the steam engine. In the eighteenth century John Dyer, author of the pastoral *Grongar Hill*, had turned his muse less happily on to the multiple spinning machine:

> A circular machine, of new design,
> In conic shape: it draws and spins a thread
> Without the tedious toil of needless hands.
> A wheel, invisible, beneath the floor,
> To ev'ry member of the harmonious frame gives necessary motion.
>
> (*The Fleece*, 1757)

Erasmus Darwin, grandfather of Charles, celebrated Thomas Savery's steam pump with all the incongruous neoclassical conventions of personification and helpful nymphs. For some, all will be forgiven for the sake of his prophecy of the age of the steam-powered "flying chariot." A footnote explains that "there seems no probable method of flying conveniently but by the power of steam, or some other explosive material, which another half-century may probably discover."

> Nymphs! You erewhile on simmering cauldrons play'd
> And called delighted Savery to your aid;
> Bade round the youth explosive steam aspire,
> In gathering clouds, and winged the wave with fire;
> Bade with cold streams the quick expansion stop,
> And sunk the immense of vapour to a drop–
> Pressed by the ponderous air the Piston falls
> Resistless, sliding through its iron walls;
> Quick moves the balanced beam, of giant birch,
> Wields his large limbs, and nodding shakes the earth.
> Lifts with strong arm her dark reluctant waves;
> Each caverned rock, and hidden den explores,
> Drags her dark coals, and digs her shining ores [. . .]
> Soon shall thy arm, unconquered steam! afar
> Drag the slow barge, or drive the rapid car;

> Or on wide waving wings expanded bear
> The flying chariot through the fields of air.
> —Fair crews triumphant, leaning from above,
> Shall wave their fluttering kerchiefs as they move;
> Or warrior bands alarm the gaping crowd,
> And armies shrink beneath the shadowy cloud.
>
> (*The Economy of Vegetation*, 1792)

But the contrast between the painters and the poets is instructive. There is an abstraction and detachment about the visual arts that the sequential and discursive powers of poetry do not, and cannot have. Painting and poetry are not parallel arts. The difference between, say, Turner and Darwin is not just that one is a great artist and the other a tenth-rate poet; the difference is also in the nature of the two media. Blake shared with Turner the intuitive feeling that "energy is eternal delight" but he was simultaneously aware,

> How the youthful Harlot's curse
> Blasts the new born Infant's tear,
> And blights with plagues the Marriage hearse.

Turner, it is true, painted *The Slave Ship*; Hogarth engraved his *Moralities*; but the painter is not bound to social reality as is the worker with words.

With a poet such as Keats we find a new and significant development. Keats was a Londoner and a cockney most of whose life was spent within an urban and metropolitan society. Yet unlike with Blake there is little evidence of this in his poetry. We have no internal clue to tell us that the "Ode to a Nightingale" was written in broad daylight in a Hampstead garden. For the most part Keats chooses quite explicitly to set his poetry in another world: Greek mythology, the Middle Ages, or in "Faery Lands Forlorn." Only occasionally, as in "Isabella," do we get a glimpse of a familiar capitalistic and imperial industrial system:

> With her two brothers this fair lady dwelt,
> Enriched from ancestral merchandize,
> And for them many a weary hand did swelt
> In torched mines and noisy factories,
> And many once proud quiver'd loins did melt
> In blood from stinging whip;—with hollow eyes
> Many all day in dazzling river stood,
> To take the rich ored driftings of the flood.

For the vast majority of his poems, Keats chose to turn his back upon the problems of his own time and tried to create for himself worlds where his poetic ideals carry their own validity.

> And they are gone: aye, ages long ago
> Those lovers fled away into the storm.
> That night the Baron dreamt of many a woe,
> And all his warrior guests, with shade and form
> Of witch and demon, and large coffin worm,
> Were long be nightmared. Angela the old
> Died palsy twitched, with meagre face deform;
> The beadsmen, after thousand ayes told,
> For aye unsought for slept among his ashes cold.
>   (*The Eve of St. Agnes*)

Not for nothing is Keats the most potent single poetic influence upon the art of the Victorian era. It was to Keats that the pre-Raphaelites were to turn when they desired poetic subjects for their painting. Arthur Hughes painted a Gothic tryptich of *The Eve of St. Agnes*. Keats's rich sometimes cloying language was a fatal attraction and often a snare to a generation of later poets from Tennyson to Swinburne. Even Hopkins fell under his spell and finally forged many of his own idiosyncratic verse rhythms in reaction.

Like Coleridge, Keats turns to the Gothick for the material from which to create his alternative autonomous world of fantasy. As does *The Ancient Mariner*, *The Eve of St. Agnes* draws much of its attraction from its very remoteness from the world of everyday experience. It belongs to another world of color and rich visual symbolism as remote from the nineteenth century as the *The Arabian Nights*. Yet the "Gothick convention" (if it may be so called) provided both poets with something they needed, and could find nowhere else: a language in which to talk about areas of human experience for which they had no conceptual framework. The prevailing empiricist psychology of John Locke and David Hartley allowed no room for a theory of the unconscious, for irrational deeds of guilt and expiation, for the mysteries of pain and suffering with which the poets found themselves confronted. The age lacked a vocabulary and a symbolism for even approaching such matters, and so it was to the work of Blake, Coleridge, and Keats that the Victorians turned in search of a language to describe the complexities of the irrational. In an unpublished notebook of 1829, Coleridge attempted to describe what he meant by the "phantasmagoric allegory." Its "prominent characters" are "its breadth, or amplitude, and its rapid Aurora borealis-like Shifting yet still within a loosely predetermined

Sphere and with a unity of direction." "The Allegoric," he goes on, "does not exclude the Literal, nor one Allegory another." Suddenly we see a glimpse of another stage in the evolution of a word. *Phantasmagoria* has, of course, the same root as *fantasy*. It is a word that will crop up repeatedly in the course of this study. It was, for instance, a collection of German horror stories called *Phantasmagoriana* that inspired Mary Shelley to write *Frankenstein.* "Phantasmagoria" was the comic title-poem that gave its name to a collection of sixteen humorous and whimsical poems published by Lewis Carroll in 1869.

It was, however, a new word first coined in 1802 to serve the needs of the exotic and apocalyptic leanings of the new age of steam and revolution, visions, and technology. The "Phantasmagoria" at the Lyceum in London was an application of the newly invented magic lantern, involving back projection on to a transparent screen, with double slides to add movement. It was just one of a growing gallimaufry of such amazing optical entertainments of the period. Philip James de Loutherberg, the painter and Royal Academician, had helped to create a popular demand for the visually spectacular with his "Eidophusikon" as early as 1781—involving color, light, and music. But this, with its tiny stage, four feet by eight, was rapidly dwarfed by a series of panoramas with subjects ranging from Boulogne to Agincourt. Turner had produced one of the Battle of the Nile, and Girtin his "Eidometropolis": a panoramic view of London from the South Bank. A public taste for the amazing and spectacular had facilitated the rise of a whole new visual technology. In the Strand, for instance, Reinagle and Barker exhibited "the Bay of Naples and the recent eruption of Vesuvius"— a favorite theme that was even staged in the theatre with aquatic spectacles, ballets, and visions of Satan in Pandemonium, or at Astley's Amphitheatre, where disasters and victories were shown daily.[55] Off Hanover Square was Merlin's Mechanical Museum, whose exhibits included The Temple of Flora, Merlin's Cave, the Antique Whispering Busts, the Vocal Harp, the Bird Cage for Ladies, the Aerial Cavalcade, and the Artificial Flying Bat.[56] In 1822 Bullock produced a panorama of the North Pole, in his Egyptian Hall, complete with live figures, and the following year Louis Daguerre (inventor of the Daguerreotype) opened his "Diorama" in Regent's Park, with elaborate lighting, scenery, and a revolving auditorium.[57] The thirst for mechanical spectacles of this kind continued unabated into the 1830s, and never really died away until it was finally overtaken by the cinema at the end of the century, but by the beginning of Victoria's reign, the grandiose visions of Martin, Turner, and their rivals were becoming less popular in an age for which mere bigness had a decreasing appeal.

The visual taste for the apocalyptic had its direct equivalents in literature. Philip James Bailey's forty thousand line epic, *Festus*, whose metaphysical ambitions seemed to begin where *Faust* and *Paradise Lost* gave up, had its prose counterpart in the great set pieces of novels like Bulwer Lytton's *The Last Days of Pompeii* (1834). The ending is pure Martin:

> Suddenly, as he spoke, the place became lighted with an intense and lurid glow. Bright and gigantic through the darkness, which closed around it like the falls of hell, the mountain shone—a pile of fire! Its summit seemed riven in two; or rather, above its surface there seemed to rise two monster shapes, each confronting each, as Demons contending for a World. These were of one deep bloodhue of fire, which lighted up the whole atmosphere far and wide; but, *below*, the nether part of the mountain was still dark and shrouded, save in three places, adown which flowed, serpentine and irregular, rivers of the molten lava. Darkly red through the profound gloom of their banks, they flowed slowly on, as towards the devoted city. Over the broadest there seemed to spring a cragged and stupendous arch, from which, as from the jaws of hell, gushed the sources of the sudden Phlegethon. And through the stilled air was heard the rattling of the fragments of rock, hurtling one upon another as they were born down the fiery cataracts—darkening, for one instant, the spot where they fell, and suffused the next, in the burnished hues of the flood along which they floated! [. . .]
>
> The sudden illumination the bursts of the floods of lava, and the earthquake [. . .] chanced when Sallust and his party had just gained the direct path leading from the city to the port; and here they were arrested by an immense crowd, more than half the population of the city. They spread along the field without the walls, thousands upon thousands, uncertain whither to fly. The sea had retired far from the shore; and they who had fled to it had been so terrified by the agitation and preturnatural shrinkings of the element, the gasping forms of the uncouth sea things which the waves had left upon the sand, and by the sound of the huge stones cast from the mountain into the deep, that they had returned again to the land, as presenting the less frightful aspect of the two. Thus two streams of human beings, the one seaward, the other *from* the sea, had met together, feeling a sad comfort in numbers; arrested in despair and doubt.[58]

In the scale and epic scope of its fantasy, the early years of the nineteenth century far overshadow the Victorian period, but the gradual shift in sensibility away from apocalyptic epics was not merely a matter of size. The intensely personal nightmare visions of Henry Fuseli were, perhaps, more prophetic of the way in which taste was to develop. Coleridge's use of the word *phantasmagoria* in his old age illustrates quite strikingly how the magic-lantern show of thirty years before had been *internalized*. It referred now not to external scenes of blood and thunder, fire and volcanoes, but to the rapidly shifting images of a fevered brain, creating and living in its own dreamworld. It is one of the earliest words for what the twentieth century was to call *surrealist*. For Coleridge it clearly carried something of the other associations of that word, but in that jotted note he also links phantasmagoria with another ancient and in many ways opposite literary form, the *allegory*.

In contrast with the wild and chaotic flux of the phantasmagoria, an allegory is the most tightly disciplined of literary kinds. To show one set of happenings under the guise of another, keeping both external probability and internal correspondence between the two or more levels of the story, requires a very tightly controlled structure. It implies a universe not of arbitrariness and accident, but one charged with hidden meaning and significance. In observing Coleridge's apparent paradox it is hard not to be reminded that he had himself, more than thirty years before, written the

1.7 Noel Paton: "Death and Life-in-Death" (1863).
Illustration to S. T. Coleridge's The Ancient Mariner, *Part III.*

supreme example of such a genre. *The Ancient Mariner* is perhaps the most famous juxtaposition of the two forms in the language. Though it is unique, it also illustrates better than any other work the new spirit of the Romantic age, with its yearning for the grandiose and the exotic, and its quest for a cosmic significance in human life. One way of seeing the roots of Victorian fantasy, as it were, in microcosm, is to look at the way in which the Victorians approached and attempted to interpret *The Ancient Mariner*. For many, it summed up the phantasmagoria of a dreamworld that some have argued is the aim (conscious or unconscious) of nearly all Victorian art. Yet a dreamworld need not necessarily imply escapism, as some contemporaries were quick to recognize. Dreams can be, and often are, loaded with the most complex of hidden meanings. "In myths and fairy tales," writes Jung, "as in dreams, the psyche tells its own story."[59] We have already mentioned the amazing number and variety of Victorian illustrated editions of *The Ancient Mariner*: each suggesting new interpretations and significances to the poem. Doré's have a brooding mysticism that spills over into languor and paralysis, with a strong sense of the "otherness"

1.8 Noel Paton: "The Spirit from the Land of Mist and Snow" (1863).
Illustration to S. T. Coleridge's The Ancient Mariner, *Part V.*

of the Mariner's ordeal. Paton's technically more naïve version is also more revealing, ranging from the macabre eroticism of Death and Life-in-Death, to the brooding Spirit in the Antarctic—adapted with a strangely literal intensity from Blake's *Ancient of Days*. Patten Wilson's decorative arabesques look forward to the graceful yet grotesque shapes of Kay Neilson and Arthur Rackham. In each the tension between apparent irrationality and hidden meaning manages to imply the existence of "other worlds," mysterious and yet almost familiar, lying just beyond the frontiers of our normal world—and somehow connected with it.

"There is a curtain," wrote E. Nesbit, just over a hundred years after Coleridge, "thin as gossamer, clear as glass, strong as iron, that hangs for ever between the world of magic and the world that seems to us to be real. And when once people have found one of the little weak spots in that curtain [. . .] almost anything may happen."[60]

1.9 Patten Wilson: "The Water Snakes."
Illustration to S. T. Coleridge's The Ancient Mariner, *Part IV.*

Chapter 2

Christmas as Scrooge's

The *internalization* of fantasy in the early nineteenth century meant, in effect, the evolution of a new language. The worlds of dreams and nightmares, madmen and children were areas of human experience which had hitherto been all too often ignored or even denied. Their recognition helped to open up a new view of the human mind in which conventional distinctions between aesthetics and psychology were blurred by a growing awareness of the unconscious in shaping our mental processes. As we have seen, it is possible to trace something of this evolution by looking at various key figures in the development of late eighteenth-century sensibility, yet such men as Walpole and Beckford, or their successors of the next generation like Coleridge or Keats, John Martin or Pugin, at best perhaps arbitrarily selected to illustrate a point, only give us a part of the picture. A new "language" of the mind does not come into being through a few innovators alone, however important they may be; it must also reflect a genuine shift in the climate of feeling in a whole society. If we are to try and understand such a cultural sea change we must look to a quite different stratum of its literature, and at the world from which this literature sprang.

It is fatally easy to generalize about Victorianism and to construct a model of fantasy to fit. For instance it is tempting to argue that the peculiarly rich development of fantasy within the period is in some way the product of social repression and inhibition. In an impressionistic and personal little book,[1] *The Victorian Age in Literature*, G. K. Chesterton for example summarizes the prevailing mood of the mid-century as the "Victorian Compromise." What gave the era its distinctive flavor, at once urban and yet culturally provincial, self-searching and yet smug, he argues, was that it rested upon a peculiar emotional and intellectual compromise between forces whose conflict would otherwise have threatened the stability of the whole social order. In short, for the sake of certain immediate practical advantages, it was as if Victorian society tacitly agreed to pretend that quite incompatible beliefs and aims could successfully coexist. Such an argument clearly deserves respect if only because, as he himself reminds us, Chesterton was born a Victorian, and he can convey a sense of what it actually felt like to be one that is difficult for even the most scholarly historian to recapture. He was also a prolific creator of fantasies. His argument summarizes what many late Victorians, from Thomas Hardy to Edmund Gosse, came to feel about their own upbringing. As a modern literary historian has put it, "Despite the resounding clash of individual wills, there was until late in Victoria's reign, a desire for cultural synthesis urgent enough to inspire from even the most rebellious a concession to an established social morality."[2] Certainly it is difficult for us to sympathize with the accepted bases of Victorian society unless we grasp that England in the 1840s was engaged in one of the greatest moral and social cleanups that, short of actual physical revolution, any society has known. During the 1830s there had been a series of wide-reaching political reforms—extending the franchise and attempting to check some of the cruder forms of electoral corruption. Slavery was abolished; a few of the worst excesses of child and female labor conditions were tackled, and in many occupations working hours were limited for the first time. Even the labyrinthine processes of ecclesiastical reform were put in motion. At a voluntary level a multitude of interconnected Evangelical societies had sprung into existence by the 1840s, concerning themselves with everything from cruelty to animals to prostitution.[3] Like all revolutionary cleanups it involved repression. That was the price to be paid, and for many Victorians it undoubtedly seemed a cheap one. It is easy for the twenty-first century, preoccupied with its own troubles, to look back with nostalgia to Victorian Britain as an age of peace, order, and increasing prosperity, and to ignore the fact that for those actually living at the time it was a period of intense anxiety and self-doubt. Carlyle, Dickens, Kingsley, Eliot, Morris, Ruskin, and a host of others betray constant fears for the fate of their society. Indeed, the fear of actual revolution was never very far from the minds of many of the middle class until well into the 1850s, and as fears of the Chartists and radical agitation slowly abated they were replaced by a no less profound "ontological insecurity" produced by increasing social mobility and the threats to the traditional religious world picture posed by evolution and the materialism of the physical sciences. It is against this background of social and personal anxieties that we must see the tensions between the need for reform and the need for a social consensus. Such a viewpoint perhaps explains better than any other the phenomenon of Victorian tenacity to a series of moral half truths—what Conrad, with pessimistic clarity was to call "a few simple notions of goodness"—as well as the sense of apparently permanent unease and weariness that afflicted so many eminent and energetic Victorians. Later ages may have been quick to label it *hypocrisy* without asking what were the social and intellectual conditions that made such hypocrisy for many people the preferable choice. For all its faults, and its fundamental instability, what Chesterton calls "the Victorian Compromise" was one that managed to hold Dickens, Browning, and Tennyson for much of their lives. If a few, like Matthew Arnold, saw through it, they had little to put in its place, and its strength might be nowhere better illustrated than by the degree of anguish needed finally to drive Eliot and Newman, in their own very different ways, out into the cold.

Yet the picture of Victorian society as a repressive one, based on an impossible compromise and therefore a hypocritical and even collectively schizophrenic—though, as we have seen, it clearly contains some elements of truth—can also be dangerously misleading. There were plenty who were prepared to speak out not merely against individual abuses, but against the fundamental tenets of society itself, and the idea of the world of Dickens, Carlyle, Ruskin, and Thackeray as complacent or self-satisfied is absurd. It was probably the most profoundly self-critical age in English history. Writers were quick to campaign on matters of public and social importance. John Martin and Kingsley were both fanatical advocates of better sewage and water supplies—especially for London. Dickens led in the fight for better education. Thomas Hood was the author of *The Song of the Shirt*, exposing (like the omnipresent Kingsley) the sweatshops of the East End.

Similarly, the notion of a silent consensus over sex, plausible enough as a generalization, begins to break down rapidly when we start to look at individual examples. It is true that the fantasies of Lear and Carroll show every sign of latent repressions, arguably homosexual in the case of Lear, even (perhaps) pedophiliac in Carroll, but the moment we start to look at Kingsley or George MacDonald the theory is much more difficult to sustain. Steven Marcus in *The Other Victorians* has shown not merely the rise of a shadow pornographic literature of the period, often directly parodying the major writers, but also the part which sexual references, overt and oblique, play in the psychology of the major literature itself.[4] In much of Dickens, indeed, it is clear enough. There is more overt sexuality in Steerforth's relationship with Rosa Dartle, in *David Copperfield*, for example, than there is in the work of any novelist writing earlier in the century. Neither does the fantasy of the period sublimate or evade sexuality, as one might expect if it were primarily the product of sexual repression.

MacDonald's *Phantastes* opens with an obliquely suggested (but clear) seduction, and contains what one modern Freudian critic has called the sexiest song in Victorian literature.[5] Nor could Kingsley be accused in any sense of needing to compensate for repressive sexual inhibitions. We have already mentioned his erotic drawings: though private by their very nature, as presents for his wife, they were hardly furtive. Perhaps more significantly for any social thesis on the roots of fantasy, he was also publicly outspoken on the subject—as, for instance, in his comments on a particular strike that it was the sexual license of the millowners with their factory girls that was "the unspoken cause, among brothers and sweethearts, of fearful indignation, which only found vent in political agitation."[6] When Mrs. Gaskell caused scandal among her readers by dealing with illegitimacy in *Ruth*, and even condoning a "fallen woman," Kingsley wrote at once, as a stranger, to offer her his support.[7]

Our earlier metaphor of fantasy, therefore, as the *underside* or *obverse* of the Victorian imagination cannot be taken simply to mean that fantasy is always an escape or refuge from a repressive social code. There are too many variables and too many levels involved. In most societies evidence for some kind of social compromise can be found: one might argue that, to a greater or less degree, it is the permanent condition of any complex society. Though it may be superficially attractive to link evidence for repressions in Lear and Carroll, for instance, a detailed examination of their work suggests they were very different kinds of repression[8]—as we shall see in a later chapter. Similarly Dadd, painter of grotesque and erotic fairies, seems to be a very different case from either—or from other "fairy" illustrators such as Cruikshank, John Leech, or Richard Doyle, who show no particular signs of hidden repressions. We do not know the causes of Dadd's madness, but it was apparently hereditary.[9] It is true, however, that the period did produce one of the most potent myths of repression in fantasy in Robert Louis Stevenson's *Dr. Jekyll and Mr. Hyde*—where the worthy and benevolent Jekyll contains within himself; unassimilated, the alter ego of the evil and terrifying Hyde, who finally overwhelms and destroys the respectable doctor. Yet to argue as Chesterton does in support of his thesis that the story is a paradigm of what the Victorian age did not understand about itself is surely difficult to sustain.[10] It is quite clear, even if only from the symbolism of Hyde's name, that Stevenson knew very well what he was about in creating his story. To talk of the "age" as having a common collective consciousness (that would have to exclude Stevenson) is simply a misuse of metaphor. Evidence for psychological naïveté—and there is certainly plenty in the literature of the period—can be matched by equal evidence of psychological subtlety and penetration. Richard Reis has similarly criticized Robert Lee Wolff for his unwarranted assumption that MacDonald was an example of an unconscious mythmaker who did not understand the forces behind his art.[11] If the nineteenth century was fascinated by its dreams and nightmares, there is every indication that many of the dreamers were well aware of what dreams were made of.

It is in fact much more rewarding to see this polarity of fantasy and imagination straightforwardly in terms of literary genre. Sociological and psychological accounts of this great flowering of fantasy in Victoria's reign are entertaining in almost direct proportion to their speculativeness, but their real weakness is that the more one looks at the detailed interconnections between the writers the more such macrotheories look redundant. With the exception of Lear, the great creators of fantasy knew each other personally—often as friends. Carroll read *The Water Babies* before publication and when he was at work on *Alice in Wonderland*; he himself sent his completed manuscript to MacDonald for advice on publication. Kipling and Nesbit exchanged books and frequently borrowed ideas directly from one another, as well as from the earlier writers, accepting their place in what was by then a recognized genre.[12] Yet its foundations were older than Kingsley or Lear. Behind the great writers of fantasy were two very different cultural traditions: an English one of vigorous popular journalism in satire and cartoon which had never been tied to naturalistic conventions; and, as we shall see, from Germany a quite different, but equally non-naturalistic one, of mysticism and folktales. From such figures as Cruikshank or Hood down to a host of minor entertainers, often anonymous, an older English tradition of symbolic names and stylization lived on and flourished. Dickens was able to use such expressive names as Mr. Jingle, the Cheerible brothers, or Sir Leicester Deadlock, because he found ready made a comic tradition as old as the medieval *humors*. Yet there is a difference in the Victorian forms. What strikes us immediately about a Dickens episode, a Cruikshank or a Phiz illustration, is the endless busy detail. It is overflowing with life. So far from being a simplification or limitation of experience, they seem rather to suffer from a superabundant richness that can only be captured and contained by the conventions of the cartoon—just as Chesterton's own splendid story, *The Man Who was Thursday*, was itself clearly the product of exuberance rather than repression. Here, if anywhere, in this exuberant overspill of reality, lie the real roots of Victorian fantasy.

Thus we encounter the paradox that in what is often taken to be the great age of realism, humor and satire commonly achieved literary expression within conventions that were essentially unrealistic and fantastic. Reviewing Dickens's *The Battle of Life* in a long article for *Frazer's Magazine* in 1847 entitled "A Grumble about the Christmas Books," Thackeray argues that unreality was an essential attribute of the new genre he was discussing:

> If I judge Mr. Dickens's present volume rightly, it has been the author's aim, not to produce a prose tale of mingled fun and sadness, and a close imitation of life, but a prose poem, designed to awaken emotions tender, mirthful, pastoral, wonderful. [. . .] The action of the piece you see clearly enough, but the actors speak and move to measure and music. The drolls are more violently funny; the serious heroes and heroines more gracefully and faultlessly beautiful. Such figures are never seen among real country people. [. . .] these charming little books of Mr. Dickens's are chorals for Christmas executed in prose.[13]

That Thackeray picks out the poetic and the stylized as the essential qualities of the form tells us much about its origins in the popular literature of the 1820s and 1830s. Following on the success of Rudolph Ackermann's *Forget Me Not* in 1825 there had been a vogue for similar annuals with collections of poems and short stories with a family appeal intended specifi-

2.1 Thomas Hood: "The Angel of Death," from The Volunteer, *an antiwar antiheroic poem in* Whims and Oddities II *(1827). It illustrates a typical Hood pun:*
There stood the leader of our foes
With vultures for his cronies
No Corsican, but Death himself
The Bony or all Bonies.
To complete the antiwar message, both flags are British not French.

cally for the lucrative Christmas market. Quite the most outstanding were those of Thomas Hood (1799–1845) who had started his career as a comic writer with two volumes called *Whims and Oddities* in 1826 and 1827, and had then edited a Christmas anthology, *The Gem*, in 1828. His first *Comic Annual* in 1830 was a new and original departure: previous annuals had carried comic material, but the prevailing tone had been lightly sentimental. Hood's new annual was a vehicle for wit and satire, but the tone was zany, fantastic, and grotesque—even at times savage. Visually, it drew upon an older satiric tradition of "tail-piece" illustration. Thomas Bewick (1753–1828) had illustrated natural history books not merely with his famous woodcuts of birds and animals themselves, but also with little cartoons at the foot of the page which drew satiric human parallels.

2.2 A tail piece from Bewick's Water Birds (1805).
Accompanying the section on the Black-Backed Gull. He describes gulls as being "greedy and gluttonous, almost indiscriminately devouring whatever comes their way, whether of flesh or putrid substances, until they are obliged to disgorge their overloaded stomachs."

A tail piece of a gourmet vomiting, for instance, illustrates a seagull's regurgitation.[14] Hood's *Comic Annuals* were filled with elaborate puns and extravagant conceits. They continued regularly throughout the 1830s, the last volume appearing in 1842, only three years before his death. From the first they inspired a host of imitators. Louisa Sheridan's *Comic Offering or Ladies' Melange of Literary Mirth*, which ran until 1835, kept to the same format and binding, and was a blatant parody of Hood's style and puns. More startling in origins was the *New Comic Annual* produced by Hood's own publishers, Hurst Chance & Co., in identical size and layout which was clearly intended to deceive the reader into believing it was by Hood himself. The dedicatory poem at the beginning actually refers to Hood by name in the first line. Though the *Comic Annuals* were full of jokes, puns,

2.3 "Skeleton Keys." Illustration loosely attached to a macabre punning poem about being imprisoned and hanged from Louisa Sheridan's Ladies Comic Offering *(1833). A publication closely modeled on Hood's* Comic Annuals.

cartoons, and comic verse, they were never bawdy (Hood prided himself on his "wholesomeness") but frequently macabre—occasionally, with an underlying moral seriousness.

In a changed key, and worked into an organic whole, these were elements that were to reappear in the first real Christmas book, Dickens's *A Christmas Carol* in 1843. In spite of a host of imitators, including himself, Thackeray was in no doubt that it was Dickens who had "invented" the genre—and there is circumstantial confirmation of this from Thackeray's earlier review for *Frazer's*, "Our Batch of Novels for Christmas 1837," in which the books dealt with are all ordinary fiction, with no suggestion of any particular seasonal content. By 1847, however, the formula was clearly well established. Thackeray selects, so he tells us, "8 or 9 of the 25 or 30 volumes" on offer for Christmas 1846. We have, for instance, *A Christmas in the Seventeenth Century*, by Mrs. Percy Sinnett; *A New Year's Day: A Winter's Tale*, by Mrs. Gore, illustrated by Cruikshank; *January Eve: a Tale of the Times*, by G. Soane Esq., B.A.; *The Good Genius that Turned Everything into Gold; or, the Queen Bee and the Magic Dress. A Christmas Fairy Tale*, by the Brothers Mayhew, illustrations by Cruikshank; *The Yule Log for Everybody's Christmas Hearth*, by the author of *The Chronicles of the Bastille*, yet again illustrated by fast working Cruikshank; and Fisher's *Drawing Room Scrap Book*, by the

Hon. Mrs. Norton. Dickens, as aforementioned, has produced *The Battle of Life*, and there is a newly translated volume of *Wonderful Stories for Children*, by Hans Andersen. Having singled out these last two for praise, and damned the rest, Thackeray begins a caustic review of *Mrs. Perkins's Ball*—only to break off in mock horror at the discovery that it is by himself. Though the second of the books listed above is maudlin rather than magical, the contents of the rest are only too predictable:

> "Curses on all fairies!" I gasp out; "I will never swallow another one as long as I live. Perdition seize all Benevolence! Be hanged to the Good and the True! Fling me every drop of the milk of human kindness out of the window!—horrible, curdling slops, away with them! Kick old Father Christmas out of doors, the abominable old impostor! Next year I'll go to the Turks, the Scotch, or other Heathens who don't keep Christmas. Is all the street to come for a Christmas Box? Are the waits to be invading us by millions, and yelling all night? By my soul, if anybody offers me plum-pudding again this season, I'll fling it in his face!"[15]

It was perhaps predictable too that when Thackeray himself was tempted away from the rather heavy comic realism of *Mrs. Perkins's Ball*, it was to parody this avalanche of Christmas fantasias in a "pantomime" of his own: the highly successful *The Rose and the Ring* of 1853, which effectively brings to an end the decade in which all the best examples of the genre appeared.

Though this popular tradition depended on many illustrators, including Leech, Doyle, and Thackeray himself, visually it had been to an astonishing degree the creation of one man: the indefatigable Cruikshank. If Bewick had popularized the use of the realistic comic tail piece, Cruikshank had given shape to the fantasy of his age by his brilliant illustrations to Grimms' fairytales in 1823. He had been brought up in the tradition of the eighteenth-century caricaturists William Hogarth and James Gillray, and had begun his career as a cartoonist during the Napoleonic wars. When he turned to fairies he naturally adapted the grotesques of caricature and satire that he was used to.[16] The ravings of Napoleon Buonaparte became the model for the raging Rumpelstiltskin. The figures of political infighting were simply mythologized. During the 1830s and 1840s Cruikshank became one of the best known as well as most prolific of artists, and his name began to appear more prominently than the author's on title pages. His own *Comic Almanac* joined the stream of other comic books of the mid-1830s, and he was the illustrator of Dickens's *Sketches by Boz*. Though his pictures often appeared to be spontaneous sketches, they were in fact carefully prepared and full of significant detail in the manner of Hogarth. His series of drawings on "The Drunkard's Children" is a direct imitation of Hogarth's *Moralities*. Eventually his obtrusive moralizing and fanatical teetotalism caused a breach even with Dickens who, in an article on "Frauds and Fairies" complained that he was despoiling childhood memories.[17]

Hood himself had been trained as an engraver and illustrator in this tradition, though most of his short working life was spent as a not very successful journalist, often in poor health, and always pushed for money. His draughtsman's apprenticeship, however, meant that like so many of the Victorian fantasists he could illustrate his own work. The basic cast of mind revealed by his puns is both visual and concrete. Yet though his surprisingly antipatriotic "Angel of Death," for instance, is essentially a visual pun, a closer inspection reminds us that its ingredients, the cannon and the two ensigns, are themselves symbols. He was also capable of highly abstract and unvisualizable puns, such as the lines from "The Ballad of Faithless Nellie Gray":

> [H]ere I leave my second leg,
> And the Forty Second Foot.

Hood's basic form of fantasy, the pun, as Empson has shown, demands a very special and complex mental set, bringing together things which the mind normally manages to keep clearly separate.[18] For our own sanity, we do not usually think of a numbered infantry regiment as a quantity of real feet. As we shall see, there are similarities between Hood's outrageous punning and Lear's, whose creation of a genre of nonsense by words and pictures is apparently much less complicated, but who, in fact, often hinges his limericks on concealed and unsuspected puns, sometimes of a very bizarre order. The man who wrote of himself in 1840 that "no gentleman alive has written so much comic and spitten so much blood within six consecutive years" was very much a loner, but a glance at Hood's work may for all that suggest ways in which he was—exaggeratedly perhaps—symptomatic of his uncertain age.

Ruskin was one of the first to see a link between the spirit of Cruikshank and Hood. In his *Appendix to Modern Painters* on "Modern Grotesque" he acknowledges the "innate and incommunicable" style of the caricaturist, but goes on to see in his work something of the spirit of the age.

> When the powers of quaint fancy are associated (as is frequently the case) with stern understanding of the nature of evil, and tender human sympa-

thy, there results a bitter or pathetic spirit of grotesque, to which mankind at the present day owe more through moral teaching than to any branch of art whatsoever.

In poetry the temper is seen, in perfect manifestation, in the works of Thomas Hood; in art it is found both in various works of the Germans— their finest and their least thought of; and more or less in the works of George Cruikshank, and in many of the illustrations of our popular journals.[19]

A recent biographer of Hood has gone on to link this spirit of the grotesque directly with the pun—a verbal equivalent of the Cruikshank cartoon:

> Punning was inveterate to Hood's nature. Both in speaking and in writing he punned continually and, it would seem, compulsively. His punning indicated that his mind possessed a fundamental, unresolved dichotomy: he perceived the comic in the tragic and the tragic in the comic. But this discovery of incongruity caused him distinct unease. Since equivocation came easily to his nature, Hood was, through puns, provided with a defense mechanism by which he could shy away from the full implications of his vision. In his social poems his marked reluctance to affirm in a straightforward manner his beliefs on controversial subjects reveals a basic insecurity; through punning, the outlet his gifts permitted him, he reconciled his embarrassment before unease. Rarely did he stare boldly in the face of a problem, social, political, or other—hence the puns and anticlimactic endings of so many works.[20]

There are two very interesting ideas here. The first is that Hood was strongly, even compulsively, aware of unresolved contradictions in his society, and that his puns are in some way an expression of this conflict. This is surely a fruitful extension of the argument already advanced by Chesterton and others which we have been examining in this chapter. The second assumption, however, is more odd: namely, that equivocation and ambiguity are not so much a literary device as an admission (conscious or unconscious) of personal weakness and insecurity. According to this scheme of things, puns are examples of pathology rather than rhetoric. Unrewarding as I find this kind of psychological argument *ad hominem*, nevertheless it does highlight an important fact about Hood's style. Irony and puns are only possible within a group who use words in exactly the same sort of way. Hood's fiercely ironic satires of poverty and injustice were in a tradition that goes back through the eighteenth century at least as far as Swift. They depend as do Swift's on the reader's ability to gauge tone with familiarity and precision. The more pluralistic a society becomes, the more difficult irony becomes. There is a final irony in the way in which Hood's puns and jokes are dependent upon the very consensus of language and values that he, like so many of his socially aware contemporaries, wished to attack.

The variety and range of Hood's output reveals an alteration between crude comic brutality and a much more sensitive social awareness. A writer who can move from the Gothic and grotesque *Haunted House*, or *Eugene Aram*, to the puns of *Nellie Gray*, the social satire of *Miss Kilmansegg and her Precious Leg*, or the bitter social conscience of *The Bridge of Sighs* or *The Song of the Shirt*, however insecure he may have been personally (and how many writers are not?), clearly had also a certain professional and literary confidence. He would have been delighted, but not altogether astonished, to find that children in Soviet Russia learned some of his social poems in translation—just as he was to discover how widely read his poems were when he went to Germany in the 1830s.

Appropriately enough, the full range of Hood's extraordinary sensibility is best exhibited in the "Golden Legend" of *Miss Kilmansegg and her Precious Leg*, which first appeared in parts in the *New Monthly* magazine in 1840, and was then reprinted complete in the *Comic Annual* of 1842. Morality, social satire, buffoonery, and the grotesque are here all intertwined into a single poem of mock epic proportions: some 2,388 lines altogether. The illustrations, by John Leech, Cruickshank's most successful pupil, exactly capture the tone of savage caricature. Its target is one that has consistently inspired fantastic satire from Ben Jonson to Dickens: gold, and the worship of gold in all its forms. The name of the heroine, of course, "killman's egg" is a reference to the legend of the Golden Goose, as the text makes clear:

> For money had stuck to the race through life
> (As it did to the bushel when cash so rife
> Pozed Ali Baba's brother's wife)—
> And down to the Cousins and Cozlings,
> The fortunate brood of the Kilmanseggs,
> As if they had come out of golden eggs,
> Were all as wealthy as "Goslings."[21]

The pace of the verse, with its sustained wit (only sometimes appearing as outright puns), and constant inventiveness, is astonishing—as is the range of feeling, from broad comedy and biting satire to occasional pathos. With all its humor, *Miss Kilmansegg and her Precious Leg* is not primarily a comic poem, but an attack on a society maimed and dehumanized by greed. Miss Kilmansegg is an heiress, born to enormous, and, above all, *conspicuous* wealth. Her christening, for instance, is but the first act of a life of ritually displayed pride and status—translated into its universal currency:

> Gold! and gold! and besides the gold,
> The very robe of the infant told
> A tale of wealth in every fold,
> It lapp'd her like a vapour!
> So fine! so thin! the mind at a loss
> Could compare it to nothing except a cross
> Of cobweb with banknote paper.[22]

> Gold! still gold! it rain'd on the nurse,
> Who, unlike Danae, was none the worse;
> There was nothing but guineas glistening!
> Fifty were given to Doctor James,
> For calling the little Baby names,
> And for saying Amen!
> The Clerk had ten,
> And that was the end of the Christening.[23]

The child grows up, pampered and surrounded by the symbols of wealth even in her games. Her doll is of solid gold, and

> The yearly cost of her golden toys
> Would have given half London's Charity Boys
> And Charity Girls the annual joys
> Of a holiday dinner at Highbury.[24]

When she is still a child, however, her horse ("Banker" "by Bullion out of an Ingot mare") bolts when she is riding in the park, and, as a result of the ensuing accident she has to have her leg amputated. To emphasize the maiming effect of her wealth, Hood now produces his crowning symbol of vulgar ostentation, at once fantasy and satire: her missing leg is replaced by an artificial one of pure gold:

> So a Leg was made in a comely mould,
> Of Gold, fine virgin glittering gold,
> As solid as man could make it—
> Solid in foot, and calf, and shank,

A prodigious sum of money it sank;
In fact 'twas a Branch of the family Bank,
And no easy matter to break it.

All sterling metal—not half-and-half,
The Goldsmith's mark was stamp'd on the calf —
"Twas pure as from Mexican barter!
And to make it more costly, just over the knee,
Where another ligature used to be,
Was a circle of jewels, worth shillings to see,
A newfangled Badge of the Garter!

"Twas a splendid, brilliant, beautiful Leg,
Fit for the Court of ScanderBeg,
That Precious Leg of Miss Kilmansegg!
For, thanks to parental bounty,
Secure from Mortification's touch,
She stood on a member that cost as much
As a Member for all the County![25]

2.4 John Leech: "Her Organ of Veneration."
Illustration to Thomas Hood's Miss Kilmansegg and her Precious Leg *(1842).*

As was intended it should, her fame is spread far and wide by this golden limb, which is prominently displayed on social occasions. When she appears at a Ball as Diana, her tunic "is loop'd up to a gem in front / To shew the Leg that was Golden!" As in *Volpone*, gold has now subverted every human desire. A woman's leg was considered so sexually suggestive that it would normally have been highly indecent to reveal it at all in public, let alone at a Ball (we are entering the age of the crinoline), yet the exhibitionism of her wealth is only applauded. An added irony is introduced by her fancy dress appearance as Diana—the Goddess of Chastity. Naturally inflamed with desire for gain more sordid and artificial than mere sex, suitors of every walk of life pursue her ardently, but in the best tradition of Victorian morality she chooses disastrously, and marries a spendthrift foreign Count who, equally naturally, is only after her money. Eventually, when he has succeeded in gambling away her entire fortune, he tries to persuade her to part with the precious leg itself in order to sell it. When she refuses, he beats her to death with the golden leg and disappears with it.

> Gold, still gold! hard, yellow, and cold,
> For gold she had lived, and she died for gold —
> By a golden weapon—not oaken;
> In the morning they found her all alone —
> Stiff, and bloody, and cold as stone —
> But her Leg, the Golden Leg was gone,
> And the "Golden Bowl was broken!"[26]

Over and over again the refrain of gold, and its corrupting influence is driven home by direct reference and imagery alike. The physical grotesqueness of the golden symbol that (literally) upheld her is constantly emphasized. At their engagement, for instance,

> [I]nstead of the lock that lovers beg,
> The Count received from Miss Kilmansegg
> A model, in small, of her Precious Leg —
> And so the couple were plighted![27]

At her death the coroner's jury finally bring in the verdict of "suicide": "Because her own Leg had killed her!" It is more than just another of Hood's bad jokes.

Hood's work is best understood within a tradition of popular journalism rather than high art, but his pity and indignation are none the less real for being expressed through puns and grotesque fantasy. His influence on his contemporaries was widespread and lasting. On a visit to Germany, when driven out of England by debt and in search of somewhere cheap to live abroad, he found that his books were already widely known. In America no less a person than Poe acclaimed his "marked originality" as "a glowing grotesquerie, uttered with a rushing *abandon* vastly heightening its effect." "The field in which Hood is *distinctive*," he added, "is a borderland between Fancy and Fantasy. In this region he reigns supreme. Nevertheless, he has made successful and frequent excursions, although vacillatingly, into the domain of the true Imagination."[28] Once again we find the fantasy/imagination antithesis being used by a contemporary to distinguish between two very different kinds of sensibility: as it were, the satire of *Miss Kilmansegg and her Precious Leg* and the realism of *The Song of the Shirt*. Yet Hood's own ambivalence—if ambivalence it is—is mirrored by Edgar Allan Poe's. Is it really for his striving towards true imagination that Poe admires him? Or is it rather for the peculiar intensity of his fantasy? When Poe himself uses the word *imagination* in his *Tales of Mystery and Imagination* it is this very element of the fantastic that predominates—and reveals where his own deepest interests lay.

As mentioned 1843, the year after Hood's last *Comic Annual*, saw the publication of the first real Christmas book, Dickens's *A Christmas Carol*. Though written in response to particular circumstances of the day and in a tone that is unmistakably Dickens's alone, it stands in a tradition of popular literature that goes back through Hood and beyond. Its plot is so well known that it is easy for us to forget what an extraordinary story it actually is. Chesterton himself has called attention to one aspect of this—the curious phenomenon of Victorian spirituality:

> [I]n spite of a certain ethical cheeriness that was almost *de rigueur*—the strange fact remains that the only sort of supernaturalism the Victorians allowed their imaginations was a sad supernaturalism. [. . .] When we think [. . .] of the uncountable riches of religious art, imagery, ritual and popular legend that has clustered round Christmas through all the Christian ages, it is a truly extraordinary thing to reflect that Dickens (wishing to have in the *Christmas Carol* a little happy supernaturalism by way of a change) actually had to make up a mythology for himself.[29]

As we shall see, such a view of *A Christmas Carol* is by no means the whole story, but in general the observation is an acute one. Thackeray was quick to notice in his *Grumble about Christmas Books* that Dickens was not alone in this amazing spiritual vacuum of a supposedly religious age. The world of the Christmas books of Hood, Dickens, and Thackeray belonged to a popular literature whose emotional set was light years away from the earnest piety of Evangelical, Broad, or High Churchman alike. Even if we discount the subliterary world of the proliferating tract societies, literally hundreds of "religious" novels were published during the 1840s and 1850s. Kingsley, Thomas Hughes, F. D. Maurice, Manning, and Newman all wrote one or more. Yet, as Newman had perceptively recognized, the medieval synthesis that had produced the mixture of genuine piety and vulgar comedy of the Feast of Fools or the Townley Shepherds' Play had been rejected by a weakened and insecure Protestantism as corruption and blasphemy.[30] After the emotional wholeness and vigor even of Blake or Coleridge, there is all too often something petty, partial, or inhibited about the accepted Christianity of mid-Victorian England. It is little wonder that many of the finest and most sensitive spirits found themselves drawn, in spite of its obvious defects, towards the less truncated vulgarities of Roman Catholicism. Pugin, Newman, Manning, Faber, Hopkins, and even, finally, a broken Oscar Wilde made the journey at a social cost almost inconceivable to the more pluralistic twentieth century.

Just as Hood's Christmas recipe of sentimentality and bizarre satiric fantasy was the product not so much of a religious sensibility as a strongly felt humanitarianism, so Dickens's greatest Christmas myth was first and foremost a response to contemporary revelations about the state of the poor. Earlier in 1843 he had been deeply disturbed to read a Government Blue-book on the conditions of children's employment (the same report that had moved Elizabeth Barrett Browning to write her poem, *The Cry of the Children*) and he had contemplated bringing out "a very cheap pamphlet called An Appeal to the People of England on Behalf of the Poor Man's Child."[31] In October of that year, however, he was invited to speak at the first annual soirée of the Manchester Athenaeum—sharing the platform with such people as Benjamin Disraeli. The Athenaeum was an institute founded to bring culture and education to the working classes, and Dickens in his speech proceeded to expound his passionate belief that education was the answer to England's desperate social problems.

Sometime during that evening in Manchester the idea of *A Christmas Carol* was born. It was composed during long walks about the London streets ("fifteen and twenty miles many a night when all the sober folks had gone to bed . . .") in the intervals of writing *Martin Chuzzlewit*. By the end of November it was finished, and, with a publishing speed not uncommon for those days, Chapman and Hall had it on sale, complete with four hand-colored illustrations by John Leech, by December 17. By Christmas Eve it had sold six thousand copies and was reprinting.

Since *A Christmas Carol* has remained one of the most consistently successful pieces of fantasy ever written, it is worth looking in some detail at just how the fantastic elements serve the basic plot in a way that conventional realism could not do. The story, in essence, hinges upon a problem that was to interest a number of the greatest novelists of the century:

George Eliot and Leo Tolstoy among them.[32] Is "conversion" possible? Is it really the case that a person can suddenly and dramatically change his entire outlook and way of life, as it were overnight? Elsewhere this was to be a theme demanding some of the most lengthy and subtle analyses of realistic fiction; here, the new medium, constituting what Thackeray called a "prose poem," enabled Dickens to work by a hitherto impossible concentration and compression by a series of powerful and emotionally compelling images. The opening scenes of Scrooge alone in his flat above the counting house on Christmas Eve, prepared to quarrel with the "humbug" and hypocrisy of the whole world, is rapidly contrasted with flashbacks to his own youth with the Ghost of Christmas Past, the uneasy present, and especially what is happening in the lives of those most directly affected by him (such as the Crachits), and finally the sinister, dismal, and sordid future with the last Ghost. This technique of concentrating on the juxtaposition of a succession of highly emotive images enables the narrative to move at a great pace, yet at the same time convey an enormous amount of factual information. We see, for instance, the young Scrooge left alone at boarding school over Christmas with nothing but his books, *Ali Baba* and *Robinson Crusoe*, the very diet of fantasy that had delighted Dickens himself as an unhappy child. On a second occasion (implying others in between) he is reprieved at the last moment by his sister, who explains "Father is so much kinder than he used to be. . . ." Encapsulated in the two scenes, and the odd remark, is a whole vision of miserable and isolated childhood. These cheerless vistas are suddenly thrown into even starker relief by the next scene: a nostalgic Christmas to end all nostalgic Christmases at Fezziwig's Ball. Finally, we are shown, by the briefest of glimpses, Scrooge's own ill-fated love affair, and the girl's eventual happy marriage to another poorer, but more warm-hearted, man. The "magic" of the ghost has, in effect, produced a history of Scrooge's own life in a series of "spots of time," comparable in form though not in direction of development, with those of Wordsworth's *Prelude* (not to be published for another seven years) and, like those, used as a means of *psychological* exploration.

The strength of *A Christmas Carol* lies quite simply in its psychological credibility. Supernatural marvels are barren tricks unless they show us aspects of character that we would not otherwise see. The loveless boy Scrooge from an unhappy home, abandoned in his formative years in neglect at the grimmest of schools, is himself unable to give or receive love as an adult. Instead he turns increasingly to the security and, above all, the power that money appears to offer. Money as power is a central theme of Victorian fiction. As Ruskin was to put it:

What is really desired, under the name of riches, is, essentially, power over men; in its simplest sense, the power of obtaining for our own advantage the labour of servant, tradesman, and artist; in wider sense, authority of directing large masses of the nation to various ends [. . .] the art of becoming "rich," in the common sense [. . .] is "the art of establishing the maximum inequality in our own favour."[33]

The will to dominate rather than money per se is thus the key to Scrooge's character—and in this he does *not* change. In the first encounters described at the beginning of the book his delight is always to shock and horrify those with whom he has contact. Bob Crachit can be bullied. The nephew and the benevolent gentleman who seek him out are not merely repulsed, but turned away with a quite flamboyant exhibition of surly misanthropy:

Merry Christmas! Out upon merry Christmas! What's Christmas time to you but a time for paying bills without money; a time for finding yourself a year older, and not an hour richer; a time for balancing your books and having every item in 'em through a round dozen of months presented dead against you? "If I could work my will," said Scrooge indignantly, "every idiot who goes about with 'Merry Christmas,' on his lips, should be boiled with his own pudding, and buried with a stake of holly through his heart. He should!"[34]

2.5 John Leech: "You Don't Believe in Me," Observed the Ghost.
Illustration to Charles Dickens's A Christmas Carol *(1843).*

Scrooge's hatred of mankind and its preposterous benevolence never lacks the rhetorical flourish. Even when he is confronted by Marley's ghost, he does not easily relinquish the conversational initiative, and argues vigorously that the apparition is merely a hallucination with some obvious physical explanation. His utilitarian ethics and sceptical materialism are all of a piece.

> "You don't believe in me," observed the Ghost.
> "I don't," said Scrooge.
> "What evidence would you have of my reality, beyond that of your
>   senses?"
> "I don't know," said Scrooge.
> "Why do you doubt your senses?"
> "Because," said Scrooge, "a little thing affects them. A slight disor-
> der of the stomach makes them cheats. You may be an undigested
> bit of beef, a blot of mustard, a crumb of cheese, a fragment of
> underdone potato. There's more of gravy than of grave about you,
> whatever you are!"[35]

This initial power struggle is repeated with the Ghost of Christmas Past—who, indeed, is eventually "extinguished" by the agonized Scrooge. That he does not similarly resist the second and third Spirits is more due to his growing interest and involvement in what is happening than because he is actually cowed by them.

2.6 John Leech: "Extinguishing the Ghost of Christmas Past."
Illustration to Charles Dickens's A Christmas Carol.

Moreover, Scrooge's attempt to *psychologize* Marley's Ghost is significant in more ways than one. Marley, we notice, never actually disproves Scrooge's claim, and the whole series of visitations and visions can, as he stoutly argues, be interpreted as an *inner* psychological experience. This view, indeed, is actually reinforced by the discovery that what the Ghost of Christmas Yet to Come shows him is not the *real* future at all, but merely projections based upon his present way of life. Tiny Tim, after all, whose death is the excuse for the tear jerking scene in the Crachit family, "did NOT die," and the whole vision is, as it were, a *double* fantasy: one fantasy within another. The Spirits, in fact, cannot be said anywhere to show Scrooge anything that he does not in one sense already know. Nevertheless, even if the argument that Marley's Ghost is merely a "crumb of cheese or a fragment of underdone potato" cannot be disproved, its obstinate

2.7 "The air was filled with phantoms, wandering hither and thither in restless haste, and moaning as they went. Every one of them wore chains like Marley's Ghost. . . . He had been quite familiar with one old ghost in a white waistcoat with a monstrous iron safe attached to his ankle who cried piteously at being unable to assist a wretched woman with an infant, whom it saw below on a doorstep."
John Leech: Illustration to Charles Dickens's A Christmas Carol.

reductionism is instantly refuted existentially: Scrooge is reduced to a terrified submission for the moment by the Ghost, who utters a "frightful cry"
and shakes his chain with "a dismal and appalling noise." What actually
changes Scrooge, however, is not fear, but a stark confrontation with the
basic needs of human life. Again, Marley's Ghost strikes the keynote that is
to be echoed throughout the story:

> "Business!" cried the Ghost, wringing its hands again. "Mankind was my
> business. The common welfare was my business; charity, mercy, forbear-
> ance, and benevolence, were, all, my business. The dealings of my trade
> were but a drop of water in the comprehensive ocean of my business!"[36]

Scrooge is taken back, almost without comment by the Ghost itself, to relive
certain key moments in his former life; he is then shown his present life—
and finally where it will inevitably lead. As we have observed, he is, in one
sense, told nothing new at all; he is merely shown his life as a whole—as a
cumulative development, in the context of Christmas. His attempt to cling
to a mechanistic and deterministic psychology is thus attacked at a quite different level from that at which it sought to provide *explanations*—that of
"charity, mercy, forbearance, and benevolence," and finally personal guilt.

This conviction that personal values are more important than any
systems of mechanistic psychology puts Scrooge's conversion into a familiar category of nineteenth-century experiences. Dickens is showing us an
experience essentially similar to events in the lives of Wordsworth, John
Stuart Mill, or Carlyle, which they came to look back on as turning points
in their lives. In his *Autobiography*, for instance, Mill tells us of how he lost
all sense of value in what he was doing—as he believed, for the good of
mankind—and it was only through reading the poetry of Wordsworth that
he was able to discover:

> a source of inward joy, of sympathetic and imaginative pleasure, which
> could be shared by all human beings; which had no connexion with strug-
> gle or imperfection, but would be made richer by every improvement in
> the physical and social condition of mankind.[37]

Mill's "conversion," like that of Scrooge, is not at first sight a religious one:
he remains this-worldly and humanistic. Moreover, however they may have
appeared to observers, such experiences are not felt by those who under-
went them to be *alterations* of the personality so much as discovery of their
true personality. Similarly, Scrooge's character is not transformed. He

retains all his old desire to shock, startle, and dominate: the purchase of the turkey on Christmas morning ("the one as big as the man"), the surprise visit to his nephew, and the raising of Bob Crachit's wages all have the authentic drama of the old Scrooge. What has been transformed is his feeling of identity with mankind: his realization that what he has lost and needs most is love.

The true paradox of Dickens's construction, of course, is that this psychological credibility is only made possible by the technique of fantasy. The prose poem relates and compresses the action, not merely to the point of being unrealistic, but into literal impossibility:

> "What's today?" cried Scrooge, calling downwards to a boy in
>   Sunday clothes, who perhaps had loitered to look about him.
> "EH?" returned the boy, with all his might of wonder.
> "What's today, my fine fellow?" said Scrooge.
> "Today!" replied the boy. "Why, CHRISTMAS DAY."
> "It's Christmas Day!" said Scrooge to himself. "I haven't missed it.
>   The Spirits have done it all in one night. They can do anything
>   they like. Of course they can. Of course they can."[38]

2.8 John Leech: "Ignorance and Want."
Illustration to Charles Dickens's A Christmas Carol.

All three visitations, it turns out, did miraculously occur on a single night, thus, as it were, foreshortening the perspective and exaggerating the speed of development, without destroying the psychological realism of Scrooge's change of heart. This is the more remarkable since, as we have pointed out, his conversion is apparently not a religious one, but humanitarian. If we compare Scrooge's experience with that, say, of Martin the Cobbler in Tolstoy's short story, *Where Love is, God is*, we can see how strikingly secular is his conversion to universal benevolence. Yet there is more to Dickens's carefully controlled secularity than meets the eye. Tiny Tim, the little child, is set in the midst of his family at Christmas, and he it is who hopes that the people in Church will remember "upon Christmas Day, who made lame beggars walk and blind men see." If we half expect a Christ Child in *A Christmas Carol*, we find only the "meagre, ragged, scowling, wolfish" children clinging pitifully and yet menacingly to the skirts of Christmas Present: Ignorance and Want. The message is clear: divine compassion and charity in the England of the 1840s, means also education in the name of enlightened self-interest.

> "Spirit! are they yours?" Scrooge could say no more.
> "They are Man's," said the Spirit, looking down upon them. "And they cling to me, appealing from their fathers. This boy is Ignorance. This girl is Want. Beware them both, and all of their degree, but most of all beware this boy, for on his brow I see that written which is Doom, unless the writing be erased. Deny it!" cried the Spirit, stretching out its hand towards the city. "Slander those who tell it ye! Admit it for your factious purposes, and make it worse. And bide the end!"
> "Have they no refuge or resource?" cried Scrooge.
> "Are there no prisons?" said the Spirit, turning on him for the last time with his own words. "Are there no workhouses?"
> The bell struck twelve.[39]

What we do not pity now, we shall have cause to fear later.

Fantasy thus performs a dual role in the story. It offers, in an amazing technical *tour de force*, a non-Christian Christmas "magic" that persuades the miser to rediscover his own roots and so effect a conversion, while, at the same time, linking this personal self-discovery directly with universal social problems without any kind of divine intermediary that might soften the stark choice. Thackeray's description of *A Christmas Carol* as a prose poem is peculiarly apt: without breaking natural or psychological realities, it concentrates and compresses them, while securing for the means a willing suspension of disbelief.

How perilous this achievement is can be seen by comparison with another of Dickens's Christmas books, *The Chimes,* that in its own day enjoyed nearly as high a reputation as *A Christmas Carol.* Though it has a social concern that is as strong, if not stronger, the mainspring of the story is somehow lacking. The supernatural or fantastic element, the spirits of the chimes themselves, remain outside the action which, indeed, is much less dynamic altogether. Trotty Veck's vision of the future, terrible and bleak as it is, and drawing on the same horrors of the sweatshop that moved Hood and Kingsley, is simply a *vision*; it does not change people or situations because it is less personal. Veck lacks the drive and robustness of Scrooge. He is never in control, and remains essentially a spectator at the end as he was at the beginning. The fantasy is enclosed in a little story within a story. This greater passivity of character, and therefore of plot, is reflected in a diminished intensity and vitality of language. Entertaining as it often is as a piece of prose, the opening of *The Chimes* seems merely idiosyncratic and "Dickensian" in the most whimsical sense beside the humorous dramatic suspense of the famous opening on Marley's death in *A Christmas Carol.*

> They were old chimes, trust me. Centuries ago, these Bells had been baptized by bishops; so many centuries ago that the register of their baptism was lost long, long before the memory of man: and no one knew their names. They had had their Godfathers and Godmothers, these Bells (for my own part, by the way, I would rather incur the responsibility of being Godfather to a Bell than a Boy): and had had their silver mugs no doubt, besides. But time had mowed down their sponsors, and Harry the Eighth had melted down their mugs: and now they hung, nameless and mugless, in the church tower.
>
> Not speechless, though. Far from it. They had clear, loud, lusty, sounding voices, had these Bells; and far and wide they might be heard upon the wind. Much too sturdy Chimes were they, to be dependent on the pleasure of the wind, moreover; for, fighting gallantly against it when it took an adverse whim, they would pour their cheerful notes into a listening ear right royally.[40]

The Chimes was published the year after *A Christmas Carol,* for Christmas 1844, and, as Dickens had hoped, it was an even greater success. Five dramatizations appeared on the London stage within weeks. Twenty thousand copies were sold inside three months. The political message, even more explicit than that of *A Christmas Carol,* aroused fierce controversy among critics—as Dickens had intended it should. Yet less critical attention was paid to the way in which this greater social realism had, paradoxically, weakened the overall reality of the plot. Deprived of the single organizing vision that had commanded willing suspension of disbelief in the first book, much of the writing in *The Chimes* remains episodic and merely clever. The fantasy removed, we are left with fancy.

> The wind came tearing round the corner—especially the east wind—as if it had sallied forth, express, from the confines of the earth, to have a blow at Toby. And oftentimes it seemed to come upon him sooner than it had expected, for bouncing round the corner, and passing Toby, it would suddenly wheel round again, as if it cried "Why, here he is!" Incontinently his little white apron would be caught up over his head like a naughty boy's garments, and his feeble little cane would be seen to wrestle and struggle unavailingly in his hand, and his legs would undergo tremendous agitation, and Toby himself all aslant, and facing now in this direction, now in that, would be so banged and buffeted, and touzled, and worried, and hustled, and lifted off his feet, as to render it a state of things but one degree removed from a positive miracle, that he wasn't carried up bodily into the air as a colony of frogs or snails or other portable creatures sometimes are, and rained down again, to the great astonishment of the natives, on some strange corner of the world where ticket porters are unknown.[41]

This is a very "Dickensian" piece, but it could come from almost any book. It was, as Thackeray acutely pointed out, the worst features of Dickens's whimsical style, devoid of their function within the overall scheme, that most attracted the legion of inferior imitators.

> "To see the faults of a great master, look at his imitators," Reynolds says in his *Discourses*; and the sins of Mr. Dickens" followers must frighten that gentleman not a little. Almost every one of the Christmas carollers are exaggerating the master's own exaggerations, and caricaturing the face of nature most shamefully. Every object in the world is brought to life, and invested with a vulgar knowingness and outrageous jocularity. Winds used to whistle in former days, and oaks to toss their arms in the storm. Winds are now made to laugh, to howl, to scream, to triumph, to sing choruses; trees to squint, to shiver, to leer, to grin, to smoke pipes, dance hornpipes and smoke those of tobacco.[42]

It is hardly surprising that when, in 1853, Thackeray himself was at last tempted into producing a Christmas fantasy, he should have sternly eschewed all possibility of comparison with Dickens, and attempted to put into practice his own prescription of 1847.

That's your proper sort of pantomime business–that's the right way in Christmas books. Haven't you seen the Clown in the play; his head cut off by the butcher and left on the block before all beholders; his limbs severally mangled and made into polonies, and yet in two minutes he says, "How are you?" (the droll dog!) as lively as ever? Haven't we seen Pantaloon killed before our very eyes, put pitilessly into his mother's mangle, brought out from that instrument utterly dead, and stretched eighteen feet in length?–and are we hurt, are our feelings outraged? No, we know Harlequin will have him alive in two minutes by a quiver of his stick [. . .] And as in pantomimes, so I say in Christmas stories, those fire-side Christmas pantomimes, which are no more natural than Mother Goose or Harlequin Gulliver.[43]

2.9 William Makepeace Thackeray: The Count of Hogginarmo is Annoyed with His Servants. Illustration to W. M. Thackeray's The Rose and the Ring.

The Rose and the Ring is indeed described by Thackeray in the prelude as being "a fire-side pantomime" in exactly this sense. It was, he says, written to accompany a series of drawings he had made for his family while staying in Italy. The image of the pantomime echoes the 1823 preface to Grimm's fairytales. We shed no tears for the Count of Hogginarmo when he is gobbled up by the ravening lions "bones, boots, and all." But as in all good pantomimes there is a moral to the story as well. In his 1847 article on Christmas books Thackeray had been very decided on the subject of morals to fairy stories.

> If a man wants to make a mere fantastic tale, nobody calls upon him to be tight and close in his logic. If he wants to moralize, his proposition should be neat and clear, as his argument is correct. I am reconciled now to the Wolf eating up Red Riding Hood (though I was sceptical in my childhood on this point), because I have given up believing that this is a moral tale altogether, and am content to receive it as a wild, odd, surprising and not unkindly fairy story.[44]

But in the hands of Thackeray—the cynical old puppetmaster of *Vanity Fair*—the element of self-parody is never very far from the surface. He cannot lose himself in his story as Dickens frequently does. The description of Dickens reading *The Chimes* aloud with tears streaming down his face exhibits a totally different kind of sensibility. Reflecting a growing sophistication of popular taste in the 1850s, *The Rose and the Ring* not merely advances propositions that are neat and clear, but contrives to satirize both its own moral confidence, and the conventions of the fairy story itself.

But by 1855 the conventions of the fairy story were themselves changing. The most important single influence was probably the volume of Hans Andersen's *Wonderful Stories for Children,* which Thackeray had praised so enthusiastically in his 1847 review. It was only one of five translations of Andersen's stories to appear that year—indicating both his enormous popularity and the growing market for fairy stories as a genre. Up to this time such stories had been retold, rather than made up—even Robert Southey's *The Three Bears* is now known to be a reworking of an earlier tale.[45] Now, at the same time as Andersen's original stories were finding a public, two English writers also tried their hands at totally original creations. So far as is known, John Ruskin's *The King of the Golden River* is the first original English fairy story. Though it had actually been composed by the youthful Ruskin for the twelve-year-old Effie Gray in 1841, it was not published until ten years later for a public that he hoped had been made more receptive by Andersen. The basic plot, with two evil brothers, Schwartz and Hans, and their kindly younger one, Gluck, is conventional enough, nevertheless, the story is unmistakably nineteenth-century in tone, with a clear moral, and a certain restrained wit in the telling. Quite the most memorable and original character, however, is the South West Wind, who is possibly the first magical personage in fiction to show that combination of kindliness and eccentric irascibility that was to appear so strongly in a whole tradition of subsequent literature, including Thackeray's Fairy Blackstick, Nesbit's Psammead, and even Tolkien's Gandalf.

> He had a very large nose, slightly brass-coloured; his cheeks were very round, and very red, and might have warranted a supposition that he had been blowing a refractory fire for the last eight and forty hours; his eyes twinkled merrily through long silky eyelashes, his moustaches curled twice round a like a corkscrew on each side of his mouth, and his hair, of a curious mixed pepper and salt colour, descended far over his shoulders. He was about four feet six in height, and wore a conical pointed cap of nearly the same altitude, decorated with a black feather some three feet long. His doublet was prolonged behind into something resembling a violent exaggeration of what is now termed a "swallow tail" but was much obscured by the swelling folds of an enormous black, glossy looking cloak, which must have been very much too long in calm weather, as the wind, whistling round the old house, carried it clear out from the wearer's shoulders to about four times his own length.[46]

2.10 Richard Doyle: "The South West Wind Esq." Illustration to John Ruskin's The King of the Golden River. *Note the rustic frame to the picture.*

In payment for his inhospitable reception by the two elder brothers on a wet and gusty night, he promises to return at twelve—which he does, with complete punctuality.

> The two brothers sat up on their bolster, and stared into the darkness. The room was full of water, and by a misty moonbeam, which found its way through a hole in the shutter, they could see in the midst of it an enormous foam globe, spinning round, and bobbing up and down like a cork, on which, as on a most luxurious cushion, reclined the little old gentleman, cap and all. There was plenty of room for it now, for the roof was off!
>
> "Sorry to incommode you," said their visitor, ironically. "I'm afraid your beds are dampish; perhaps you had better go to your brother's room. I've left the ceiling on, there."[47]

In 1846, however, another book had appeared that is a much more clear ancestor of *The Rose and the Ring*. Francis Edward Paget's *The Hope of the Katzekopfs*, is of the same brand as *The King of the Golden River* in its clearly defined moral with allegorical undertones. To those who know *The Rose and the Ring*, other elements of the plot are immediately familiar. When a long hoped-for son is born to the Fairy King and Queen, they do not invite the bad tempered fairy Abracadabra to the christening. Naturally, she comes nonetheless, and gives the baby prince the name of Eigenwillig ("self-will"). In due course he lives up to his name. Eventually Abracadabra retrieves the situation by literally drawing him out—into a long thin elastic string. Pulling him through a keyhole she rolls him into a bouncy rubber ball which is sent all over the kingdom as she wishes. Both the court christening and something of the zany humor of this story are picked up by Thackeray for his fire-side pantomime, which, as he frequently stresses runs exactly according to the rules of all such stories: no matter if the actual conventions that he implies are immemorial (at least as old as Paflagonia "ten or twenty thousand years ago") are many of them less than ten years old.

What is, perhaps, most original about the plot of *The Rose and the Ring* is that the greatest moral development takes place not in any of the human characters, but in the formidable Fairy Blackstick herself—the originator of all the magic in the story. Before the tale opens at all she has tried, and become tired of, the normal devices of supernatural justice.

> She had scores of royal godchildren; turned numberless wicked people into beasts, birds, millstones, clocks, pumps, bootjacks, umbrellas, or

other absurd shapes; and in a word was one of the most active and offi-
cious of the whole College of fairies.

But after two or three thousand years of this sport, I suppose Blackstick grew tired of it. Or perhaps she thought, "What good am I doing by
sending this Princess to sleep for a hundred years? by fixing a black
pudding on to that booby's nose? by causing diamonds and pearls to drop
from one little girl's mouth, and vipers and toads from another's? I begin
to think I do as much harm as good by my performances. I might as well
shut my incantations up and allow things to take their natural course.

"There were my two young goddaughters, King Savio's wife, and
Duke Padella's wife: I gave them each a present, which was to render
them charming in the eyes of their husbands, and secure the affection of
those gentlemen as long as they lived. What good did my Rose and Ring
do those two women? None on earth. From having all their whims
indulged by their husbands, they became capricious, lazy, ill-humoured,
absurdly vain, and leered and languished, and fancied themselves irre-
sistibly beautiful, when they were really old and hideous."[48]

When she is invited, in the normal course of events, to the christenings of
the baby Prince Giglio, son of King Savio of Pafiagonia and the Princess
Rosalba, daughter of King Calvafiore of Crim Tartary, she merely wishes

2.11 William Makepeace Thackeray: "His Royal Highness the Prince of Crim Tartary."
One of Thackeray's own illustrations to The Rose and the Ring—*satirizing both*
the conventions of the fairy story and the sanctity of monarchy.

each of them "a little misfortune" and sails out of the window. As is only proper with fairy wishes, they come true. On the death of Savio, the throne of Paflagonia is usurped by his brother, Valoroso, and Calvafiore is shortly afterwards murdered and replaced by the rebellious Duke Padella. The two new monarchs have learnt the lesson with regard to capricious fairies and Blackstick is not invited to the christenings of Angelica and Bulbo, their respective offspring. Unblessed with misfortune in any shape, they grow up, petted and spoiled, in the lap of luxury, while Giglio and Rosalba, reduced to menial roles, learn humility through suffering. The Dickensian theme of the need for education is repeated with comic exaggeration. Rosalba, now the Princess Angelica's maid and companion, scrapes together her education by attending Angelica's lessons with her, while Giglio, who has spent an idle and dissolute youth, has to make up for lost time by strenuous application, living in fear of discovery under the assumed name of "Giles."

> So he sat down and worked away, very, very hard for a whole year, during which "Mr. Giles" was quite an example to all the students in the University of Bosforo. He never got into any riots or disturbances. The professors all spoke well of him, and the students liked him too; so that, when at examinations he took all the prizes, viz:—

The Spelling Prize	The French Prize
The Writing Prize	The Arithmetic Prize
The History Prize	The Latin Prize
The Chatechism Prize	The Good Conduct Prize

> all his fellow students said, "Hurray! Hurray for Giles! Giles is the boy— the student's joy! Hurray for Giles!" And he brought quite a quantity of medals, crowns, books, and tokens of distinction home to his lodgings.[49]

The payoff for this prodigious feat of learning comes only a few pages further on, when Giglio, throwing off his disguise, confronts the vanguard of the vast Paflagonian Army under its veteran commander, Captain Hedzoff who calls on the Prince to surrender his sword: "we are thirty thousand men to one!"

> "Give up my sword! Giglio give up his sword!" cried the Prince; and stepping well forward on the balcony, the royal youth without preparation delivered a speech so magnificent, that no report can do justice to it. It was all in blank verse (in which, from this time, he invariably spoke, as more becoming his majestic station). It lasted for three days, and three nights, during which not a single person who heard him was tired, or

remarked the difference between daylight and dark. The soldiers only cheering tremendously, when occasionally, once in nine hours, the Prince paused to suck an orange, which Jones took out of the bag [. . .] and at the end of this extraordinary, this truly gigantic effort, Captain Hedzoff flung up his helmet, and cried, "Hurray! Hurray! Long live King Giglio!"

Such were the consequences of having employed his time well at College![50]

In the manner of all good fairy stories, however, virtue is not left to be its own reward, and in the battle that follows Giglio is equipped by the Fairy Blackstick with nothing but the best. His suit of armor is not merely dazzling to the eyes, it has the added advantages of being waterproof, gun proof, and sword-proof. "Besides the fairy armour, the Prince had a fairy horse, which would gallop at any pace you please; and a fairy sword, which would lengthen and run through a whole regiment of enemies at once."[51] Not unnaturally, his opponent, King Padella, feels the injustice of the odds against him, and sensibly gives up at once. "If," says he to Giglio, "you ride a fairy horse, and wear fairy armour, what on earth is the use of my hitting you?" The point is well taken by the magnanimous Giglio, a satisfactory peace is forthwith concluded, Giglio marries Rosalba, and the virtuous live happily ever after.

The Rose and the Ring is in many ways no more than Thackeray claimed it to be: a Christmas entertainment for the family. It has, for instance, none of the urgency or power of *A Christmas Carol.* Yet, technically, it marks an important change in Victorian sensibility. The elements of self-parody, the use of fantasy both to present a *serious* moral, and, simultaneously to satirize the magical means by which the virtuous (and hard working!) are rewarded, and the wicked and idle punished, show a real change of tone from the earlier popular literature of both Hood and Dickens. As if to make the separation of categories doubly plain, Hood's poems were posthumously collected and bound in two twin volumes, marked *comic* and *serious* respectively. Dickens mingled his serious message with passages of comedy, but the basic earnestness of that message is similarly never tampered with. By contrast, Thackeray's technique looks forward to the much more complex and ambiguous comedy of Kingsley in *The Water Babies*, which parodies the very moral it wished to affirm, and is always ready to satirize an uncritical acceptance of its own message. From the 1850s onward fantasy is more self-conscious, more free, flexible, and reflexive, inviting the reader to accept, but to think about the nature of this or her acceptance. Thackeray points the way toward the role fantasy was to play in bridging the divided halves of the Victorian psyche. The next developments in fantasy were to come from a very different stratum of the literary world, but the works of Kingsley, Carroll, Lear, and MacDonald owe much to the vigorous and popular journalistic tradition which preceded them.

Chapter 3

Dreams and Nightmares

Monsters under the Hill

Mary Shelley's *Frankenstein* was the climax of two very different tendencies in Romanticism, combining a fascination with the bizarre and unnatural, with a quest for greater psychological realism. According to legend, her story originated with what must be the most sensational recitation ever given of Coleridge's *Christabel*. Lord Byron had first come across the poem from Walter Scott in 1815, and at his request had been given a manuscript copy by Coleridge. The following summer he met Percy Bysshe Shelley in Geneva. With Shelley were two women: Mary Godwin, with whom he had just eloped, and Claire Clairmont, her stepsister, who had already seduced Byron in London, and by whom she was already pregnant. With Byron was a party that included his personal physician and secretary, Polidori, an Italian Scot whose sister was later to be mother to the Rossettis.[1] The *New Monthly Magazine* takes up the story: "It appears that one evening Lord Byron, Mr. P. B. Shelley, the two ladies and the gentleman before alluded to, having perused a German work, which was entitled *Phantasmagoriana*, began relating ghost stories; when his lordship having recited the beginning of *Christabel*, then unpublished, the whole took so strong a hold of Mr. Shelley's mind, that he suddenly started up and ran out of the room. The physician and Lord Byron followed, and discovered him leaning against a mantelpiece with cold drops of perspiration trickling down his face."[2] He was duly revived (by another account) with "a douche of cold water and a whiff of ether." Apparently while he was listening to the terrifying description of the Lady Geraldine undressing, Shelley had been suddenly overcome by the hallucination of eyes instead of nipples in Mary's breasts. The upshot was a competition at writing horror stories. Polidori produced a novel called *The Vampyre*, and Mary, *Frankenstein*.

Unfortunately for the legend, it appears from other records that they actually began writing their stories on June 17, the night before these dramatic events, but Mary Shelley's account of her difficulties in beginning suggest that Coleridge's poem may indeed have acted as a trigger.

So Christabel (or perhaps one should say, Geraldine) was, as it were, stepmother to the most famous monster of the century—if not of all time. But, as befits such parentage, the exact nature of Frankenstein's monster is more ambiguous than his popular reputation usually allows. In one sense, of course, *Frankenstein* is what it is assumed to be, a horror story, and a worthy founder of the tradition of twentieth-century horror films that bear the name—worthy, that is, in that the horrors are always faintly disappointing, never delivering quite the *frisson* they promise. In another, and much more interesting sense, however, it can be read as a story of maternal deprivation, with a theme that links it with Rousseau, Wordsworth, Freud, Spock, and Bowlby. The monster is not innately depraved: he desires love, but because he never receives it, even from his creator, he is unable to give it. He is the product of a bad environment in a true Godwinian sense, made and destroyed by harsh and unjust circumstances beyond his control. In short, he is the first *psychologized* monster. On the one hand, we can sympathize with him, and understand why he is as he is; on the other, we are never allowed to forget that he is a deadly and ruthless killer, possessed of superhuman powers of strength, endurance, and—hatred. Mary Shelley's novel epitomizes the Romantic process of *internalization*: being a monster is a quality of mind.

There has recently been a huge revival of interest in *Frankenstein*—partly aided by Kenneth Branagh's 1994 hugely enjoyable film, *Mary Shelley's Frankenstein*—and the book has been given a variety of intriguing interpretations, ranging from feminist to philosophical,[3] but one of the biggest problems the book faces is that the complexity of reference is never matched by the probability of the story itself.

A modern critic, George Levine, greeted a new edition of *Frankenstein* with the comment that "it is so extraordinarily silly a book that it seems either pretentious or absurd to treat it [. . .] as a text to be edited. [. . .] By most standards of reasonable literary judgement, *Frankenstein* should have died shortly after its first popular success."[4] One recalls a similar tone in F. R. Leavis's baffled strictures on *Wuthering Heights*. Both critics seem nonplussed by the combination of evident power and absurd irrationality that seems to characterize so many of the great myths of Gothic literature. Both actually use the same description, "one of the great freaks of English literature," of the two books. It is as if the whole Gothic convention somehow eludes the normal methods of criticism, and achieves its psychological power by some means deeper and more primitive than mere probability or truth to life. There is a sense of having encountered a quality outside the normal scope of literature as it is commonly understood. "After all," remarks Levine, "what are we really to do with a book whose initial dramatic moment is of a man in a dogsled mushing across the Arctic Ocean, pausing to look up at the captain of a ship only recently unlocked from the ice, and speaking with drawing room politeness: 'Before I come on board your vessel [. . .] will you have the kindness to inform me whither you are bound?'" It is, he concludes, "uproarious camp." Perhaps so. But let us look at the passage in question:

> About two o'clock the mist cleared away, and we beheld, stretched out in every direction, vast and irregular plains of ice, which seemed to have no end. Some of my comrades groaned, and my own mind began to grow watchful with anxious thoughts, when a strange sight suddenly attracted our attention, and diverted our solicitude from our own situation. We perceived a low carriage, fixed on a sledge and drawn by dogs, pass towards the north, at the distance of half a mile: a being which had the shape of a man, but apparently of gigantic stature, sat on the sledge, and guided the dogs. We watched the rapid progress of the traveller with our telescopes, until he was lost among the distant inequalities of the ice.
>
> This appearance excited our unqualified wonder. We were, as we believed, many hundreds of miles from any land. [. . .] In the morning, however, as soon as it was light, I went upon deck, and found all the sailors busy on one side of the vessel, apparently talking to someone in the sea. It was, in fact, a sledge, like that we had seen before, which had drifted towards us in the night, on a large fragment of ice. Only one dog remained alive; but there was a human being within it, whom the sailors were persuading to enter the vessel. He was not, as the other traveller seemed to be, a savage inhabitant of some undiscovered island, but an European. When I appeared on deck, the master said, "Here is our captain, and he will not allow you to perish on the open sea."
>
> On perceiving me, the stranger addressed me in English, although with a foreign accent. "Before I come on board your vessel," said he, "will you have the kindness to inform me whither you are bound?"
>
> You may conceive my astonishment on hearing such a question addressed to me from a man on the brink of destruction, and to whom I should have supposed that my vessel would have been a resource which he would not have exchanged for the most precious wealth the earth can afford.[5]

Camp this may be for some, but, as Levine himself observes, what we are left with are certain overwhelming images. The plot is unimportant; we forget it quickly enough. What we recall is the *image* of a vast shape speeding over the ice on its mysterious and unexplained errand, and of the *image* of his pursuer so obsessed with his purpose that nothing else can concern him. It is this preponderance of image over plot that is the hallmark of the Gothic convention. Dismiss the plot of *The Castle of Otranto*: what we remember is the huge hand and helmet. Who can remember the plot of *The Mysteries of Udolpho*? It is the image of Emily alone on the darkened battlements, or before the mysterious picture that we recall, as we do the ghastly bleeding nun in Lewis's *The Monk*.

I suggested earlier that the Gothic convention provided, in effect, a *language* to describe certain areas of human experience for which no other then existed. But in what sense are we describing a language here? The metaphor is clearly not the right one, for it seems to imply something sequential—order, development, plot. The very words put it into the wrong mental set. What we are apparently faced with here is a very peculiar paradox: a literary medium that doesn't tell us a story, so much as offer verbal *pictures*. The Gothic did not work by sequential arguments against the excessive rationality of the eighteenth-century system builders, but by flashes that haunt the waking mind like the images of dreams. Coleridge's *Christabel* is, in this sense, the complete antithesis of *The Ancient Mariner*. It should not be treated as unfinished narrative poem at all, but simply for what it is: a series of powerful and interlinked images. One might perhaps describe it, in this way, as the purest exercise in the Gothic mode ever attempted. Similarly, those critics who, like Levine, complain that *Frankenstein* has no ending are beside the point. What ending *could* there be after that opening vision of the monstrous pursuit across the ice?

This was a question that was being asked of other even more monstrous and disturbing visions as the century progressed. In 1812 Baron Cuvier, Europe's most eminent anatomist, startled the scientific world by announcing that a pair of jaws over four feet long, that had been dug up in a chalk mine at Maestricht in 1770, had belonged to an extinct monster of truly gigantic proportions. The remains of other vast creatures, apparently dating from before the Flood, were coming to light in quarries and chalk pits in southern England. In 1822 Gideon Mantell, a general practitioner from Lewes in Sussex, had his attention drawn by his wife to some fossil teeth in a pile of chalk by the roadside, and realized from their size that they could belong to no known animal. By 1825 he was able to publish a description of the complete animal—naming it, from the similarity of the teeth to those of the modern iguana, an "Iguanadon."[6] In Oxford, the Professor of Geology, the Rev. William Buckland had published the year before an account of another huge skeleton found in a local quarry which he called simply a "Megalosaurus."[7] Though the term was not coined until 1841, the great age of Dinosaur discovery had begun. Monsters, more vast and variegated than the most fantastic imagination could dream of, were now suddenly being found under people's very feet. They were in a few years to reshape man's whole way of thinking about his world—and about himself.

On Tuesday, April 11 1848, the Theological Examiners at Cambridge asked the question: "Give the date of the deluge." The correct answer, as candidates would have been expected to know off pat, was "2348 B.C., or 1656 after the Creation of the world."[8] What the discoveries of the prehistoric monsters had put at stake in the most dramatic way was a time change of dizzying magnitude. As we can see from those Cambridge examiners, even as late as the 1840s it was still possible for educated people to accept the time scale worked out from biblical chronology by Archbishop Ussher in the seventeenth century. He had, with remarkable precision, discovered that the world was created at 9 a.m. on October 23, 4004 B.C. For a short while it looked as if men like Buckland were right in believing that geology was merely confirming scripture by showing the remains of the great beasts that had perished in Noah's flood, but it was not possible to maintain such a position for very long in spite of E. Nesbit's grandfather, Anthony Nesbit, who in his *Essay on Education* (1841) claimed that the prehistoric animals had become extinct because Noah had left them out of the ark. Increasingly geological evidence showed that the strata in which the fossils were discovered were hundreds of millions of years old. "Catastrophist" geological theories, such as that of the Flood, were demolished by Lyell's *Principles of Geology* (1830–1833); Mantell's *Wonders of Geology* followed in 1838. In less than a generation, the monsters from underground had shattered an entire world picture and confronted man with dark, unimaginable vistas of prehuman history.

For the theologically minded there were special problems. On the "principle of plenitude" it was argued that at the Creation God had made every possible species so as to leave no links incomplete in the Great Chain of Being.[9] For many, it was inconceivable that a good God had doomed whole species to complete extinction. For a time some clung to the hope that examples of these creatures might be discovered still living in remote parts of the world. But worse possibilities than extinction of individual species were to follow. Because the Mosasaurus, the first prehistoric monster to be described by Cuvier, had been (correctly) interpreted as a giant lizard, the other discoveries of Buckland and Mantell were also seen as lizard-like.[10] But in 1841 Richard Owen, Professor at the Royal College of Surgeons in London, in an address to the British Association, showed that the Iguanadon, Megalosaurus, and Hylaeosaurus (the gigantic "Wealden Lizard" with scaly armored plates, discovered by Mantell in 1832) were structurally quite different from lizards, and, indeed, from all existing reptiles. They were, argued Owen, a new and hitherto unknown class of animals for which he proposed the name *Dinosauria* or "terrible lizard." As even Tennyson had realized in *In Memoriam* (1850), the evidence for the disappearance of whole classes of animals was there for all to read, and though Darwin's *Origin of Species* was not published until 1859, it had been substantially completed by the mid-1840s. For such devout biblical literalists as the zoologist Philip Gosse, the choice between science and religion was an agonizing one—which he finally solved by what might perhaps be described as the greatest piece of Victorian fantasy of all. In his book *Omphalos* (1847) he argued that though we knew by divine revelation that the world *was* created some six thousand years ago, it was created complete with an instant *past*: with sedimentary strata, fossils, and all the evidence "of the slow development of organic forms."[11] The actual point of creation is therefore scientifically undetectable, and can only be known by special revelation. For scornful reviewers of the day, this was simply an argument that "God hid the fossils in the rocks in order to tempt geologists into infidelity"; Kingsley commented that he could not "believe that God had written on the rocks one enormous and superfluous lie." It is slightly surprising that science fiction writers have been so slow to take up such an ingenious idea.

By this time the prehistoric monsters, terrifying or fascinating according to the individual's standpoint, had captured the imagination of Victorian Britain. The earliest calculations, indeed, had made them even more vast and fabulous than they turned out to be. Comparing the teeth and clavicle of the Iguanadon with the present day iguana suggested the former might be 100 feet in length, comparisons of the femora and the claw bone gave figures of 75–80 feet, and the largest specimen, by these calculations, would be over 200 feet long.[12] The scientific debate over their exact size, however, is less important for our purposes than the popular impact of these discoveries. In 1852, when the Crystal Palace was moved from Hyde Park to its permanent site at Sydenham, Prince Albert suggested that there should be replicas of some of the newly discovered monsters put up in the grounds. The sculptor commissioned, Benjamin Waterhouse Hawkins, thought at first in terms of the great extinct mammals like the Mastodon, but once he had encountered Owen's descriptions of the Mesozoic giants he was fired with the ambition to "revivify the ancient world" of the great dinosaurs. On the islands in the six-acre lake at Sydenham he constructed life size models of what it was believed the Iguanodon, Hylaeosaurus, Megalosaurus and others had looked like. The largest weighed thirty tons— and it is a tribute to Hawkins's thoroughness and workmanship that they are still there today. To celebrate the completion of the project, a dinner for twenty-one leading scientists was held inside the shell of the almost completed Iguanodon, with Owen in place of honor, literally at the head. The new dinosaur park was opened by Queen Victoria and Prince Albert in the presence of forty thousand spectators in June 1854. Owen and Hawkins had created a wildly inaccurate but popular image of the great saurians that was to last for more than a generation.

3.1 "Hawkins's Workshop at the Crystal Palace, Syndenham."
Illustrated London News, December 31, 1853.

*3.2 Gustave Doré, "And God Said: Let the Waters Generate Reptile
with Spawn Abundant" (*Paradise Lost *VII.387–88).*

These discoveries, spectacularly illustrated by the Crystal Palace models, had a predictable effect on contemporary art and literature. If we compare the monsters created by the early Victorian artists with those of the
late eighteenth century, the difference is startling. The weird creatures of
James Jefferys (1751–1784) or the better known sea monsters of John
Hamilton Mortimer (1740–1779) are clearly descended from the half-
human species of classical mythology—fauns, centaurs, and tritons. Though
they have scales and claws and often tails, their scale is essentially a human
one. They even have human faces. In contrast, for the Victorian artists the
wildest outsize dreams of the Romantics were suddenly a reality. Images of

horror which had always leaned toward the slimy and scaly became more specifically reptilian. Martin, for instance, was quick to reinterpret the monsters of *Paradise Lost* in terms of the new realism. Nor was his interest a dilettante one. Mantell, who had just obtained the fossils of a newly discovered Iguanodon at Maidstone, noted in his diary for September 27, 1834:

> Among the visitors who have besieged my house today was Mr. John Martin (and his daughter) the most celebrated, most justly celebrated artist, whose wonderful conceptions are the finest production of Modern art. Mr. Martin was deeply interested in the remains of the Iguanodon etc. I wish I could induce him to portray the Country of the Iguanodon: no other pencil but his should attempt such a subject.[13]

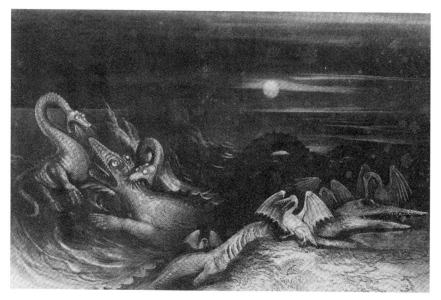

3.3 John Martin: The Great Sea Dragons as They Lived.

Mantell must have guessed that Martin was not likely to miss such a chance. The first edition of Mantell's *Wonders of Geology* in 1838 had a frontispiece by Martin entitled "The Country of the Iguanodon." Almost at the same time, Martin produced another even more dramatic mezzotint of "The Great Sea Dragons as they Lived" for Thomas Hawkins's *The Book of the Great Sea Dragons: Ichthyosauri and Plesiosauri* (1840). Other illustrators followed where Martin led. Forty years later his great rival in the fantastic, Gustave Doré, commissioned variously to illustrate Dante, Milton, and the Bible, freely adapted the vast and grotesque images of Martin and Hawkins to suit his needs. Similarly, it was small wonder that John Tenniel, when he undertook (somewhat reluctantly) to illustrate *Through the Looking Glass* in 1871, should have given the Jabberwocky the leathery wings of a ptero-dactyl and the long scaly neck and tail of a sauropod. Aubrey Beardsley's *Questing Beast*, for his illustrations to Malory, or H. J. Ford's illustrations to the *Fairy Books* of Andrew Lang show the same tradition continuing through various forms of stylization to the end of the century and beyond.

3.4 John Tenniel: "Jabberwocky" from Lewis Carroll's Through the Looking Glass.

Similar examples of the wave of popular interest in dinosaurs created by the Crystal Palace models can be found in contemporary literature. Dickens's Megalosaurus, "forty feet long or so, waddling like an elephan-tine lizard up Holborn Hill" in the muddy simile at the beginning of *Bleak House* in 1852, is well known. Yet this kind of reference, with its vivid sense of the humorous grotesque, nevertheless only serves to illustrate how far Dickens is in mood from those who came to find in the dinosaurs and other prehistoric creatures the true image of the monsters of the mind.

3.5 Anon.: "The Ice Monster" from Charles Kingsley's Madam How and Lady Why.

Francisco Goya's painting, *The Sleep of Reason brings forth Monsters*, has been taken as the visual archetype of the Romantic interest in irrational and unconscious mental states.[14] If so, the nightmare creatures of the fossils, and the chilly but unmistakable hints of mutation and extinction of species they implied, gave to these irrational fascinations a local habitation and a name without exorcising their terrors. The anonymous illustrator of Kingsley's *Madam How and Lady Why* manages to sum up the popular associations of geology with a drawing of a glacier as an "ice monster." Martin's battling monsters of the deep stand out white against a background darkness scarcely penetrated by the light of the setting sun (or it is moon?) behind them. They seem to stand out momentarily against the abyss of time in which they wallow—an image to be paralleled by that of the far future in H. G. Wells's *The Time Machine* (1895).

Not until the second half of the century, however, do we find any real literary synthesis of the psychological tradition of the striking Gothic image with the new and fantastic forms suggested by the fossil discoveries and the accompanying wave of evolutionary theorizing. Kingsley's Doasyoulikes in *The Water Babies* (1863), who degenerated into apes unable to say "Am I not a man and a brother?" must be among the first evolutionary fables.

3.6 Arthur Hughes: "Goblins."
Illustration to George MacDonald's The Princess and the Goblin.

Significantly, it is degeneration, not progress, that interests him. In the same mode, but more original was George MacDonald, whose "volutionary models seem to owe more to Lamarck than Darwin, but very little directly to either. The Goblins, in *The Princess and the Goblin*, for instance, were once "very much like other people" but had either been driven or chosen to go underground, and there "they had greatly altered in the course of generations" in their new environment. "They were now, not ordinarily ugly, but either absolutely hideous, or ludicrously grotesque both in face and form."[15] The transformation of the Goblins, however, was nothing to what had happened to their animals, the "cob's creatures":

> The original stocks of these horrible creatures were very much the same as the animals now seen about the farms and homes in the country, with the exception of a few of them, which had been wild creatures, such as foxes, and indeed wolves and bears, which the goblins, from their proclivity towards the animal creation, had caught when cubs and tamed. But in

the course of time all had undergone even greater changes than had passed upon their owners. They had altered—that is, their descendents had altered—into such creatures as I have not attempted to describe except in the vaguest manner—the various parts of their bodies assuming, in an apparently arbitrary and self-willed manner, the most abnormal developments. Indeed, so little did any distinct type predominate in some of the bewildering results, that you could only have guessed at any known animal as the original, and even then, what likeness remained would be more one of general expression than of definable conformation. But what increased the gruesomeness tenfold was that, from constant domestic, or indeed rather family association with the goblins, their countenances had grown in grotesque resemblance to the human. No one understands animals who does not see that every one of them, even amongst the fishes, it may be with a dimness and vagueness infinitely remote, yet shadows the human: in the case of these the human resemblance had greatly increased: while their owners had sunk towards them, they had risen towards their owners.[16]

3.7 Arthur Hughes: "Cob's Creatures."
Illustration from George MacDonald's The Princess and the Goblin.

There is more than a hint here, we notice, that the monstrosity of both the Goblins and their creatures was due in part to an actual interbreeding between them. Behind this essentially allegorical theory of evolution was the notion that each individual creature, animal or human, is in a constant process of spiritual development or degeneration that could be shown symbolically on the Great Chain of Being. We get the first hint of this in *At the Back of the North Wind*, published in 1871, the year before *The Princess and the Goblin*. North Wind appears to a wicked nurse in the shape of a great grey wolf, explaining afterwards to little Diamond, "I had to make myself look like a bad thing before she could see me. If I had put on any other shape than a wolf's she would not have seen me, for that is what is growing to be her own shape inside of her."[17] In *The Princess and Curdie* (1882) this symbolic theory has been greatly elaborated. Curdie is given the power by the Princess's mysterious Grandmother to detect people's true selves by their touch. He can feel the paws of the beast in the hands of the evil courtier, or, as in the case of the hideous and misshapen "dog," Lina, the hand of the child in the paw of the beast.

> Since it is always what they *do*, whether in their minds or their bodies, that makes men go down to be less than men, that is, beasts, the change always comes first in their hands—and first of all in the inside hands, to which the outside ones are but as the gloves. They do not know it of course; for a beast does not know that he is a beast, and the nearer a man gets to being a beast the less he knows it. Neither can their best friends, or their worst enemies indeed, see any difference in their hands, for they only see the living gloves of them. But there are not a few who feel a vague something repulsive in the hand of a man who is growing a beast.[18]

Later in the story, Lina leads a whole company of grotesquely mutant creatures to Curdie's aid.

> One of them, for instance, was a like a boa constrictor walking on four little stumpy legs near its tail. About the same distance from its head were two little wings, which it was forever fluttering as if trying to fly with them. Curdie thought it fancied it did fly with them, when it was merely plodding on busily with its four little stumps. How it managed to keep up he could not think, till once when he missed it from the group: the same moment he caught sight of something at a distance plunging at an awful serpentine rate through the trees, and presently, from behind a huge ash, this same creature fell again into the group, quietly waddling along on its four stumps.

Watching it after this, he saw that, when it was not able to keep up any longer, and they had all got a little space ahead, it shot into the wood away from the route, and made a great round, serpenting along in huge billows of motion, devouring the ground, undulating awfully, galloping as if it were all legs together, and its four stumps nowhere. In this mad fashion it shot ahead, and, a few minutes after, toddled in among the rest, walking peacefully and somewhat painfully on its few fours.[19]

3.8 Helen Stratton: "Curdie with the 'Uglies.'"
Illustration to George MacDonald's The Princess and Curdie.

Collectively, these creatures are called the "oddities" or the "Uglies." They are clearly in some kind of a transitional state, and, at the allegorical level it is not difficult to find a significance in the particular animal described imagining it is flying when it is really walking, or in its desire to conceal its real, or more effective, way of moving from the rest. In this, and the other cases, it is clear that, as Kingsley had claimed in *The Water Babies*, the outward form reflected the inner being—unlike in *Frankenstein*, where the outward form created the warped inner being.

Finally, in *Lilith* (1895), MacDonald's last book, we find Mr. Raven (who is in our world a librarian, but in the "other" world a bird) explaining:

Every one, as you ought to know, has a beast-self—and a bird-self, ay, and a creeping serpent-self too—which it takes a good deal of crushing to kill! In truth he has also a tree-self and a crystal-self, and I don't know how many selves more—all to get into harmony. You can tell what sort of man he is by his creature that comes oftenest to the front.[20]

Clearly this is, in some senses, an extension of the moral evolutionary chain of Being from the earlier books, but the stress is now on harmony of coexisting "selves," rather than a progression from one state to another. Man is the microcosm of the universe. We have to come to terms with the beasts or monsters that are within us—or, at least, with some of them. There is no suggestion, for instance, that Mr. Raven the bird is any different *morally* from Mr. Raven the man. Each self is, rather, an expression of a different aspect of an immensely complex, but unified, personality—who is finally discovered to be Adam, the first and representative human being.

Among E. Nesbit's earliest children's books is *The Book of Dragons* (1900). Her fantasies, which began to appear after her more realistic work

3.9 H. R. Millar: "The Moving Stone Beast."
Illustration to E. Nesbit's The Enchanged Castle *(1907).*

of the 1890s and continue into the early years of the twentieth century, show a similar use of monsters as symbols of the unconscious, though their actual forms are very different from those of MacDonald. The most obvious non-literary influence is Hawkins's dinosaurs at the Crystal Palace. Yalding Castle, the *Enchanted Castle* of the story of that name, is somewhere in the West of England, but on its grounds are enormous lifesize hollow concrete replicas of dinosaurs:

> The antediluvian animals are set in a beechwood on a slope at least half a mile across the park from the castle. The grandfather of the present Lord Yalding had set them there in the middle of the last century, in the great days of the late Prince Consort, the Exhibition of 1851, Sir Joseph Paxton, and the Crystal Palace. Their stone flanks, their wide ungainly wings, their lozenged crocodile like backs show grey through the trees a long way off.[21]

At first the children are merely amazed by them, but then they discover that for those are under the influence of the magic ring, the dinosaurs can be seen to come alive at sunset and wander round the park. There follows the usual unforeseen complications for Nesbit's children who have been caught up in magic, but at the climax of the story it becomes clear that these creatures are, in some mysterious way, parts of a beneficent whole whose ascending order, like MacDonald's, leads ultimately towards a vision of divine "light."

> From that height one could see far out over the quiet park and sleeping gardens, and through the grey green of them shapes moved, approaching.
> The great beasts came first, strange forms that were when the world was new—gigantic lizards with wings—dragons they lived as in men's memories—mammoths, strange vast birds, they crawled up the hill and ranged themselves outside the circle. Then, not from the garden but from very far away, came the stone gods of Egypt and Assyria—bullbodied, birdwinged, hawk-headed, cat-headed, all in stone, and all alive and alert; strange, grotesque figures from the towers of cathedrals—figures of angels with folded wings, figures of beasts with wings wide spread; sphinxes; uncouth idols from Southern palm-fringed islands; and, last of all, the beautiful marble shapes of the gods and goddesses.[22]

In *The Magic City* (1910) this theme is repeated in a minor and semi-comic key in the person of the Great Sloth.

"In the extreme north of Polistarchia," said Mr. Noah instructively, "lies a town called Somnolentia. It used to be called Briskford in happier days. A river then ran through the town, a rapid river that brought much gold from the mountains. The people used to work very hard to keep the channel clear of the lumps of gold which continually threatened to choke it. Their fields were then well-watered and fruitful, and the inhabitants were cheerful and happy. But when the Hippogriff was let out of the book, a Great Sloth got out too. Evading all efforts to secure him, the Great Sloth journeyed northward. He is a very large and striking animal, and by some means, either fear or admiration, he obtained a complete ascendancy over the inhabitants of Briskford. He induced them to build him a temple of solid gold, and while they were doing this the river bed became choked up and the stream was diverted to another channel far from the town. Since then the place is fallen into decay. The fields are parched and untilled. Such water as the people need for drinking is drawn by great labour from a well. Washing has become shockingly infrequent."[23]

Though the name sounds like that of the extinct mammal, the Giant Sloth, H. R. Millar's illustrations make it clear that this creature is some kind of sauropod, not unlike the *dinosaurus* of Yalding Castle. This primeval aspect of the Great Sloth is clearly important, since, as the name implies, he seems to have the function of some kind of collective *id* for the Halma men of Somnolentia. Finally, he is persuaded to wish for a pumping machine "to draw up water for eight hours a day." At once the machine appears and he finds himself compelled to use it for the prescribed time.

The room that had been full of feather bed was now full of wheels and cogs and bands and screws and bars. It was full, in fact, of a large and complicated machine. And the handle of that machine was being turned by the Great Sloth itself.

"Let me go," said the Great Sloth, gnashing its great teeth. "I won't work!"

"You must," said a purring voice from the heart of the machinery. "You wished for me, and now you have to work me eight hours a day. It is the law;" it was the machine itself which spoke.

"I'll break you," said the Sloth.

"I am unbreakable," said the machine with gentle pride.[24]

This magic world is entered only by performing an act of creation, however small. One of its most fundamental laws is that whatever is wished for will come—and then it must be used. As the Great Sloth discovers, such a law of slavery to fundamental desires is a mixed blessing; it also symbolizes an important psychological insight. At one stage in the book someone with a

3.10 H. R. Millar: "'Let Me Go,' Said the Great Sloth."
Illustration to E. Nesbit's The Magic City.

mechanical bent wishes for a car, which is fine; at another, someone threatens to wish for machine guns. The arms race leading up to the First World
War was governed by exactly the same laws, we notice. Human creativity is
a very dangerous blessing.

We discover just how dangerous from some of Nesbit's other monsters.
Not all are of the primitive and elemental kind. Perhaps her most terrifying
are the Ugly Wuglies of *The Enchanted Castle*, created by the children as
an audience for a play.

> The seven members of the audience seated among the wilderness of
> chairs had, indeed, no insides to speak of. Their bodies were bolsters and
> rolled up blankets, their spines were broom-handles, and their arm and
> leg bones were hockey sticks and umbrellas. Their shoulders were the
> wooden cross pieces that Mademoiselle used for keeping her jackets in
> shape; their hands were gloves stuffed out with handkerchiefs; and their

faces were the paper masks painted in the afternoon by the untutored brush of Gerald, tied on to the round heads made of the ends of stuffed bolstercases. The faces were really rather dreadful. Gerald had done his best, but even after his best had been done you would hardly have known they were faces, some of them, if they hadn't been in the positions which faces usually occupy, between the collar and the hat. Their eyebrows were furious with lamp black frowns—their eyes the size, and almost the shape, of five shilling pieces, and on their lips and cheeks had been spent much crimson lake and nearly the whole of a half-pan of vermilion.[25]

The disaster occurs, of course, when one of the actors, who happens to be wearing the magic ring, wishes to step up the volume of clapping. "I wish those creatures we made were alive. We should get something like applause then." The scene then develops with a true nightmare logic.

Mademoiselle began it: she applauded the garden scene—with hurried little clappings of her quick French hands. Eliza's fat red palms followed heavily, and then—someone else was clapping, six or seven people, and their clapping made a dull padded sound. Nine faces instead of two were turned towards the stage, and seven out of the nine were painted, pointed paper faces. And every hand and every face was alive [. . .] the hall was crowded with live things, strange things—all horribly short as broomsticks and umbrellas are short. A limp hand gesticulated. A pointed white face with red cheeks looked up at him, and wide red lips said something, he could not tell what. The voice reminded him of the old beggar down by the bridge who had no roof to his mouth. These creatures had no roofs to their mouths, of course—they had no—
     "Aa pp re o me me oo a oo ho el?" said the voice again. And it had said it four times before Gerald could collect himself sufficiently to understand that this horror—alive, and most likely to be quite uncontrollable—was saying, with a dreadful calm, polite persistence:—
     "Can you recommend me to a good hotel?"[26]

With all but one of these dreadful creatures the magic later wears off (the ring has a complicated and very confusing "time switch" mechanism for the duration of its wishes) but one, through an accident, goes on to be fully "human." In the *Frankenstein* tradition his hideous outward appearance means that he has become a highly unpleasant character, and with Nesbit's socialist tendencies in mind it comes as no surprise to learn that this monster is a "well-known city man," Mr. U. W. Ugli.
     As is much of *The Enchanted Castle*, the Ugly Wuglies are the stuff of dreams—or, more properly, nightmares—terrifying in their impossible real-

3.11 H. R. Millar: "A Limp Hand was Laid on his Arm."
Illustration to E. Nesbit's The Enchanted Castle.

ism. Unlike the dinosaurs, there is no suggestion of their representing primitive qualities in people, or in life as a whole. They are in the Frankenstein mold: artificial and unnatural. They represent creativity gone wrong: fabricated things from odds and ends, wholly to be feared and hated. Yet Nesbit's attitude towards her Ugly Wuglies is at least reassuring: we all know these nightmares *are* nightmares, created by mistaken use of the magic ring. The book's moral and metaphysical structure keeps such monsters in their place. But behind Nesbit's determination that children should *not* be frightened by irrational fears there lies a very different tradition of Victorian children's literature.

One of the most spectacularly terrifying examples of a gruesome breed is *The New Mother* (1882), by Lucy Clifford, wife of the Professor of Mathematics at University College, London. A thinly disguised allegory, the story tells how two children, called Blue Eyes and Turkey, are warned by their kind and loving mother that if they continue to be naughty and disobey her she will have to "go away" and "send home a new mother, with glass eyes and a wooden tail." At first they are suitably awed by this threat, but at last they are tempted by a mysterious, and clearly diabolic, little girl to break a looking glass deliberately. They do so. Sadly their mother packs

her bags, kisses them good bye, and goes away to join their father—never to
return. The hideous new mother arrives, complete with the glass eyes and
the heavy dragging wooden tail. When the children attempt to bar the door
against her, she just lifts her massive tail and smashes her way in. The terrified children run away into the forest. "All night long they stayed in the
darkness and the cold, and all the next day and the next, and all through
the cold dreary days and the long dark nights that followed." The story
concludes:

> They are there still, my children. All through the long weeks and months
> they have been there, with only green rushes for their pillows and only the
> brown dead leaves to cover them, feeding on the wild strawberries in the
> summer, or on the nuts when they hang green; on the blackberries when
> they are no longer sour in the autumn, and in the winter on the little red
> berries that ripen in the snow. They wander about among the tall dark firs
> or beneath the great trees beyond. Sometimes they stay to rest beside the
> little pool near the copse, and they long and long, with a longing that is
> greater than words can say, to see their own dear mother again, just once
> again, to tell her that they'll be good for evermore—just once again.
>
> And still the new mother stays in the little cottage, but the windows
> are closed and the doors are shut, and no one knows what the inside
> looks like. Now and then, when the darkness has fallen and the night is
> still, hand in hand BlueEyes and the Turkey creep up near the home in
> which they were once so happy, and with beating hearts they watch and
> listen; sometimes a blinding flash comes through the window, and they
> know it is the light from the new mother's glass eyes, or they hear a
> strange muffled noise, and they know it is the sound of her wooden tail
> as she drags it along the floor.[27]

The story is exceptional in a number of ways, not least in that Mrs. Clifford
is a writer of unusual power and originality, but it illustrates dramatically
the kind of monsters lurking in Victorian children's stories that Nesbit
sought to exorcise, not by ignoring them, but by taming and using them
within a very different metaphysical framework. It was the same spirit that
made her keep a skull in the house for the children to handle and look at,
so that they might accept human bones as natural objects, and not be
frightened by superstition. But Mrs. Clifford's story also tells us something
else about her age and its monsters. The nineteenth century is characteristically the great age of *realistic* fiction. Its conscious creative energies were
largely channeled by artistic theory and commercial pressures alike into
rationality and naturalism. As was suggested in the last chapter, this could,

and often did, result in the suppression and dissociation of other, deeper and less articulate elements. Ostensibly *The New Mother*, is a fable to emphasize the importance of Christian obedience. Obedience to parents and obedience to God are of a piece. The moral is not an unusual one for a certain type of Evangelical fiction, as we shall see in a later chapter. But there is, one suspects, another much less conscious element in the story from which it derives much of its power. The taboo on mirror-breaking, for example, clearly draws on something much more archetypal than normal Evangelical zeal. Moreover, no one who recognizes the parallels in mood with Kipling's *Ba Ba Blacksheep* (1890), the semi-autobiographical account of how his mother left him at the age of five in the hands of a monstrous and bullying "Auntie" to return to her husband in India for five years, can fail to see what is being done in this story, and the depth of inarticulate childhood fears on which it is attempting to play. The age of steam, utilitarianism, realism, and a simplified code of morality was haunted by monsters from dreams and nightmares, from irrational fears, and from the vast abyss of the past which the new sciences had uncovered. Fantasy gave form to those dim but potent specters, or, as in the case of Kipling's *The Brushwood Boy*, or M. R. James's chilling ghost story, *Oh Whistle and I'll Come to You, my Lad*, showed their elusiveness. Prince Albert's instinct was a profound one when he commissioned Hawkins to build the concrete monsters at the Crystal Palace. The Victorian age needed its concrete monsters if it was to keep at bay others, much less controllable.

Under the Hill

One of the strangest of William Morris's short stories to appear in his *Oxford and Cambridge Magazine* in 1856 is *Lindenborg Pool*. The narrative is technically odd in that it is enclosed within a "double frame." Though neither of the outer narratives is clear, or more than fragmentary, the main events take place within a time change suffered by a fictional "I" who is introduced by the "real" (?) author at the beginning. The effect of this story within—a story is both to heighten the mystery of what follows, and to distance it. We never see more than through a glass, darkly—by implication perhaps, through the "leaden waters of that fearful pool" itself. The "I" of the inner story discovers one stormy May day beside the mysterious pool of the title that he is no longer in the nineteenth century but a priest of the thirteenth century being taken to a castle to shrive a dying Baron of notoriously evil reputation. The scene at his castle is strangely sinister.

> [D]ismounting, (I) found myself in the midst of some twenty attendants, with flushed faces and wildly sparkling eyes, which they were vainly trying to soften to due solemnity; mock solemnity I had almost said, for they did not seem to think it necessary to appear really solemn, and had difficulty enough apparently in not prolonging indefinitely the shout of laughter with which they had first greeted me. "Take the holy Father to my Lord," said one at last, "and we will go with him."[28]

The castle is sumptuously luxurious in its appointments, which has the effects of increasing the priest's vague feeling of foreboding, and with this luxury is an overwhelming impression of bisexuality and perversion among its inhabitants.

> Moreover it increased my horror that there was no appearance of a woman in all these rooms; and yet was there not? there, those things—I looked more intently; yes, no doubt they were women, but all dressed like men;—what a ghastly place![29]

This sense of perversion in all his surroundings reaches its climax with the discovery that the grunting inarticulate "Baron" is nothing more than an enormous pig, swathed in the bedclothes.

> I held it up, that which I counted so holy, when lo! great laughter, echoing like thunder-claps through all the rooms, not dulled by the veiling hang- ings, for they were all raised up together, and, with a slow upheaval of the rich clothes among which he lay, with a sound that was half snarl, half grunt, with helpless body swathed in bedclothes, a huge swine that I had been shriving tore from me the Holy Thing, deeply scoring my hand as he did so with tusk and tooth, so that the red blood ran quick on to the floor.
> Therewithal he rolled down on to the floor, and lay there helplessly, only able to roll to and fro, because of the swathings.
> Then right madly skirled the intolerable laughter, rising to shrieks that were fearfuller than any screams of agony I ever heard; the hundreds of people through all those grand rooms danced and wheeled about me, shrieking, hemming me in with interlaced arms, the women loosing their long hair and thrusting forward their horribly grinning unsexed faces toward me till I felt their hot breath.[30]

There is a clear connexion implied between the desecration of religion and the perversion of sexuality. Adjectives like *thrusting* applied to the *unsexed* women reinforce the suggestions of unnatural relationships. The whole cas- tle is charged with an atmosphere of unnamed vice, and as the priest quits it "in reckless fury" there falls upon it a fate like that of Sodom.[31] All that is left as the sun rises is the "deep black lake" of Lindenborg Pool.

With monsters human rather than animal, Morris is a true inheritor of the Gothic mode. His work relies on the power of individual moments or scenes rather than on the plot. Here, as in the somber and moving poem, *The Haystack in the Floods*, there is a sketchy legendary and historical background, but it is not important. What is unusual in this fantasy, however, both for Morris and for his period, is the suggestion of unnamed vice and sexual unwholesomeness. For the most part the Gothic romances of Morris and Tennyson have a sexuality that is dreamy, languid, remote, and stylized; here, in spite of the protective "double frame" and the archaisms, these images of wheeling unsexed faces have a disturbing power. They reveal the existence of other currents beneath the surface of Victorian fantasies.

One quality that *Frankenstein* failed to inherit in any substantial measure from *Christabel* was the association of brooding metaphysical evil and sexual corruption. Despite both marvels and horrors, it always preserves a veneer of rationality, investing the double-edged blessings of power in Science rather than the Devil. The sinister Geraldine of Coleridge's poem does not find an adequate counterpart until we get to Poe's *Ligeia* in the 1840s. It was in America, at the very time when the scientific interest in monsters was coming to a climax, that the Gothic quest for the dramatic moment or scene was most effectively combined with a metaphysical sense of evil. What Poe called "the Imp of the Perverse" helped to make sexual corruption not so much a social phenomenon in Victorian literature as a concrete embodiment or symbol of the powers of Darkness. His *Tales of Mystery and Imagination* are, in this sense, perhaps the final and in many ways the most perfect expression of the Gothic spirit. With a few notable exceptions, like *The Gold Bug*, and *The Murders in the Rue Morgue*, the stories are essentially plotless. All is concentrated upon a single fantastic situation from which every last ounce of drama is wrung. *The Pit and the Pendulum*, for instance, is one of the supreme examples of such a set piece. Even in that story, however, the nominal framework is still a rational one: the unnamed hero has been condemned to die, slowly, at the hands of the Spanish Inquisition. In a story like *The Masque of the Red Death*, however, the final trappings of realism are swept aside, and the story's wealth of detail serves not to increase its probability, but to stress the unreality and symbolic nature of the fantasy. We are given neither country nor date for the setting. With the entire land devastated by the "Red Death," the most terrible and mysterious of plagues, the ruler, Prince Prospero, has retired

with a thousand knights and ladies of his Court to the shelter and seclu-
sion of a castellated abbey (which he, Beckfordlike, has designed himself).
Here they are immured, and pass their time in masques and voluptuous
entertainments (again, somewhat reminiscent of Beckford's twenty-first
party at Fonthill Splendens). Beyond the lavishness of the entertainments
are other qualities only to be hinted at. In the costumes of the revellers, for
instance, "were much of the beautiful, much of the wanton, much of the
bizarre, something of the terrible, and not a little of that which might have
excited disgust."[32] At the stroke of midnight a new masked guest is discovered—dressed as the Red Death himself. "His vesture was dabbled in
blood—and his broad brow, with all the features of the face, was sprinkled
with the scarlet horror."[33] When the furious Prince attempts to unmask the
interloper it is discovered that beneath the mask is an empty void. It is the
disease itself that has come as the uninvited guest.

> And one by one dropped the revellers in the blood bedewed halls of their
> revel, and died each in the despairing posture of his fall. And the life of
> the ebony clock went out with that of the last of the gay. And the flames
> of the tripods expired. And Darkness and Decay and the Red Death held
> illimitable dominion over all.[34]

Poe's sinister revelers, dancing in defiance of the plague, are appropriate forerunners of the courtiers in Morris's castle. Yet even where the
details of corruption are given form as an expression of metaphysical evil,
those forms, as in so much Victorian fantasy, remain vague and unspecified
in their horrors. Thus Mr. Hyde, in *Dr. Jekyll and Mr. Hyde*, has "Satan's
signature" unmistakably upon his face, but in what that signature consists
is not clear even to the observant Mr. Utterson.

> Mr. Hyde was pale and dwarfish; he gave an impression of deformity with-
> out any nameable malformation, he had a displeasing smile, he had
> borne himself to the lawyer with a sort of murderous mixture of timidity
> and boldness, and he spoke with a husky, whispering and somewhat bro-
> ken voice,—all these were points against him; but not all of these together
> could explain the hitherto unknown disgust, loathing and fear with
> which Mr. Utterson regarded him.[35]

Oscar Wilde, in *The Picture of Dorian Gray* (1891), appears to be slightly
more explicit than Stevenson, but on closer inspection that detail turns out
to be almost entirely a matter of oblique metaphor.

A exclamation of horror broke from the painter's lips as he saw in the dim light the hideous face on the canvas grinning at him. There was something in its expression that filled him with disgust and loathing. Good heavens! it was Dorian Gray's own face that he was looking at. The horror, whatever it was, had not yet entirely spoiled that marvellous beauty. There was still some gold in the thinning hair and some scarlet on the sensual mouth. The sodden eyes had kept something of the loveliness of their blue, the noble curves had not yet completely passed away from chiselled nostrils and from plastic throat. [. . .] It was from within, apparently, that the foulness and horror had come. Through some strange quickening of inner life the leprosies of sin were slowly eating the thing away. The rotting of a corpse in a watery grave was not so fearful.[36]

In *The Great God Pan* by Arthur Machen, the references to unnamed evil are made almost entirely in terms of the beholder's reactions.

Austin took the manuscript, but never read it. Opening the neat pages at haphazard his eye was caught by a word and a phrase that followed it; and sick at heart with white lips and a cold sweat pouring like water from his temples, he flung the paper down.[37]

But in the same paragraph this dramatic reticence is defended as necessary.

We know what happened to those who chanced to meet the Great God Pan, and those who are wise know that all symbols are symbols of something, not of nothing. It was, indeed, an exquisite symbol beneath which men long ago veiled their knowledge of the most awful, most secret forces which lie at the heart of all things; forces before which the souls of men must wither and die and blacken, as their bodies blacken under the electric current. Such forces cannot be named, cannot be spoken, cannot be imagined except under a veil and a symbol, a symbol to the most of us appearing a quaint, poetic fancy, to some foolish tale. But you and I, at all events, have known something of the terror that may dwell in the secret place of life, manifested under human flesh; that which is without form taking to itself a form.[38]

The deliberate inversion of the normal religious formula makes it quite clear what kind of "incarnation" he is thinking of. At one point in the story Machen also hints at the possibility of evolution in reverse that, as we have seen, fascinated so many Victorian writers, but once again the details are left to our imaginations. We are told merely of "the blackened face, the hideous form upon the bed, changing and melting before your eyes from woman to man, from man to beast, and from beast to worse than beast. . . ."[39] Only at one point in all Machen's dealings with evil are we given a more detailed glimpse of such decay.

> I looked, and a pang of horror seized my heart as with a white hot iron. There upon the floor was a dark and putrid mass, seething with corruption and hideous rottenness, neither liquid nor solid, but melting and changing before our eyes, and bubbling with unctuous oily bubbles like boiling pitch. And out of the midst of it shone two burning points like eyes, and I saw a writhing and stirring as of limbs, and something moved and lifted up what might have been an arm. The doctor took a step forward, raised the iron bar and struck at the burning points; he drove in the weapon, and struck again and again in a fury of loathing.[40]

The difference between this, and other accounts, however, as we discover in the final pages of *The Three Imposters*, is that it is part of an elaborate fiction created by a practiced liar for still more diabolical and sadistic ends.

Though sexuality is rarely explicit in Machen's visions of evil, it is always present just beneath the surface. The transformation of a lovely young girl into a hopeless grinning idiot that begins the chain of demon-possession, though it is actually achieved by a brain operation, is presented as a form of sexual violation or rape. Moreover, the connections he suggests between such Possession and the old nature cults of Pan, with their blatant sexual rituals, make explicit much that was left unsaid in the Victorian attitudes towards traditional supernatural forms, such as fairies. When, indeed, one looks at the lascivious little grotesques and the suggestive poses and gestures of Fuseli's fairies in his painting of *Titania and Bottom* from *A Midsummer Night's Dream*, it is hard to see why the fairy story was ever thought of as being sexually "innocent" in the nineteenth century. Many of the traditional tales, such as *The Sleeping Beauty*, or the *Frog Prince*, had obvious sexual content, and were often only retold in their modern, "cleaned-up" form for the first time during this period. In the original version of *The Sleeping Beauty*, for instance, the prince does not merely kiss the sleeping princess, he "awakens" her in both senses by rape[41]—just as Porphyro, it is delicately hinted by Keats, did Madeleine in *The Eve of St. Agnes*. It has been suggested that much of the revived popularity of fairy stories in Victorian times was due to the fact that they were one of the few accepted ways in which stories about sexual fantasies could be told. Certainly, if we include murder of children, or lovers, along with themes of rape and incest, we can see how much greater the actual range of license permitted in such stories was, compared with the more realistic conventions of the novel. This is a point underlined by the acceptability of many of Hans Andersen's stories which, so far from drawing on traditional sources, mirror the unhappy course of his own love affair with the Copenhagen actress Louise Collin. Yet even in cases like this, few sexual fantasies are wholly original. His own poignantly autobiographical tale of *The Swineherd* has an older counterpart where the gardener does not merely extract kisses from the princess, but seduces her and actually gets her with child.[42] The growing interest in *The Arabian Nights* from the latter part of the eighteenth century, which we noticed in Coleridge, was often fed by similar kinds of interest. E. W. Lane produced an edited English translation in 1840, and in the 1880s a complete and unexpurgated version was published by the great Victorian traveler, linguist, and libertarian, Sir Richard Burton. In some cases the strong sexual undertones to stories were elaborated or made more explicit by illustrators. We have already mentioned the fascination with the bizarre and unnatural that reveals itself in Fuseli's dwarfs and hermaphrodites—and is much more explicit in some of his private sketches, like that of the two lesbians looking in a mirror—and this is a tradition that continues through Victorian times. Even without the unmistakable suggestiveness of Beardsley, or the more confused eroticism of Dadd, there are disturbing enough undertones in the works of some of the most popular illustrators, such as Doyle and Cruikshank. Both were attracted by fairy stories as a medium of expression, and there are a number of pictures by both artists which seem to have been done for their own sake and do not relate to any identifiable stories. One, by Doyle, is of a gigantic ogre in a forest, another is of a tiny girl (perhaps a fairy?) being menaced by a gigantic stag beetle—almost certainly the same picture as that mentioned by C. S. Lewis which gave him nightmares as a child.[43] The suggestions of rape or sexual assault seem too clear to be ignored.

By mid-century, indeed, it is clear that fairies could, and often did, offer a surrogate language of sexuality. One of the most striking examples, as well as one of the most widely influential, was Christina Rossetti's *The Goblin Market* (1859). Laura and Lizzie, two sisters, are tempted by the goblins to come and taste their fruit:

> Morning and evening
> Maids heard the goblins cry:
> "Come buy our orchard fruits,
> Come buy, come buy:
> Apples and quinces,
> Lemons and oranges,

Plump unpecked cherries,
Melons and raspberries,
Bloom-down-checked peaches,
Swart-headed mulberries
Wild free-born cranberries,
Crab-apples, dewberries,
Pine-apples, blackberries."

"Buy from us with @ golden curl"

3.12 Dante Gabriel Rossetti: "Buy from Us. . . ."
Illustration to The Goblin Market *by his Sister, Christina Rossetti.*

Their *orchard fruits* are "wild and free born," outside the rule of law or convention in their blatant appeal to the senses, and in the ambiguous language by which they are described. Clearly the goblins are offering "forbidden fruit" in every sense, and both the sisters seem well aware that the fruit is both sinister and dangerous:

"No," said Lizzie: "No, no, no;
Their offers should not charm us,
Their evil gifts would harm us."

When the animal-like goblins finally tempt the "sweet tooth Laura" to buy and eat, in exchange for a golden curl of her hair, the resulting ecstasy brings neither satisfaction nor satiety:

> She dropped a tear more rare than pearl,
> Then sucked their fruit globes fair or red.
> Sweeter than honey from the rock,
> Stronger than man-rejoicing wine,
> Clearer than water flowed that juice;
> She never tasted such before,
> How should it cloy with length of use?
> She sucked and sucked and sucked the more
> Fruits which that unknown orchard bore;
> She sucked until her lips were sore;
> Then flung the emptied rinds away
> But gathered up one kernel stone,
> And knew not was it night or day
> As she turned home alone.

She goes in search of more, but now, unlike her sister Lizzie, she can no longer see the goblins. Gradually she pines away with desire. Lizzie brings to mind a parallel case:

> [O]f Jeanie in her grave,
> Who should have been a bride;
> But who for joys brides hope to have
> Fell sick and died.

In despair for her sister's life, Lizzie eventually decides to go to the goblins herself. They fall on her in delight, but will not sell her their fruit—urging her instead to eat with them as a "welcome guest." When she will not, they turn on her viciously, scratching, biting, and pressing the ripe fruits to her face and lips. Battered and bruised, but stained with the magic fruit juices which she has not tasted, Lizzie returns to Laura with joy and "inward laughter."

> She cried, "Laura," up the garden,
> "Did you miss me?
> Come and kiss me.
> Never mind my bruises,
> Hug me, kiss me, suck my juices
> Squeezed from goblin fruits for you,
> Goblin pulp and goblin dew.

> Eat me, drink me, love me;
> Laura, make much of me;
> For your sake I have braved the glen
> And had to do with goblin merchant men."

Laura does so.

> She kissed and kissed her with a hungry mouth.
> Her lips began to scorch,
> That juice was wormwood to her tongue,
> She loathed the feast.

There follows the crisis of the disease, with Lizzie watching by Laura's bed, but in the end the juice proves to be the antidote to its own poisonous effects, and she makes a full recovery.

Clearly, some of the emotional charge to this extraordinary poem is personal. It is possible, for instance, that Christina's sister Maria has prevented her from a disastrous elopement shortly before and the final lines "there is no friend like a sister" are an expression of her gratitude afterwards.[44] Nevertheless, much of the imagery is unmistakably and openly sexual. Jeanie "fell sick and died" for "joys brides hope to have." The besieged Lizzie, "white and golden," is compared first with a lily, and then to "a royal virgin town" under attack. Though the main theme of temptation, fall, and eventual salvation through the steadfast and sacrificial love of another, is plain enough in abstract terms, it leaves many of the problems of detail unanswered. If Laura's "fall," with its luscious pleasures and bitter aftertaste can be well enough understood in sexual terms, Lizzie's "sacrifice," although it is couched in much the same kind of language, is much less clear. What can she bring back that will save her sister and yet leave her unsullied? The allegorical answer to this "hair-of-the-dog" cure is, of course, *love*. The poem is a contrast between unreal and real, selfish and selfless loves. Laura desired sensual pleasure, Lizzie wanted to save her sister. Yet if this is all, then the imagery is inappropriate. Some elements of Lizzie's sacrifice might be eucharistic, but her urging "eat me, drink me, love me" is more than Christ-like, suggesting a passion that is almost incestuous. Conjectural conclusions about the author's feelings are beside the point here: the poem itself gains much of its power from its resistance to simple allegory, and its hints of deeper more complex relationships. Physical sex may be only one example of the "poison to the blood" that can only be cured by more of itself. Like so many fantasies of the period, it is not difficult to find in *The Goblin Market* an image of a divided mind, and a divided society, terrified to come to terms with its own deepest needs and desires. The original forbidden fruit, we recall, was from the tree of knowledge, and its sexual connotations were secondary: it was a mark of the Fall that one aspect of that knowledge was treated as if it were the whole. There are goblins of the mind, as George MacDonald knew, and we ignore them at our peril.

The hidden antithesis of Victorian prudery was, naturally, the flourishing subculture of pornography—which, though it has many forerunners, is often first identified as a separate genre in Victorian times. It is not my purpose to discuss it here. It has already been dealt with, excellently, by such writers as Steven Marcus in *The Other Victorians*, and in any case, most pornography, except in the most pathological sense, does not fall into the realm of fantasy. There is, however, one exception of sufficient significance to warrant some discussion since it presents an extraordinary, if inverted, parallel to William Morris's perverted court in *Lindenborg Pool*. It is also the climax of the use of the fairy story for an exploration of the erotic.

Aubrey Beardsley's *Under the Hill* was left incomplete at the time of his death in 1898. We know that he had lavished loving care upon it, writing and rewriting almost every sentence, and constructing around it a series of his most elaborate drawings. Fragments of the story, rigorously expurgated, had appeared with some of the drawings in *The Savoy* for January and April 1896. Though, like Coleridge with *Christabel*, he left some tantalizing hints (and some sketches) for its completion,[45] what survives is in the very best tradition of the Gothic fragment: a series of powerful and memorable images to which any shaping plot is essentially subservient and even irrelevant. Links with the episode of Shelley and the Godwin girls at the creation of *Frankenstein* seem to be explicitly hinted at in the frontispiece of a Herm with eyes instead of nipples. The "hill" of the title is in the same tradition of *double entendre* and unconscious suggestion. It is the Venusberg of the Wagnerian legends, but the title of the first chapter at once suggests another meaning as well: "How the Chevalier Tannhäuser entered into the Hill of Venus." Beneath the hill is a land of erotic fantasy of every conceivable taste whose delights are laid bare in Beardsley's lapidary and mannered prose. Almost every device of heterosexual, homosexual, hermaphrodite, and voyeuristic pleasure is exhibited, or pruriently hinted at in an extraordinary miscellany of sexual activities. The delights of Venus's own hill which Tannhäuser subsequently penetrates are no less extravagantly described:

> Cosmé's precise curls and artful waves had been finally disarranged at supper, and strayed ringlets of the black hair fell loosely over Venus's soft, delicious, tired, swollen eyelids. Her frail chemise and dear little drawers

were torn and moist, and clung transparently about her, and all her body
was nervous and responsive. Her closed thighs seemed like a vast replica
of the little bijou she had between them; the beautiful tétons du derriere
were firm as a plump virgin's cheek, and promised a joy as profound as
the mystery of the Rue Vendôme, and the minor chevelure, just profuse
enough, curled as prettily as the hair upon a cherub's head.[46]

Yet to describe this kind of whimsical exoticism purely in terms of pornography is to miss its point. Pornography is (and has always been) essentially a
commercial product, written for a specific market and with a definite end
in view. It aims to titillate, arouse, and plunge its reader into a world of
totally unreal sexuality. It fails in so far as it calls attention to its own
techniques. Beardsley's studied and stilted prose, in contrast, achieves a
quite different kind of unreality, constantly calling attention to its own
whimsy, daring, or cleverness. Venus has just entertained Tannhäuser to a
feast—or rather, an orgy—of gargantuan proportions. For a floorshow they
have watched a specially devised masque of decadence corrupting Arcadian
innocence, concluding with a welter of pederasty, sodomy, and the more
grotesque varieties of group fornication. While there are doubtless those
who can find erotic pleasures in any kind of voyeurism, most people seeking their kicks from books prefer to find their particular proclivity presented straight, and by itself. Here it is to be found in satiric juxtaposition,
and the result after a very few pages has the same effect as Beardsley's erotic
drawings: fascinating, but uninviting. We do not usually like being laughed
at in our fantasies. The essence of pornography is to involve the reader in
make believe; the effect of Beardsley's work is to distance the reader and
alienate him from the make believe, even while it may compel admiration
for its sheer virtuosity. This in itself, of course, constitutes a kind of second
level pornography for the self-conscious taste too sophisticated for simple
identification. It is a performance, a comic performance at that. The toilet
of Venus is a set piece:

> The tray was freighted with the most exquisite and shapely pantoufles,
> sufficient to make Cluny a place of naught. There were shoes of grey and
> black and brown suede, of white silk and rose satin, and velvet and
> sarcenet; there were some sea-green sewn with cherry blossoms, some of
> red with willow branches, and some of grey with bright-winged birds.
> There were heels of silver, of ivory, and of gilt; there were buckles of very
> precious stones set in most strange and esoteric devices; there were rib-
> bons tied and twisted into cunning forms; there were buttons so beautiful
> that the buttonholes might have no pleasure till they closed upon them;
> there were soles of delicate leathers scented with maréchale, and linings

of soft stuffs scented with the juice of July flowers. But Venus, finding none of them to her mind, called for a discarded pair of blood-red maroquin, diapered with pearls. They looked very distinguished over her white silk stockings. As the tray was being carried away, the capricious Florizel snatched as usual a slipper from it, and fitted the foot over his penis, and made the necessary movements. That was Florizel's little caprice. Meantime, La Popeliniere stepped forward with the frock.

"I shan't wear one tonight," said Venus. Then she slipped on her gloves.[47]

3.13 Aubrey Beardsley: "The Toilet of Venus." Illustration to her Under the Hill.
We miss much of the force of this picture if we do not recognize the parody of Beardsley's illustrations to Pope's Rape of the Lock *(1896).*

The passage begins as an elaborate inventory, relying heavily on names to conjure up the impression of costliness and luxury, and in this context the suggestion of a sexual attraction between buttonholes and buttons seems at first like no more than a slightly perverse conceit. It is only when we reach Florizel's "little caprice" with the "slipper" that the full implications of this ritual toilet begin to appear, and are confirmed by Venus's decision to dispense with her dress (and Beardsley's picture makes it clear she is bare breasted) but to wear gloves. Both in words and pictures Beardsley is fascinated with the satiric possibilities of grotesque exaggeration. If the purpose of evening dress is to titillate by artful revelation and concealment, then Venus's apparel shall outdo all others. The effect is almost as if Ben Jonson's *Volpone* (which Beardsley also illustrated) had been written by Sterne, nor should we miss the self-parody of Beardsley's illustrations to Pope's *Rape of the Lock* (1896).

Moreover, there is something familiar about this world of sensual pleasures under the hill. It is, of course, the world of the baron's court from the *Lindenborg Pool*. It so happens that the passages I have quoted have both been heterosexual, but much of *Under the Hill* is about homosexual or hermaphroditic pleasures, and there is little doubt what the reaction would have been had Morris, rather than Tannhäuser, arrived at the Venusberg and gained entrance. The association of gorgeous clothing and furnishings with sexual perversion and licence is the same in both. Beardsley is, as it were, telling the other side of the story. If we set the two stories together, we shall learn a great deal about the more hidden Victorian fantasies. Yet Beardsley's perversity, though it always depends on shock, is rarely content merely to shock. There is, for instance, almost no scatological device left unexploited:

> "That's Felix," said the Goddess, in answer to an enquiry from the Chevalier; and she went on to explain his attitude. Felix always attended Venus upon her little latrinal excursions, holding her, serving her, and making much of all she did. To undo her things, lift her skirts, to wait and watch the coming, to dip a lip or finger in the royal output, to stain himself deliciously with it, to lie beneath her as the favours fell, to carry off the crumpled, crotted paper—these were the pleasures of that young man's life.
>
> Truly there was never a queen so beloved by her subjects as Venus. Everything she wore had its lover. Heavens! how her handkerchiefs were filched, her stockings stolen! Daily, what intrigues, what countless ruses to possess her merest frippery? Every scrap of her body was adored. Never, for Savaral, could her ear yield sufficient wax! Never, for Pradon, could she spit prodigally enough! And Saphius found a month an intolerable time.[48]

What strikes the reader first about this, and other similar passages, is simply the element of public schoolboy smut.[49] But these very elements of schoolboy naughtiness—the posing, the grotesque humor, and the delight in shocking—are not an end in themselves. The Court of Venus is, logically, the place of every kind of venereal pleasure, and therefore of every kind of perversion. In that sense the fantasy is not escapist, but strongly realistic. If all possible forms of sexuality, concentrated and juxtaposed, are ultimately uninviting to all except those whose particular pleasure is watching the variety of others' pleasures, the full scope of Beardsley's multiple perversity is complete.

As has been remarked of Samuel Butler's anti-Victorianism: a Victorian is still a Victorian, even when he is standing on his head. There is a sense in which Beardsley alone of the artists of his generation achieved complete freedom of expression with regard to sex. Yet the effect of his writing remains peculiarly Victorian. He is self-conscious in a way that say, Swift, never was. His work depends upon a tension between convention and personal feeling quite as much as that of the deeply inhibited Lewis Carroll. Beardsley was frequently immoral; he was incapable of being amoral. In view of his final conversion to Roman Catholicism, and his deathbed repudiation of all his indecent drawings, it is surely significant that he chose to write on the Tannhäuser legend at all.[50] Though he himself did not get so far, the original story goes on to tell of how Tannhäuser leaves the Venusberg and goes on pilgrimage to Rome to seek forgiveness from the Pope for his sins. The Pope replies that it is as impossible for him to find forgiveness as for the staff he has in his hand to blossom. Tannhäuser leaves Rome in despair and returns to the Venusberg. Meanwhile, three days after his departure the Pope's staff begins to put forth shoots and green leaves. Messengers are dispatched in search of Tannhäuser, but he is never heard of again. How Beardsley intended to treat the whole theme it is impossible to say, but since he had already completed the drawing of Tannhäuser returning to the Venusberg before his death it is clear that, at one stage at any rate, he had a conception of the entire work in his mind. However it is handled, the story has questions about morality and forgiveness that it is difficult to avoid. Perhaps it was this that prevented Beardsley from finishing it. What we are left with is a familiar phenomenon: a series of powerful images or fragments; strange, grotesque, and obscene, perhaps, but nevertheless compelling in a way that mere pornography is not. It is the apotheosis of one strand of Victorian fantasy: the tension between the monstrous fragment and the organic and unified whole.

Chapter 4

Consensus and Nonsense:
Lear and Carroll

For some, fantasy was a means of creating other worlds in order to escape from this one. If it is clear that repression and inhibition played little part in the works of Kingsley and MacDonald, Morris or Beardsley, the same cannot be said for Edward Lear (1812–1888) or Charles Lutwidge Dodgson—better known as Lewis Carroll. For them the popular tradition, with its zany humor, and delight in puns, irony, and double meanings offered the seeds of a new art form. In childhood, dreams, and the frontiers of consciousness, in the marvelous, the grotesque, and the monstrous they discovered the possibility of quite different rules from those of the prevailing consensus: the rules of "Nonsense."

In spite of his considerable, though modest, achievement as a landscape painter, Lear always felt himself to be a marginal kind of man, standing somehow on the edge of a world he could observe, but never fully participate in. It is not difficult to find causes enough of insecurity in his personal background. He was the twentieth of a family of twenty-one children, who (not surprisingly perhaps) felt himself rejected by his mother, and was largely brought up by an elder sister. When he was only five or six years old he had his first of many attacks of epilepsy. It seems to have been a family disease, since one of his sisters also suffered from it. For the child the fits were terrifying, and—worse—isolating. They persisted throughout his life, sometimes several in a day, and though he always had enough warning to retire when he felt them coming on (so that no one outside his family seems to have been aware of them) the strain of perpetual secrecy enhanced his feelings of morbid abnormality. Masturbation was widely believed to be the cause of epilepsy, and Lear blamed his own attacks on lack of "will power."[1] Other sources of sexual relief had no less alarming

109

repercussions, and soon after his twentieth birthday he seems to have caught syphilis.[2] It is hardly surprising that in spite of his highly emotional nature (apparently capable of both heterosexual and, more often, homosexual attachments) he should have felt that marriage was impossible. "No," he wrote to a friend in 1853, "I don't mean to marry–never."

> You should, but there's time enough yet for you–6 or 8 years perhaps. In my case I should paint less and less well, and the thought of annual infants would drive me wild. If I attain to 65, and have an "establishmt" with lots of spoons &c. to offer I *may* chain myself:–but surely not before. And, alas! and seriously–when I look around my acquaintance– and few men have more, or know more intimately, do I see a majority of happy pairs? No, I don't.[3]

The personal fears and obsessions are all there, as are the flashes of the zany humor, but the comment on the miseries of marriage (whether or not relevant to his own decision to remain single) also shows us something else: a standing outside the conventions of the Victorian compromise, with its heavy insistence on the domestic bliss of hearth and home. It was a quality that was to break surface in Lear's writing over and over again. We see it in him as a young man in his sense of being a social failure at Knowsley where he was for a time tutor to the Earl of Derby's children. Lear was both oppressed by the social conventions and the rigid rules demanded by the etiquette of his aristocratic employer's world, and yet timidly defiant with the knowledge that his being an intellectual misfit was also the mark of the artist. To Tennyson, the poet, he complained that

> all the combotherations of artists' ways *do not, & will not* dovetail with country houses in Anglosaxonland. [. . .] If one were but a chimney pot, or a pipkin, or a mackerel, or anything respectable & consistent there would be some comfort; but the years go by without making the use of one's faculties one ought to do, & so I feel disgusted I do.[4]

Only from others do we learn of how he was adored by the children of the household,[5] and how, for a few of the more perceptive adult visitors, he was one of the chief attractions of Knowsley. We see his sense of alienation on a much wider philosophic ground in his growing hatred of the religious bigotry he had come to associate with orthodox Christianity. He loathed the "exclusion clauses" of the Athanasian Creed and the whole religious establishment that underpinned the parallel exclusion clauses of the social establishment.

I begin to be vastly weary of hearing people talk nonsense—unanswered,— not because they are unanswerable, but because they talk in pulpits. [. . .] Are not the priests of the age blind indeed not to discern that, though from the unassailable vantage ground of custom they may oppress the human intellect for a long long while, yet that some day the hour will come for them to go the way of all other priesthoods? [. . .] A broader creed [. . .] will assuredly come to pass whether Bishops and priests welcome the changes or resist them. Not those who believe that God the Creator is greater than a Book, and that millions unborn are to look up to higher thoughts than those stereotyped by ancient legends, gross ignorance, and hideous bigotry—not those are the Infidels,—but those same screamy ganders of the church, who put darkness forward and insist that it is light.[6]

Lear's life, in short, was a physical embodiment of the personal exclusion clause that he felt had been imposed on him by fate at birth. For most of his seventy-six years he was a wanderer, rarely staying in the same place for more than a few months together. Using his vocation as an artist and his poor health as excuse, he was able to opt out of his society in the most literal way—by traveling. Most of the exotic places he mentions in his limericks, India, the Aegean, the Near East, Egypt, Italy, the Balkans, he had actually visited in his ceaseless journeyings. Until his old age he never had a house, or even a real home of his own—and when he finally decided to settle, it was, typically, on the fringes of British expatriate society in Italy. In spite of a large number of close friends—whose devoted friendship he could never quite believe in—and his wide popularity, even eventual lionization by tourists, he was never able to shed his feelings of loneliness and isolation. Exile, wanderings, loneliness and rejection figure continually in his poems; from the light hearted "Owl and the Pussy-cat" and "The Jumblies" (from the *Nonsense Songs, Stories, Botany and Alphabets* of 1871) to the more restless and yearning "Dong with the Luminous Nose" (1877) and "My Aged Uncle Arly" (his last poem, published posthumously in 1895) there is the same desire to escape and "sail away." Of all these poems, "The Dong" seems best to express the romantic isolation of the outcast.

> When awful darkness and silence reign
> Over the great Gromboolian plain,
> Through the long, long wintry nights;—
> When the angry breakers roar
> As they beat on the rocky shore;—
> When the Storm clouds brood on the towering heights
> Of the Hills of the Chankly Bore:—

Then, through the vast and gloomy dark,
There moves what seems a fiery spark,
A lonely spark with silvery rays
Piercing the coal black night,—
A meteor strange and bright:—
Hither and thither the vision strays,
A single lurid light.
Slowly it wanders,—pauses,—creeps,—
Anon it sparkles,—flashes and leaps;
And ever as onward it gleaming goes
A light on the Bong tree stems it throws.
And those who watch at that midnight hour
From Hall or Terrace, of Lofty Tower,

Cry, as the wild light passes along,—
"The Dong!—the Dong! The wandering Dong through the forest
  goes!
"The Dong! the Dong!
"The Dong with a luminous Nose!"

4.1 Edward Lear: "The Dong with the Luminous Nose."

The grotesqueness is important. Lear always had a picture of himself as "more or less hideous"; in another deeply personal poem, "The Courtship of the Yonghy Bonghy Bo," the lovely lady Jingly Jones rejects him because she is already married, commenting for good measure on his appearance: "Though you've such a tiny body / And your head so large doth grow." In particular he always makes fun of enormous noses—like his own:

There was an Old Man in a Barge
Whose nose was exceedingly large,
But in fishing by night,
It supported a light
Which helped that Old Man in a Barge.

Here in the "Dong," allied with the personal feelings of isolation because of physical abnormality, is the fact that the abandoned Dong *chooses* his grotesque role:

> Playing a pipe with silvery squeaks,
> Since then his Jumbly Girl he seeks,
> And because by night he could not see,
> He gathered the bark of the Twangum Tree
> On the flowery plain that grows.
> And he wove him a wondrous Nose,—
> A Nose as strange as a Nose could be!
> Of vast proportions and painted red,
> And tied with cords to the back of his head.
> —In a hollow rounded space it ended
> With a luminous Lamp within suspended,
> All fenced about
> With a bandage stout
> To prevent the wind from blowing it out;—
> And with holes all round to send the light,
> In gleaming rays on the dismal night.

The heartbroken wanderer assumes the mask of the clown; the artist advertises his inner humiliation by communicating; Lear chooses his place as poet laureate of Nonsense. In 1863, when Greece crowned her new king,[7] Lear wrote to a friend asking him to "write to Lord Palmerston to ask him to ask the Queen to ask the King of Greece to give him a 'place' as 'Lord High Bosh and Nonsense Producer' . . . with permission to wear a fool's cap (or miter)–three pounds of butter yearly and a little pig,–and a small donkey to ride on."[8] Behind Lear's claim to the "fool's cap," or the Dong's carefully woven Nose, is something of the bitterness of Alfred De Vigny seeing the artist as the captured albatross casually tormented by the ignorant sailors: *Ses ailes de geant l'empechent de marcher.*

Vivien Noakes, one of Lear's best biographers, has suggested a threefold division of his nonsense writings. "The first, begun at Knowsley or even earlier and going all through the rest of his life, comes under the original classification of the happy and inconsequential." It includes the limericks, the botany, and cookery, and the nonsense he put into letters to amuse his friends. "Humour, though not an essential ingredient of nonsense, is often found in this group," he adds. The second group of stories and poems either have happy endings, or sad ones so nonsensical as not to be disturbing. It is in the third group, argues Noakes, that "the detachment is beginning to break down."[9] As in "The Daddy Long-legs and the Fly," "the world has all gone wrong." The verses are no longer primarily for children, but are expressions of his own deepest personal feelings.

Yet this division, simple and plausible as it seems at first sight, is not entirely satisfactory. Noakes's insistence that "the violence and distortion" of the limericks "leaves us unmoved" because they have the detachment essential to "pure nonsense" is an extension of Lear's own disclaimer of satire or any ulterior meaning that accompanied the publication of his first *Book of Nonsense* in 1846. But the detachment of pure nonsense is a chimera. In 1846 there was no established genre of nonsense, and Lear was much more concerned to guard his rhymes against topical or satirical interpretations than he was to define a new art form. As Noakes himself admits, incongruity is only meaningful against the background of a stable and organized world; without narrative or logical consistency it tends to drift into a mere dream.[10] As we have seen, "The Dong with the Luminous Nose" has a clear narrative: what is incongruous is the emotion that is poured into this absurd story. The reader receives, in effect, two entirely separate sets of signals, demanding quite different emotional levels of response. But if the "Dong" expresses a personal vein of alienation at its deeper level, it is a vein that nevertheless runs throughout his work in a less concentrated and intense form. The so-called "detachment" is always equivocal. In the limericks, for instance, the crowd, with its pressures toward conformity, is always threatening, criticizing, prophesying disaster, and persecuting the eccentric. "The Old Man of Whitehaven" belongs to the first, 1846 collection:

> There was an Old Man of Whitehaven,
> Who danced a quadrille with a Raven;
> But they said—"It's absurd, to encourage this bird!"
> So they smashed that Old Man of Whitehaven.

The only solution is that of the "Old Person of Basing"—and it was Lear's own:

> There was an Old Person of Basing,
> Whose presence of mind was amazing;
> He purchased a steed, which he rode at full speed,
> And escaped from the people of Basing.

By Lear's *Second Book of Nonsense* in 1872 the attitude to the crowd had become much more pointed and aggressive:

There was an old man in a garden,
Who always begged every one's pardon;
When they asked him, "What for?"—He replied "You're a bore!
And I trust you'll go out of my garden."

4.2 Edward Lear: "The Old Person of Stroud."

As have the solutions:

There was an old person of Stroud,
Who was horribly jammed in a crowd;
Some she slew with a kick, some she scrunched with a stick,
That impulsive old person of Stroud.

The only safe people are the dull and stupid:

There was an old man of Hong Kong,
Who never did anything wrong;
He lay on his back, with his head in a sack,
That innocuous old man of Hong Kong.

—or the old person of Shoreham, whose habits were marked by decorum:

He bought an Umbrella, and sate in the cellar,
Which pleased all the people of Shoreham.

Even direct political satire is present in some of the later limericks. One in the 1872 book, for instance, is specifically aimed at Gladstone's whistle stop election tours:

> There was an old man at a Station,
> Who made a promiscuous oration;
> But they said, "Take some snuff!—You have talk'd quite enough
> You afflicting old man at a Station!"

Though no one knows the origin of the name, we know that Lear did not invent the limerick. The earliest examples known are in a book called *Anecdotes and Adventures of Fifteen Gentlemen* published in 1820. Interestingly, it contains both the kind of limerick we associate specifically with Lear, where the rhyme of the last line is a repeat of the first, and also what is sometimes thought of as the more *modern* limerick, where the last line introduces a quite new rhyme:

> There was an old soldier of Bicester
> Was walking one day with his sister;
> A bull, with one poke,
> Toss'd her up in an oak,
> Before the old gentleman miss'd her.

Whether Lear ever actually saw the *Adventures of Fifteen Gentlemen* and its companion volumes, about *Fifteen Young Ladies* and *Sixteen Wonderful Old Women*, is not certain; if he did, it seems odd that it was not the old soldier of Bicester that triggered off Lear's interest in the form, but the much weaker *Old Man of Tobago*,[11] which appeared alongside it:

> There was an old man of Tobago
> Lived long on rice gruel and sago;
> But at last, to his bliss,
> The physician said this—
> To a roast leg of mutton you may go.

Poor and weak as this may be by later standards, it seems to have offered Lear what he needed—a form capable of endless variations of a rather subtle kind. It is sometimes held that Lear's limericks are themselves crude and feeble by later standards of wit and ingenuity. True as this is in a narrow sense, the very fact that the more complicated triple rhyme form predates Lear should cause us to hesitate before automatically assuming his limericks to be of a less sophisticated genre. Lear's limericks are never cerebral in the sense of being witty or clever, indeed, he studiously avoids the punch line at the end beloved of so many masters of the form. What he does, instead, is to highlight certain unexpected combinations of words by their position—usually in the middle of lines rather than at the end—and by their juxtaposition. Thus, in the case of the Old Person of Basing, the phrase *presence of mind* is suddenly linked with *escaped*. Hitherto there has been no suggestion of anything sinister about the people of Basing, but in the final repetition of the word at the end of the last line it has acquired a new and ambiguous quality. Are the good citizens of Basing in some obscure way very dangerous, or is it their very harmlessness that drives the perceptive Old Person to such precipitous flight? Is his presence of mind to be contrasted with the lack of the same quality in them? Either way, it's sucks to Basing. One is reminded of John Betjeman's "Come kindly bombs and fall on Slough." In the *Old Person of Stroud* a similar sequence of words obtrudes itself: *horribly jammed, slew/scrunched*, and finally *impulsive*. The word that sticks in the mind is the unexpectedly savage *scrunched*: but what then do we make of that final understatement, "impulsive"? *Impulse* was a key word in Romantic thought. For Wordsworth it was a touchstone of spontaneity:

> One impulse from a vernal wood
> May teach you more of man;
> Of moral evil and of good,
> Than all the sages can.
> (The Tables Turned 1798)

Lear's own use of the word is ironically in this "strong" Romantic sense. It carries all the flavor of its Latin root meaning: "an application of a sudden force, causing motion"; by the late eighteenth century the suggestions of this definition had acquired a more precise connotation in Dynamics: that of "an infinitely large force enduring for an inappreciably short time but producing finite momentum; such as the blow of a hammer." Thus Lear is being both pedantically correct in his use of the word, and at the very same time parodying Wordsworth by suggesting the eruption of violent and spontaneous forces in the psyche, rather than beneficent ones. But then, Wordsworth, it seemed, never got horribly jammed in the "crowd" in the way that Lear did.

The trains of ideas suggested by such juxtaposed word sequences are as complex as anything to be found in the other, more obviously witty, tradition of limericks, but their effect is sometimes only grimly comic. As we have seen, they frequently imply the movement of subconscious associations, rather than calculation, but this impression can be misleading. The complex sea changes of contexts and meanings are sometimes just zany, but just as often conceal sly etymological puns. Words like *runcible*, scroobious, and *ombliferous* are "pure" nonsense words; others are apparently converted into nonsense by context. Elizabeth Sewell claims that such lines as "You luminous person of Barnes," "That incipient old man at a casement," and "That intrinsic old man of Peru," fall into this category.[12] Yet recourse to the O.E.D. casts grave doubts. The old person of Barnes had "garments covered with darns":

> But they said, "Without doubt, you will soon wear them out,
> You luminous person of Barnes!"

4.3 Edward Lear: "The Old Person of Barnes."

The accompanying picture reinforces the image of a man of shreds and patches and holes. *Luminous*, we discover, can mean not merely "giving off light," but also "well-lighted" in the sense of a well-lit room; the man in the picture is undoubtedly well lighted. Similarly, the Old Man at a casement "held up his hands in amazement";

> When they said, "sir! you'll fall!" he replied, "Not at all!"
> That incipient Old Man at a casement.

There may be shades of a real portmanteau word, *inslipient*, here, but the root meaning of *incipient* is, of course, "beginning." His reply, "Not at all!" is strictly correct if he is only just beginning. Presumably he is a forerunner of Carroll's Humpty Dumpty. The Old Man of Peru actually has what looks like a double pun: "he tore off his hair, and behaved like a bear." Having torn off his hair, as the picture makes clear, the old man is certainly *bare*, and he is left with no extrinsic appendages; all he is left with is (literally) what is "in himself." Even more interesting, however, than these examples is the case of the word *promiscuous*, which is something of a favorite with

Lear. Apart from its obvious sexual connotation (which was newly acquired in Lear's time) it still carried its old force of "mixed" or "confused and indiscriminate" as its main meaning. Kingsley, in *Alton Locke* (1862), makes his shoemaker, in what may be intended as a slightly pompous archaism, refer to "ancient times [. . .] when any poor man as had a petition could come promiscuously to the King's royal presence."[13] Thus, to call the oration of the old man at the station promiscuous, or to describe how the Two Old Bachelors "over Crag and Precipice" "rolled promiscuous down," is merely to repeat the kind of game we have noticed above, but this time Lear is playing with fire. He is using a long and (to a child) exotic word apparently nonsensically, and in fact correctly. But what are we to make, in the light of Lear's own "syphilitic infections," of the association between "promiscuous" and "afflicting" in relation to Gladstone—the well-known street prowler and rescuer of prostitutes?

Just as it was the simplest limericks that apparently allowed Lear most scope for word play, so in the accompanying drawings there is a deftness of caricature and economy of line that is unequalled in his *serious* landscape work. To consider either pictures or poems apart from each other is to lose much of their suggestive vigor. Consider the expressions of the person from Barnes and the puzzled pair confronting him. At a comic level, the two art forms are as much a unity as Blake's in the *Songs of Innocence and Experience*; it has, perhaps, only been equalled by Thurber.

Thus, to describe the limericks as being "detached" in content, and "pure nonsense" is untrue. They are as mixed a form as the longer poems, revealing in miniature both the private obsessions and the sheer love of incongruity that characterize the longer, more serious poems. Moreover, it is important to remember that these two qualities cannot be separated in this kind of schematic way. Lear's love of incongruity and delight in word play and word abuse is not the less a sense of fun for being intimately bound up with his private guilt, fears, and obsessions. The human psyche is not divisible. There is no doubt, I believe, that Lear's entirely innocent use of promiscuous is also at the same time playing on the nonexistent sexual innuendo. He is, if you like, trying to get the adult reader to be half-shocked in order to show, by this false reaction, what a dirty mind the *reader* has; some comedians use the same technique much more blatantly today. For children, of course, *promiscuous*, like *incipient* or *intrinsic*, is simply a good nonsense word. As we suggested at the end of the first chapter, all forms of fantasy depend on laws as tightly structured as those of the real world (indeed, possibly more so, since magic has, by definition, no magic world beyond itself to hint at). Fantasy in some form appears in

almost every age; Nonsense is a product of the Victorian era. It is the true
inversion or underside of its culture in that, so far from being *free* or formless, it is the most highly organized and, in many ways, the most rigidly controlled of all forms of fantasy. Lear's turning to the limerick was not
accidental—it offered a brevity and discipline that is essential to the well-
timed non sequitur or sly irony, and creates a perfect complement to the
accompanying sketches. In the longer poems this structural tightness cannot so easily be achieved by form, and is more dependent on narrative; to
that degree they are less nonsensical. Yet it would be a mistake to argue that
Lear's nonsense is allegorical or satirical in any close structured sense.
Whereas the structure of Carroll's work is nearly always logical, in Lear's
the structure is primarily *emotional*. Not merely are the longer poems dominated and given shape by a prevailing mood or feeling, their nonsense is
almost always the result of an emotional, rather than a logical incongruity.
For the faithful hound, beloved of Victorian sentimental stories, my aged
Uncle Any has a faithful cricket; love affairs are always between preposter-
ously ill-matched people, animals, or things.

For Lear, as we have seen, this sense of things being ill-assorted or mis-
matched ran very deep. He perceived his whole world in terms of emotional incongruities, with the result that he was in the most literal sense a
person to whom nonsense "happened."

The journals of his travels are full of preposterous minor adventures. In
Greece, for example, while waiting for his guide to find a hut for the night
in pitch darkness, the exhausted Lear sat down on what he supposed to be
a bank—only to find that a dark "bovine quadruped suddenly rose up
under him and tilted him into the mud." According to his companion, as
Lear regained his feet he cheerily burst into song:

> There was an old man who said, Now
> I'll sit down on the horns of that cow.[14]

Earlier on the same tour at Elbassan, in Albania, Lear had recorded the following incident.

> No sooner had I settled to draw—forgetful of Bekir the guard—than forth
> came the population of Elbassan, one by one, and two by two, to a mighty
> host they grew, and there were soon from eighty to a hundred spectators
> collected, with earnest curiosity in every look; and when I had sketched
> such of the principal buildings as they could recognize, a universal shout
> of "shaitan!" (the Devil) burst from the crowd; and strange to relate, the
> greater part of the mob put their fingers in their mouths and whistled

furiously, after the manner of butcher boys in England. Whether this was a sort of spell against my magic I do not know; but the absurdity of sitting still on a rampart to make a drawing, while a great crowd of people whistled at me with all their might, struck me so forcibly, that come what might of it, I could not resist going off into convulsions of laughter, an impulse the Gheghes seemed to sympathize with, as one and all shrieked with delight, and the ramparts resounded with hilarious merriment.[15]

Another incident, which, one feels could only have happened to someone with an identity problem as great as Lear's, also illustrates the intense pride he took in his Nonsense, even while being uncertain of its value.

I was on my way from London to Guildford in a railway carriage containing, besides myself, one passenger, an elderly gentleman. Presently, however, two ladies entered, accompanied by two little boys. These, who had just had a copy of the *Book of Nonsense* given them, were loud in the delight, and by degrees infected the whole party with their mirth.

"How grateful," said the old gentleman to the two ladies, "all children and parents too ought to be to the statesman who has given his time to composing that charming book!"

(The ladies looked puzzled, as indeed was I, the author.)

"Do you not know who is the writer of it?" asked the gentleman.

"The name is 'Edward Lear,'" said one of the ladies.

"Ah!" said the first speaker; "so it is printed, but that is only a whim of the real author, the Earl of Derby. 'Edward' is his Christian name, and, as you may see, LEAR is only EARL transposed."

"But," said the lady doubtingly, "here is a dedication to the great grandchildren, grand nephews, and grand nieces of Edward, thirteenth Earl of Derby, by the author, Edward Lear."

"That," replied the other, "is simply a piece of mystification; I am in a position to know that the whole book was composed and illustrated by Lord Derby himself. In fact, there is no such person at all as Edward Lear."

"Yet," said the other lady, "some friends of mine tell me they know Mr. Lear."

"Quite a mistake! completely a mistake!" said the old gentleman, becoming rather angry at the contradiction, "I am well aware of what I am saying. I can inform you, no such person as 'Edward Lear' exists!"

Hitherto I had kept silence, but as my hat was, as well as my handkerchief and stick, largely marked inside with my name, and as I happened to have in my pocket several letters addressed to me, the temptation was too great to resist, so, flashing all these articles at once on my would-be extinguisher's attention, I speedily reduced him to silence.[16]

Yet for all the pride of moments like these (and there is, despite the humor, something alarming about needing to prove your identity by the name in your hat), Lear never seems to have valued his nonsense on the same level as his "serious" painting. He was paid as much as £400 for a large landscape, but in 1862 he parted with the *Book of Nonsense* outright to the publishers for £125, and considered that he had made a brilliant bargain. It was to go into nearly thirty editions in his own lifetime. He wrote to a friend, "I went into the city today to put the £125 . . . into the funds. It is doubtless a very unusual thing for an artist to put by money, for the whole way from Temple Bar to the Bank was *crowded* with carriages and people— so immense a sensation did this occurrence make. And all the way back it was the same, which was very gratifying."[17] His self-irony at this point is the more poignant because of another incident that same evening, when he went to dine with some friends. "Bye & bye, on showing the receipt for the Bk of Nonsense, they seemed to think it was nil, wh. distressed & disgusted me, & made me cross,"[18] he wrote, this time not to a friend, but to the privacy of his diary. Had it been 1846, one might argue that this strangely unbusinesslike deal was simply the result of inexperience, but by 1862 Lear had had ample time to see his growing popularity. It is clear, too, that he never thought of his nonsense writings as art. "I cannot but know," he once wrote to Holman Hunt about his painting, "that there is a vein of poetry within me that *ought to have* come out—though I begin to doubt if it ever will."[19]

This ambiguous and uncertain attitude towards nonsense may also serve to explain the enigma of Lear's and Carroll's obstinate silence about each other's work. Superficially, the parallels between them are striking. Both were shy and sensitive bachelors; both were very fond of children, and came themselves from large families; both were afraid of dogs;[20] both were of an "analytic state of mind"—Carroll indexed his entire correspondence, which, by his death had 98,000 cross-references. Both were marginal kinds of men, if in very different senses. Though Lear was mentally a rebel and internal refugee, he was in the last resort as much dominated by the society that threatened him as the more socially conventional Carroll. Both became internationally famous during each other's lifetimes as writers of nonsense. Yet neither, in letters, journals, or even recorded conversations, ever seems to have mentioned the other. This silence is the more extraordinary since they actually had many friends and acquaintances in common— including the pre-Raphaelites and Tennysons. The Tennyson family, like thousands of other Victorian middle class households, had both *The Book of Nonsense* and *Alice in Wonderland* on their shelves. However, it is possible, with the advantages of hindsight, to make the similarities appear greater than they might have seemed to the two writers themselves. For both, certainly, fantasy or Nonsense was a way of dealing with feelings of insecurity and loneliness, but we must remember that what we recognize as a genre simply did not exist before Lear's first *Book of Nonsense* in 1846—and that consisted entirely of limericks and drawings, very unlike anything of Carroll's. To a twentieth-century observer, the apparent similarities of language and style may be more those of a period than of specific individuals.[21] For instance, the made-up languages of Swift in *Gulliver's Travels* are strikingly similar to that in Fielding's *Tom Thumb the Great*, but the similarity is that both are offshoots of eighteenth-century English—a similarity not so easy to detect for eighteenth-century Englishmen. Similarly, for us today, the "Roman" costumes of the 1930s cinema look as unmistakably "1930s" as they do Roman.

It is reasonable to suppose, therefore, that a common "Victorianism" in Nonsense would not have been noticeable to Lear and Carroll and their immediate contemporaries. There is a good illustration of the existence of this invisible common ground in a letter from Canon Dodgson, Lewis Carroll's father, to his small son, which sounds to a modern ear like pure Lear:

> Then what a bawling & tearing of hair there will be! Pigs and babies, camels and butterflies, rolling in the gutter together—old women rushing up chimneys & cows after them—ducks hiding themselves in coffee cups, & fat geese trying to squeeze themselves into pencil cases.[22]

But the actual bases of Carroll's Nonsense were strikingly different from those of Lear.

The creation of the name, and the corresponding *persona* of "Lewis Carroll" is a case in point. But for the choice of Edmund Yeats, editor of a humorous paper called "The Train" we might now be dealing with the works of "Edgar Cuthwellis." On February 11, 1856, Charles Lutwidge Dodgson made the following entry in his diary:

> Wrote to Mr. Yeats sending him a choice of names:
> 1. *Edgar Cuthwellis* (made by transposition out of "Charles Lutwidge").
> 2. *Edgar U. C. Westhill* (ditto).
> 3. *Louis Carroll* (derived from Lutwidge . . . Ludovic . . . Louis, and *Charles*).
> 4. Lewis Carroll (ditto).

Yeats chose the last with sound instinct; but that Dodgson should employ a pen name at all, and that it should be a kind of remote pun, is clear indication of how different Carroll was from Lear. The shy mathematician of Christ Church needed a persona, but it had to be derived by a process of logical reasoning, however remote. Whereas Lear's nonsense is one of emotion, nostalgia, and sheer buffoonery, Carroll's is one of undeviating rationality pushed to its furthest and wildest extremes. Like Lear, Carroll found his nonsense in the everyday world around him; not, however, in its emotions or bizarre coincidences, but in the received conventions of society which had become frozen and reified, acquiring the status of objective "laws" of nature. To discover nonsense, all one had to do was to step through the framework of unquestioned assumptions that form the boundaries of our normal world. Carroll's "hemispherical problem," first broached in *The Rectory Umbrella*, a magazine he had composed for his family's amusement as a boy, illustrates literally the nonsense of convention in our daily lives:

> Half of the world, or nearly so, is always in the light of the sun: as the world turns round, this hemisphere of light shifts round too, and passes over each part of it in succession.

Supposing on Tuesday it is morning at London; in another hour it would be Tuesday morning at the West of England; if the whole world were land, we might go on tracing Tuesday Morning, Tuesday Morning all the way round, till in twenty-four hours we get to London again. But we *know* that at London, twenty-four hours after Tuesday morning, it is Wednesday morning. Where, then, in its passage round the earth, does the day change its name? Where does it lose its identity?[23]

The conventional answer to this problem, of course, is the International Date Line, but that was not agreed upon for another thirty years, in 1884. The young Dodgson goes on to suggest, almost with the air of a *reductio ad absurdum*, that an arbitrary line might be drawn on one side of which it would be Tuesday, on the other, Wednesday. He toys with the idea of allowing everyone to choose for themselves what day it is, but regretfully dismisses it as impractical. But without such a line, he points out, "there would be no distinction at all between each successive day, and no week, month, etc., so that we should have to say, 'The Battle of Waterloo happened today, about two million hours ago.'"[24] Where Lear sought to escape by moving geographically, Carroll simply moved the geography itself.

We find a more sophisticated version of this game in *Alice in Wonderland* itself. Alice's long fall down the rabbit hole has taken her to the center of the earth: she lands safely because, of course, there is no gravity to pull her further. But in Wonderland, at the center of the earth, there is also no rotation of the earth, no alternation of day and night, and therefore no *solar* time at all. What we do still have, however, is *lunar* time, based on the phases of the moon (assuming they were visible!). But the lunar month is only twenty eight days, whereas the calendar one—based on an arbitrary division of the solar year—is thirty or more. The Mad Hatter's watch, we recall from Alice's surprised comment, tells not hours, but days of the month. When he asks her "What day of the month is it?" she replies "The fourth."

> "Two days wrong!" sighed the Hatter. "I told you butter wouldn't suit the works!" he added, looking angrily at the March Hare.[25]

We already know from the previous chapter that the month is May, so the date is May 4th, which turns out to be the birthday of Alice Liddell—daughter of Dean Liddell of Christ Church, the original "Alice" for whom the story was composed. Now if we consult an almanac for May 4, 1862—the year in which *Alice in Wonderland* was first told—we find, as might be guessed, that on that day there was exactly two days' difference between solar and lunar time. In other words, the Mad Hatter's watch read the sixth.[26] In an echo of the old hemispherical problem, the Mad Tea-party had to choose not what day it was, but what hour it should be, so they chose tea-time.

"It's always six o'clock now."

Elsewhere, in *The Hunting of the Snark*, Carroll was to turn his attention to the other conventions of terrestrial geography. The Bellman, leading the expedition in search of the mysterious and elusive Snark, has armed himself with a map which is "A perfect and absolute blank":

> "What's the good of Mercator's North Poles and Equators,
> Tropics, Zones, and Meridian Lines?"
> So the Bellman would cry: and the crew would reply
> "They are merely conventional signs!"
>
> (Fit II, stanza 3)

Even with this clearheaded approach, not all is plain sailing, however, for "the bowsprit got mixed with the rudder sometimes" and the Bellman's navigational instruction is not always helpful. But Carroll's fascination with conventional signs did not stop with the rules of geography and time. Earlier, at the beginning of *Alice in Wonderland*, he had already turned his attention to the bases of numbers themselves. The fact that we normally work to the base 10 is itself no more than an arbitrary convention, the natural product of our having five digits on each hand. When Alice in the hall with the pool of tears begins to have (understandable) doubts as to her identity because of her alarming changes of size, she attempts, like Wordsworth,[27] to revert to the certainties of mathematics:

> I'll try if I know all the things I used to know. Let me see: four times five is twelve, and four times six is thirteen, and four times seven is—oh dear! I shall never get to twenty at that rate![28]

Something has gone disastrously wrong with the certainties of mathematics. Normally, we count to 10, and then start again. 10 + 1 we call 11, 10 + 2 is 12, and so on. When we reach 10 + 10 we call it *twenty* (i.e. base 2) and we start again: (base 2) + 1, etc. Now when Alice says that 4 x 5 = 12, her base is clearly not the conventional one of 10; if it were, 12 would be base + 2, and 4 x 5 = 20. *Her* base + 2 = 20, so Alice's base must be 18. Looking at 4 x 6 = 13 in the same way, we find that the base is now 21: 4 x 6 = 24 = 21 + 3 = base + 3 = 10 (our base) + 3 = 13. We have, therefore, something very extraordinary indeed: a progression or *table* in which the base *increases* by 3 each time. 4 x 7 = 14 (base 24); 4 x 8 = 15 (base 27); and so on until we reach 4 x 12 = 19 (base 39). We might expect to find that 4 x 13 = 20 (base 42). However, it does not; for 20 = 10 x 2 = base x 2—which, on a base of 42, is 84. Alice is in fact quite right, for as long as the base is increasing by 3 at each step and the product by only one, she will, of course, never reach 20.[29] Carroll has invented a new, logical, regular, and utterly lunatic multiplication table.

The non-mathematician's head reels, but the arithmetic of *Alice in Wonderland* is simple compared with what happens in *Through the Looking Glass*. *Alice in Wonderland*, for all its problems with time, is still playing with the conventions of *our* world. Through the looking glass, however, we pass from our world into its mirror-reflection. Where before, the laws of nature were the same and it was merely the situation that was altered, now the familiar laws of our existence are completely inverted as well. The basic framework is a game of chess—a strange game, perhaps, but the sort of childish game, full of mistakes, that a real Alice might play. But we are through the looking glass; everything is inverted so time runs backwards. Hatta (our old friend the Mad Hatter apparently reincarnated) is "in prison now, being punished: and the trial doesn't even begin till next Wednesday: and of course the crime comes last of all." The White Queen summarizes the problem:

> "It's a poor sort of memory that only works backwards," the Queen remarked.
> "What sort of things do you remember best?" Alice ventured to ask.
> "Oh, things that happened the week after next," the Queen replied in a careless tone.[30]

As a kind of *reductio ad absurdum*, while she is speaking the White Queen is bandaging her finger; then she screams; and finally she pricks it.

Behind the looking glass movement is similarly inverted. In a letter, Lewis Carroll tells how he stood a child (named Alice, naturally) in front of a mirror with an orange in her right hand. When asked in which hand the little girl in the mirror held the orange, Alice replied, "her left."

> "How do you explain that?" asked Carroll. Alice couldn't explain it. Instead, she wondered:
> "Supposing I was on the other side of the glass, wouldn't the orange still be in my right hand?"
> "Well done, little Alice," exclaimed Carroll. "It's the best answer I've had yet."[31]

According to Carroll, this incident was the genesis of the mirror theme in his mind. It is certainly the basis of a great deal of tricks that are played by the looking glass world on Alice, for, we must remember, though she has crossed into the inverted world of her own reflection, she herself remains *un-inverted*. This is obviously essential if she is to experience the contrast: if everything, including the observer, were simply back to front, there would be no perception of the difference possible. Alice first encounters the problem when she walks out of the house into the garden and tries to walk towards the hill. By trial and error she discovers that she can only go the way she wants by walking firmly in the opposite direction. This is familiar mirror inversion. But when she actually succeeds in meeting the Red Queen (by walking in the opposite direction, of course), something even more extraordinary happens.

Just at this moment, somehow or other, they began to run. Alice could never quite make it out, in thinking it over afterwards, how it was that they began: all she remembers is, that they were running hand in hand, and the Queen went so fast that it was all she could do to keep up with her: and still the Queen kept crying "Faster"![32]

4.4 John Tenniel: "Still the Queen Kept Crying 'Faster!'"
Illustration to Lewis Carroll's Through the Looking Glass.

But nothing moves. Much has been written and claimed about this episode—even that it anticipates Einstein and the theory of relativity—but the basic rationale is very simple. In our world, this side of the looking glass, Speed is the ratio of Distance over Time: $S = d/t$. In other words, the higher the speed at which we travel, the greater the distance traveled, and the shorter the time taken. Through the looking glass, however, the equation is, in Carroll's logic, inverted, so that $S = t/d$. The higher the speed, the *greater* the time taken, and the *shorter* the distance covered. Thus you have to run very fast indeed in order to stand still:

> The Queen propped her against a tree and said kindly, "You may rest a little, now." Alice looked round her in great surprise. Why, I do believe we've been under this tree all the time! Everything's just as it was!"
>
> "Of course it is," said the Queen: "what would you have it?"
>
> "Well, in *our* country," said Alice, still panting a little, "you'd generally get to somewhere else—if you ran very fast for a long time, as we've been doing."

"A slow sort of country!" said the Queen.

"Now, *here*, you see, it takes all the running you can do to keep in the same place. If you want to get somewhere else, you must run at least twice as fast as that!"[33]

Alice's words *all the time* are, of course, a typical Carroll pun: since time has been substituted for our space, they were actually running *in time*. Indeed, such puns are actually sanctioned by the inversions of the whole scheme. If it is possible to invert a word, the result is presumably a pun, unless it be the literal inversion of mirror writing, in which Jabberwocky is, of course, discovered. Humpty Dumpty claims, "When I use a word, it means just what I choose it to mean—neither more nor less."[34] It is he, we recall, who interprets Jabberwocky to Alice. The theme of inversion is thus taken up and explored at every level in *Through the Looking Glass*, from the most simple spacial reversals suggested by the mirror itself; to a complete mathematical and linguistic scheme of things. The only inversion that Carroll does not show us, is that of time itself. The White Queen bandaging her finger, then screaming, and finally pricking herself is an inversion of the *sequence* of cause-and-effect, but it is *not* a reversal of time. In *Sylvie and Bruno*, however, the first of Carroll's final pair of nonsense books, we find a watch that can be set to go forwards or backwards, and carries time with it accordingly.

Armed with this instrument of science fiction, Carroll, who appears more or less as himself in the story, enters a house to observe the effects of time reversal. He finds a mother with four daughters of ages "from about fourteen down to ten" who were, apparently, all coming towards the door:

(I found they were really walking *backwards*), while their mother, seated by the fire with her needlework on her lap, was saying, just as I entered the room, "Now, girls you may get your things on for a walk."

To my utter astonishment—for I was not yet accustomed to the action of the Watch—"all smiles ceased: (as Browning says) on the four pretty faces, and they all got out pieces of needlework, and sat down. No one noticed *me* in the least, as I quietly took a chair and sat down to watch them.

When the needlework had been unfolded, and they were all ready to begin, their mother said "Come, *that's* done at last! You may fold up your work, girls." But the children took no notice whatever of the remark; on the contrary, they set to work at once sewing—if that is the proper word to describe an operation such as *I* had never before witnessed. Each of them threaded her needle with a short end of thread attached to the work, which was instantly pulled by an invisible force through the stuff, dragging the needle after it: the nimble fingers of the little seamstress caught it at the other side, but only to lose it again the next moment. [. . .]

At last all the work was picked to pieces and put away, and the lady led the way into the next room, walking backwards, and making an insane remark "Not yet, dear: we must get the sewing done first." After which, I was not surprised to see the children skipping backwards after her, exclaiming, "Oh, mother, it is such a lovely day for a walk!"

In the dining-room, the table had only dirty plates and empty dishes on it. However the party—with the addition of a gentleman, as good natured and as rosy, as the children—seated themselves at it very contentedly.

You have seen people eating cherry tart, and every now and then cautiously conveying a cherry stone from their lips to their plates? Well, something like that went on all through this ghastly—or shall we say "ghostly"?—banquet.

An empty fork is raised to the lips: there it receives a neatly cut piece of mutton, and swiftly conveys it to the plate, where it instantly attaches itself to the mutton already there. Soon one of the plates, furnished with a complete slice of mutton and two potatoes, was handed up to the presiding gentleman, who quietly replaced the slice on the joint, and the potatoes in the dish.[35]

The only thing Carroll does *not* invert here is the actual speech of individual characters: a concession necessary to the intelligibility of the whole scene. Indeed, at another level, the scene is all too intelligible. The idealized middle-class family (all girls, we notice; Carroll did not like little boys) is reversed to make possible one of the things Carroll most desired. He can take his place among them invisibly, and without question, in this fantasy. Behind it lie two other unstated possibilities: the recovery of a lost little girl, Alice Liddell herself, who has in reality grown up, married, and gone out of Carroll's life; and secondly, the inversion of a whole society that frowns (as Mrs. Liddell did) on the association of bachelor dons and little girls, and creates and endorses such separations.[36] Like Lear, Carroll has no alternative society to put in the place of his world, he merely plays with the nonsense of inverting it and making it go backwards.

Yet if our understanding of the technique itself is incomplete without an attempt to see the psychological motivations behind it, it is no less truncated if we fail to see the brilliance of what Carroll *has* created of his desire to invert existence. The whole passage anticipates with uncanny visual accuracy something that could not actually be *seen* until the invention of the cine camera. Carroll was, of course, a first-class amateur photographer. It was his real entrée into such domestic scenes as that pictured in the incident: the first time he went to see the Tennysons it was on the strength of a brief introduction, and an offer to photograph the family. It would be fascinating to know if Carroll had ever seen any of the early experiments with moving pictures. Another uncanny visualization in *Sylvie and Bruno*, however, could certainly not have been based on any such experiments.

> [I]f I take this book, and hold it out at arm's length, of course I feel its *weight*. It is trying to fall, and I prevent it. And, if I let it go, it falls to the floor. But, if we were all falling together, it couldn't be *trying* to fall any quicker, you know: for if I let go, what more could it do than fall? And, as my hand would be falling too—at the same rate—it would never leave it, for that would be to get ahead of it in the race. And it could never overtake the falling floor.[37]

The mathematics of space travel and the problems of weightlessness are a twentieth-century concern; once again, Carroll's disengagement from his immediate surroundings, enables him to put one foot off the planet, even while remaining very Victorian in his balance—or logic.

Carroll's fascination with logical structure repeats itself at every level like a sequence of Chinese boxes. The verbal logic, punning, and word play is paralleled by inverted or reversed sequences in the action, and finally, with a fascination with the ambiguities of aesthetic form itself. He never repeats himself. *Alice in Wonderland* is a dream; so is *Through the Looking Glass*, but whereas the former is in geographical limbo at the still point of the turning world with dream transitions, the latter is a formal chess game; *The Hunting of the Snark* is a mock heroic epic (or as Carroll himself calls it, "an agony in eight fits"); *Sylvie and Bruno* offers us two parallel worlds with abrupt magical transitions between them, reminiscent of George MacDonald's fantasies, which Carroll certainly knew well.[38] Each form is explored with extraordinary subtlety of repetition to produce an aesthetic organization of almost fugue-like complexity. Thus the initial dream of Alice, when it is transposed into the complex mirror-images of *Through the Looking Glass*, is finally matched by a dream of *her* by the Red King.

> "He's dreaming now," said Tweedledee: "and what do you think he's dreaming about?"
>
> Alice said, "Nobody can guess that."
>
> "Why, about *you*!" Tweedledee exclaimed, clapping his hands triumphantly. "And if he left off dreaming about you, where do you suppose you'd be?"
>
> "Where I am now, of course," said Alice.

"Not you!" Tweedledee retorted contemptuously. "You'd be nowhere. Why you're only a sort of thing in his dream!"

"If that there King was to wake," added Tweedledum, "you'd go out—bang!—just like a candle!"

"I shouldn't!" Alice exclaimed indignantly. "Besides, if *I'm* only a sort of thing in his dream, what are *you*, I should like to know?"

"Well, it's no use *your* talking about waking him," said Tweedledum, "when you're only one of the things in his dream. You know very well you're not real."

"I *am* real!" said Alice, and began to cry.[39]

4.5 John Tenniel: "Tweedledum and Tweedledee."
Illustration to Lewis Carroll's Through the Looking Glass.

The dispute about who is in whose dream is never solved, only shelved by the quarrel of Tweedledum and Tweedledee. The Red King continues to sleep on undisturbed under the tree throughout the story, and right at the very end Alice continues to puzzle over which was the *real* dream, and which its mirror image. Carroll has here made use of something like Berkeley's notion that all material things, including ourselves, are given their existence in the mind of God.[40] But the Red King is not God. He is merely the mirror image of Alice, dreaming about her dreaming about him.

Yet mirror images are not identical. In the *White Knight's Song*, ostensibly a parody of Wordsworth's "Resolution and Independence," we find the lines,

And now, if e'er by chance I put
My fingers into glue
Or madly squeeze a right-hand foot
Into a left-hand shoe.[41]

As Tenniel's illustration of Alice going through the mirror reminds us, the lateral inversion of mirror reflections produces an asymmetry: right-hand shoes, or screw threads, are not interchangeable with left-handed ones; even clocks tell a different time when reflected. The little girl with the orange in her hand had raised a problem that was to fascinate Carroll all his life. One of Kant's early works, *On the First Ground for the Distinctions of Regions in Space* (1768), deals with the very question of asymmetry that so intrigued Carroll, and it is extremely likely that he had read it.[42] Kant actually cites the example of a written page: "In a written page, for instance [. . .] the very same writing becomes unrecognisable when seen in such a way that everything which formerly was from left to right is reversed and is viewed from right to left."[43] This was how the *Looking Glass* books appeared to Alice. Jabberwocky is first seen in mirror writing (Carroll had to have a special block made with reversed type to show this) and Alice has to hold it up to the mirror before she can make sense of it.[44]

Various critics have professed to find allegorical correspondences in Carroll's work.[45] Interpretations of *Alice in Wonderland* abound—all entertaining and ingenious, many with a germ of probability. The mirror writing has been seen as a parody of contemporary Oxford scholarship, while Jabberwocky itself has been taken as the story of how Benjamin Jowett, the notoriously agnostic Professor of Greek at Oxford, and Master of Baliol, came to sign the Thirty Nine Articles to save his job. Perhaps more probable is the suggestion that Tweedledum and Tweedledee are the High and Low Church factions, embattled over trivia of ecclesiastical ritual until terrified into flight by the monstrous crow of Disestablishment. Certainly the story of two (equal) warriors being frightened off their battle by a big black bird occurs as early as Ariosto's *Orlando Furioso* (1516).[46] One of the more plausible versions of the chess game holds that the Red Queen is the Church of Rome, and the White Queen, the Church of England. Where the Red Queen is confident—and certainly believes herself infallible—the White Queen is merely vague and amiable, boasting of being able to read words of one letter. When frightened by the monstrous Crow, she says she couldn't even remember her own name—a confession which gives plausibility to the theory that the Crow is Disestablishment. In matters spiritual she excels herself: being able to believe "as many as six impossible things before breakfast." We are strongly reminded of Newman's satires on the Anglican Church in his 1850 *Lectures on Certain Difficulties felt by Anglicans.* "It cannot be said to think"; he commented scornfully, "it does not know what it holds and what it does not; it is not even conscious of its own existence."[47] However, another authority believes that the White Queen is Newman himself, and the Red Queen Manning.

What is certain is that Carroll enjoyed satires, parodies, and thinly veiled allegory; during his time in Oxford he produced a number of occasional pieces of this vein—some with excruciating puns. A few of these, such as the *White Knight's Song* itself, found their way into his longer published nonsense works, often with considerably revised texts. The actual evidence would suggest that nearly all these apparently exclusive "interpretations" of Carroll's books could in fact be right; though there is ample evidence of allegory and satire, there is very little evidence of consistency. Carroll worked from episodes, not from consistent characters. Every local scandal and cause of gossip in Oxford was grist to his mill—often finding its way into his books long after the particular incident which had inspired it had been forgotten. What was important for Carroll, with this mosaic patchwork technique of construction was that with it he was able to create not merely an alternative language, but enter into alternative worlds. At its simplest these were literal "alternative worlds" such as Wonderland, or the Looking Glass World, or even the tiny world in *Sylvie and Bruno Concluded,* which was so small that one "could walk right round it in twenty minutes."

> There had been a great battle, just before his visit, which had ended rather oddly: the vanquished army ran away at full speed, and in a few minutes found themselves face-to-face with the victorious army, who were marching home again, and who were so frightened at finding themselves between two armies, that they surrendered at once![48]

At a more complex and deeper level, Carroll's alternative world in the *Alice* books *is* a theological one. But it is not that of the satiric allegorical correspondences and Oxford scandals; those, like the puns, the mathematical games, and the chess moves, belong to the superficial structure. In what is by far the best book on Carroll to date, A. L. Taylor argues convincingly that in the *Alice* books Dodgson is using a metaphorical pattern

> so elaborate and far-fetched that if found in the work of Donne or Herrick it would be called "conceit." And this is the truth of the matter: in his serious verse Dodgson was a minor nineteenth-century romantic, but in his

prose he was the latest, and greatest of the metaphysical poets. The book is not so much an allegory as a kind of plastic fable or parable, the same symbols, even Alice, being used in different ways at different times in the way that a phrase is used in music or an expression in algebra.[49]

We do not necessarily have to agree that Carroll is the greatest of the metaphysical poets to see the value of this way of looking at him. It offers us a perspective by which we can bring into focus the sheer range of events and moods in the *Alice* books—which can be so easily lost in the more piecemeal hunt for allegory. Especially in *Through the Looking Glass*, the humor and satire are intermingled with much darker and more frightening passages—such as the ending of Queen Alice's feast.

> "Take care of yourself!" screamed the White Queen, seizing Alice's hair with both her hands. "Something's going to happen!"
>
> And then (as Alice afterwards described it) all sorts of things happened in a moment. The candles all grew up to the ceiling, looking something like a bed of rushes with fireworks at the top. As to the bottles, they each took a pair of plates, which they hastily fitted on as wings, and so, with forks for legs, went fluttering about: "and very like birds they look," Alice thought to herself, as well she could in the dreadful confusion that was beginning.
>
> At this moment she heard a hoarse laugh at her side, and turned to see what was the matter with the White Queen; but instead of the Queen, there was the leg of mutton sitting in the chair. "Here I am!" cried a voice from the soup-tureen, and Alice turned again, just in time to see the Queen's broad good natured face grinning at her for a moment over the edge of the tureen, before she disappeared into the soup.[50]

What is going to happen is the end of the game. The rules by which it has been played out are now redundant. The White Queen is in the soup. Alice, the newly queened pawn, takes the Red Queen. As usual, much can (correctly) be made of the various levels of allegory and symbolism, but there is a terrifying and nightmarish quality to this apocalypse that is not explicable in terms of a chess game or even Oxford intrigues. It belongs to another, and much more primitive emotional set. Here A. L. Taylor, though he does his task better than any of his fellow critics, follows essentially the same method in attempting to work out the details of what is happening:

> After Judgement Day ("Examination"), Kingdom Come—or Creation. It is the Twilight of the Chess men, the last confusion. The Leg of Mutton sits in the Queen's chair and even the Soup ladle comes "walking up the

table to Alice and signing to her to get out of its way." Matter is triumph-
ing over mind. The last shall be first, with a vengeance! [. . .] Alice pulls
the table cloth and brings "plates, dishes, guests and candles crashing in a
heap on the floor," which looks like the end of a good many things dear
to the heart of the Catholic.[51]

Only as an afterthought does he hint at possible reasons why Alice, "gentle,
patient, and unselfish," who does all that is demanded of her, finds at the
end that "her empty plate turns into a queenly crown."[52] I suspect that to
find the roots of that extraordinary emotional force behind the last judgment and Alice's triumph we need to look not at the attenuated world of
nineteenth-century Anglicanism, which has provided so much of the overt
symbolism of *Through the Looking Glass*, but at the harsher mediaeval
world of Bosch, and its serenely beautiful counterpart in mystical poems
like *The Pearl*. In that great fourteenth-century poem, the "Pearl" of the
title is a little girl who has died and who is revealed to her grief-stricken
father in a trance. She tells him her state of bliss: she, herself, is a "Queen"
in Heaven. In our world, she explains, there can only be one Queen, but in
Heaven there is a looking-glass reversal of earthly values: there *all* are
Queens. For us, to share something, be it a plate of strawberries or the
crown of the realm, is to diminish it proportionately; such is the nature of
divine love, however, that in Heaven sharing always *enhances* and increases
what is shared. Monarchy itself is incomplete until all shall be kings and
queens. It is a conception worthy of a Dante; it is also a conception that, for
quite other reasons, reflects the logical and emotional yearnings of the
lonely mathematics don of Christ Church. When Alice forgets her name in
the wood without names, she is sure that it begins with an "L."[53]

Just as the Gothick convention offered so many writers of the late eighteenth and early nineteenth centuries an alternative language for dealing
with areas of unassimilable psychological experience, so Nonsense offered
the Victorians, like Carroll and Lear, an alternative language for coping
with the conditions of a world at once more complicated and more repressive. So far from being random, or, in that interesting and very revealing
word so beloved of some of its admirers, "pure" and meaningless,
Nonsense constituted an entire alternative aesthetic, making possible a radically different kind of art. In the attitudes of both Lear and Carroll, as well
as in the minor Nonsense writers such as Hood, we can trace the emer-
gence of this new form in the uneasy and ambiguous way in which they
regarded their own creations: both decrying them, and simultaneously
insisting that they be valued by others. We see it, for instance, in Carroll's

decision that the original printing of the *Alice* illustrations was not good enough; in the end the whole first edition was withdrawn, and given either to children's hospitals, or sent to America where inferior workmanship would not be noticed! We see it in the curious little sermons and homilies to children that so disfigure the last two Nonsense books of Carroll, *Bruno and Sylvie* and *Bruno and Sylvie Concluded*. We can see it in Lear's own evident confusion over the value of his work. In this sense, the personal unease that drove both authors in the direction of fantasy to begin with was only exacerbated by the product—however much it may have satisfied them in other ways. It was another group of fantasy writers, more confident of their part in Victorian literature, Kingsley and MacDonald, that were to bring the art form to full self-consciousness, even if their work was neither as clever, nor in the long run as popular as that of the two sad eccentrics, Lear and Carroll.

Chapter 5

Adults in Allegory Land:
Kingsley and MacDonald

During the summer of 1863, Charles Dodgson was at work in Oxford put-
ting the finishing touches on *Alice in Wonderland*. Henry Kingsley, the
novelist brother of Charles, had already seen the manuscript while staying
with the Liddells at Christchurch Deanery, and had urged him to publish.[1]
Hesitating, Dodgson sought a second opinion, and lent the script to his
friend George MacDonald, whom he had met in the 1850s through a doctor, James Hunt, who had been treating him for his stammer. MacDonald
read it to his children. When they reached the end, the eldest, six-year-old
Greville, "exclaimed that there ought to be sixty thousand volumes of it."[2]
With hindsight, the children's enthusiastic approval may seem a foregone
conclusion, but for one who clearly was still nervous of the new medium,
Dodgson's choice of literary judges was significant. MacDonald had already
published his first fantasy, what he had called an "adult fairy story."
Phantastes, in 1858. It had earned him a small but growing reputation and
a circle of admirers including Dodgson. It was by any measure a startlingly
original work, and to an English public, almost totally unaware of its
German antecedents, it was doubly so, and made MacDonald the obvious
person for Dodgson to consult about his own book. But while Dodgson
was still hesitating and revising, another fantasy was published which was
to outsell both MacDonald's and Carroll's books over the next few years:
Charles Kingsley's *The Water Babies*.

Like *Alice in Wonderland*, it was written for a specific person,
Kingsley's youngest son, Grenville.

> Sitting at breakfast at the rectory one spring morning this year, the father
> was reminded of an old promise, "Rose, Maurice, and Mary have got

their book, and baby must have his." He made no answer, but got up at once and went into his study, locking the door. In half an hour he returned with the story of little Tom. This was the first chapter of "The Waterbabies," written off without a correction. The rest of the book, which appeared monthly in "Macmillan's Magazine," was composed with the same rapidity and ease as the first chapter—if indeed what was so purely an inspiration could be called composing, for the whole thing seemed to flow naturally out of his brain and heart, lightening both of a burden without exhausting either; and the copy went to the printer's with scarcely a flaw. He was quite unprepared for the sensation it would make.[3]

Like the fantasies of both Carroll and MacDonald, it was basically a theological allegory, but whereas they, in their very different ways, used their theology to provide a hidden structure to the narrative, Kingsley's book brashly proclaimed its allegorical status in almost every line and incident. To his friend and "master," F. D. Maurice, Kingsley wrote with typical directness:

I have tried, in all sorts of queer ways, to make children and grown folks understand that there is a quite miraculous and divine element underlying all physical nature; and that nobody knows anything about anything, in the sense in which they may know God in Christ, and right and wrong. And if I have wrapped up my parable in seeming Tomfooleries, it is because so only could I get the pill swallowed by a generation who are not believing with anything like their whole heart, in the living God.

Meanwhile, remember that the physical science in the book is *not* nonsense, but accurate earnest, as far as I dare speak yet.[4]

Yet the throwaway reference to the *parable* as a "pill" to be sugared by "seeming Tom-fooleries" is deceptive. Perhaps we should be put on our guard from the fact that Tom's name itself is derived from "Tom-foolery." The whole point of sugaring a pill normally is to make it palatable by *concealing* it; Kingsley's method is the exact opposite of this: he is, in effect, constantly calling attention to the sugar.

But remember always, as I told you at first, that this is all a fairy tale, and only fun and pretence; and, therefore, you are not to believe a word of it even if it is true.[5]

It would be easy to assume, from the apparent speed and casualness with which Kingsley worked, that he simply put it down as it came to him, and that the result has little of conscious artistry in it, but his easy flowing style in fact conceals a carefully worked out structure. At the age of seventeen Kingsley had written a heavily symbolic fantasy with the title, *Psyche, a Rhapsody*. Its romantic Platonism is callow and derivative enough in detail, but in its overall design there is considerable originality; with hindsight, it is not difficult to see in the maiden's quest for love through a variety of tableaux a first working out of how fantasy might serve as a theological instrument.[6] If so, it was by means of a bold technical inversion that it was to reach its culmination in *The Water Babies*.

We have noted how *The Water Babies* flaunts its allegorical status at the reader, but if in fact he takes up the challenge and sets to work to summarize this apparently simple parable and relate it to the underlying "spiritual narrative," he discovers almost at once that something very curious has happened. Many of the best bits of the story are unaccountably missing. Unlike that equally self-advertising allegory, *The Pilgrim's Progress*, to a new illustrated edition of which he wrote an introduction in 1860, there is not a clear one-for-one correspondence between the events in the surface narrative and the underlying theme: the surface narrative is stuffed with superfluous detail that is actually quite irrelevant to the deep structure. The main story itself is rambling and ramshackle, taking every excuse for asides or digressions that cut right across any clear allegorical thread, but, as recourse to any of the numerous abridged versions will demonstrate, *The Water Babies* is a story that needs its irrelevancies and digressions. It is interesting to notice how often those who feel the need to cut or pare down the narrative to a simpler form, are the same ones who confess to disliking the barebones story anyway.[7] The full version is superior to the abridgements because it is simply a quite different kind of work. Dissolve the sugar, and something very odd indeed has happened to the pill—it is hardly there at all. *The Water Babies* is one of the very rare examples in literature of inverted didacticism. Lewis Carroll's Duchess assures Alice that "Everything's got a moral, if only you can find it."[8] Kingsley's frequent disclaimers of "a moral" are coupled with a structure that clearly implies the existence of any number: why else, for instance, should we have that pair *in loco parentis*, Mrs. Doasyouwouldbedoneby and Mrs. Bedonebyasyoudid? The very names reek of Bunyan. Yet this same structure appears on closer inspection to be parodying itself, even while being in earnest. That this might be part of a deliberate aesthetic structure becomes increasingly probable once we notice that Kingsley has modeled himself not so much on Bunyan, as on Sterne and Rabelais.

We get the first clue to this extraordinary synthesis as early as 1849. To his wife he wrote, "I have read Rabelais right through, and learnt

5.1 Noel Paton: "Mrs. Douasyouwouldbedoneby."
Illustration to Charles Kingsley's The Water Babies.

immensely from him."[9] "Were he ten times as unspeakably filthy as he is,"
Kingsley wrote to a friend the following day, "I consider [him] as priceless
in wisdom, and often in true evangelic godliness."[10] How Rabelais fits into
Kingsley's world is illustrated quite strikingly by a book he produced a few
years after, in 1854. *Glaucus* is a book for children on the wonders of the
seashore: an introduction to marine biology within a framework of natural
theology. It is an early example of the passion for underwater life that provides the setting for so much of *The Water Babies*, as well as its incidental
interest, but it is also an example of the way in which the marine world
immediately inspires in Kingsley a Rabelasian gusto of description. It is, of
course, very apt. There *is* something monstrous, grotesque, scatalogical,
and wildly comic about water life to our eyes, and it is these qualities about
the caddis fly, the lobster, of the long sea worm that instantly appealed.
The beginning of chapter III of *The Water Babies* has a series of such
comic/satiric descriptions:

> Sometimes [. . .] he went into a still corner, and watched the caddises eat-
> ing dead sticks as greedily as you would eat plum pudding, and building
> their houses with silk and glue. Very fanciful ladies they were; none of

them would keep to the same materials for a day. One would begin with some pebbles; then she would stick on a piece of green weed; then she found a shell, and stuck it on too; and the poor shell was alive, and did not like being taken to build houses with: but the caddis did not let him have any voice in the matter, being rude and selfish, as vain people are apt to be; then she stuck on a piece of rotten wood, then a very smart pink stone, and so on till she was patched all over like an Irishman's coat. Then she found a long straw, five times as long as herself, and said, "Hurrah! my sister has a tail, and I'll have one too"; and she stuck it on her back, and marched about with it quite proud, though it was very inconvenient indeed. And, at that, tails became all the fashion among the caddis baits in that pool, as they were at the end of the Long Pond last May, and they all toddled about with long straws sticking out behind, getting between each others legs, and tumbling over each other, and looking so ridiculous, that Tom laughed at them till he cried, as we did. But they were quite right you know; for people must always follow the fashion, even if it be spoon-bonnets.[11]

The ambiguity of that last remark is pure Kingsley, as is the chatty colloquial tone of the whole passage. One can sense his wonder and delight that an "accurate earnest" description of water life should open up a world best described in terms of *Gargantua* or *Tristram Shandy*.

The defenses of St. Brandan's Isle illustrate perfectly the way in which the Rabelasian technique has become fused with the delight in accurate biological detail of *Glaucus*.

And, instead of watchmen and policemen to keep out nasty things at night, there were thousands and thousands of water snakes; and most wonderful creatures they were. They were all named after the Nereids, the sea-fairies who took care of them, Eunice and Polynoe, Phyllodoce and Psamathe, and all the rest of the pretty darlings who swim round their Queen Amphitrite, and her car of cameo shell. They were dressed in green velvet, and black velvet, and purple velvet; and all were jointed in rings; and some of them had three hundred brains apiece, so that they must have been uncommonly shrewd detectives: and some had eyes in their tails; and some had eyes in every joint, so that they kept a very sharp look out; and when they wanted a baby-snake, they just grew one at the end of their own tails, and when it was able to take care of itself it dropped off; so that they brought up their families very cheaply. But if any nasty thing came by, out they rushed upon it; and then out of each of their hundreds of feet there sprang a whole cutler's shop of

Scythes,	Javelins,
Billhooks,	Lances,

Pickaxes,	Halberts,
Forks,	Gisarines,
Penknives,	Poleaxes,
Rapiers,	Fishhooks,
Sabres,	Bradawis,
Yataghans,	Gimblets,
Creeses,	Corkscrews,
Ghoorka Swords,	Pins,
Tucks,	Needles,
And so forth,	

which stabbed, shot, poked, pricked, scratched, ripped, pinked, and crimped those naughty beasts so terribly, that they had to run for their lives, or else be chopped into small pieces and be eaten afterwards. And, if that is not all, every word, true, then there is no faith in microscopes, and all is over with the Linnaean Society.[12]

We do not need a psychological theory of a deeply divided personality, such as that advanced by Susan Chitty in *The Beast and the Monk*,[13] to see how Rabelais and natural theology could come together so fruitfully in Kingsley, but the evidence from other areas of his life gives striking support for the existence of this tension. Her publication of the erotic drawings done for his wife just before and after their marriage gives us fascinating evidence about that area of their lives over which the Victorians were most reticent. Not all clergymen were as prudish as Dodgson, and Kingsley held a veneration for sex which was at times nearly as ludicrous as that of D. H. Lawrence.[14] Whether we regard this as a healthy tension or a neurotic polarity depends largely on our own standpoint: certainly Kingsley's manic

5.2 Percival Skelton: "Tom and the Lobster."
Illustration to Charles Kingsley's The Water Babies.

depressive temperament culminated in a regular series of breakdowns over the years, but it is equally possible, and perhaps more helpful, to see this peculiar closeness of the sacred and the profane in him as yet another example of the intenseness he devoted to everything he did. It was to be the source of his greatest strengths, and, occasionally, of his greatest humiliations. Whatever its roots in Kingsley's own personality, however, what we find in *The Water Babies* is a quite *conscious* use of opposing elements to produce a complex and highly organized artistic structure.

As do so many other Victorian fantasy writers, Kingsley makes use of "another world," but his underwater world is essentially a part of this one and is ready created for him. No fictional fantasy could equal the variety and peculiarity of the life he found teeming in the rivers and sea; there was no need to pass through any looking glass beyond that of the reflecting surface of the water itself to find an inversion of our own world. Simultaneously, it provided satire, *and* evidence for the wonder of creation. In this, the underwater world offered a microcosm of Kingsley's vision of nature as a whole. Nature is the theme of *The Water Babies* in an almost musical sense: it is presented to us in a series of different keys, interrelated and orchestrated to produce a structure analogous to a fugue. At a formal level, for instance, the organization of the book, with its lists, digressions, and deliberately juxtaposed incongruities is a reflection of the organic structure of natural things. Harthover House (its very name perhaps an indication of the supremacy of *Heart* and *Hearth*) is the essence of Englishness—possibly even a symbol of England itself:

Harthover had been built at ninety different times, and in nineteen different styles, and looked as if someone had built a whole street of houses of every imaginable shape, and then stirred them together with a spoon.

For the attics were Anglo Saxon.

The third floor, Norman.

The second, Cinque cento.

The first floor, Elizabethan.

The right wing, Pure Doric.

The centre, Early English, with a huge portico, copied from the Parthenon.

The Left wing, Pure Boeotian, which the country folk admired most of all, because it was just like the new barracks in the town, only three times as big.

The grand staircase was copied from the Catacombs at Rome.

The back staircase, from the Taj Mahal at Agra. This was built by Sir John's great-great-great uncle, who won, in Lord Clive's Indian wars, plenty of money, plenty of wounds, and no more taste than his betters.

The cellars were copied from the caves of Elephanta.

The offices, from the Pavilion at Brighton.

And the rest from nothing in heaven, or earth, or under the earth.

So that Harthover House was a great puzzle to antiquarians, and a thorough Naboth's vinyard to critics, and architects, and all persons who like meddling with other men's business, and spending other men's money. So they were all setting upon poor Sir John, year after year, and trying to talk him into spending a hundred thousand pounds or so in building, to please them and not himself. But he always put them off, like a canny North-countryman as he was. One wanted him to build a Gothic house, but he said he was no Goth; and another, to build an Elizabethan, but he said he lived under good Queen Victoria, and not good Queen Bess; and another was bold enough to tell him that his house was ugly, but he said he lived inside it, and not outside; and another, that there was no unity in it, but he said that that was just why he liked the old place. For he liked to see how each Sir John, and Sir Hugh, and Sir Ralph, and Sir Randal, had left his mark upon the place, each after his own taste; and that he had no more notion of disturbing his ancestors' work than of disturbing their graves. For now the house looked like a real live house, that had a history, and had grown and grown as the world grew; and that it was only an upstart fellow who did not know who his own grandfather was, who would change it for some spick and span new Gothic or Elizabethan thing, which looked as if it had been all spawned in a night as mushrooms are. From which you may collect (if you have wit enough), that Sir John was a very sound headed, sound hearted squire, and just the man to keep the country side in order, and show good sport with his hounds.

Tom, who first asked the question about the house's age, has been completely forgotten: the point is that because it grew *naturally*, and piecemeal, as different squires actually liked it, Harthover House is an honest structure a piece of living history and not a dead mechanical arrangement produced by an externally imposed plan.

It is in the labyrinths of the Harthover flues that Tom gets lost, comes down the wrong chimney, and discovers first a portrait of Christ and then Elie. Thus the suggestion that Harthover symbolizes the structure of nature (and thence the structure of the book) has religious as well as aesthetic implications. This is part of a tradition of thought that goes back to Wordsworth. Kingsley's original declared intention, we recall, to show "that there is a quite miraculous and divine element underlying all physical nature," was an expression of a feeling that had haunted him all his life. In 1842, when he was just twenty-three, he noted:

The great mysticism is the belief which is becoming every day stronger with me that all symmetrical natural objects, aye, and perhaps all forms, colours, and scents which show organization or arrangement, are types of some spiritual truth or existence, of a grade between the symbolical type and the mystic type. When I walk the fields I am oppressed every now and then with an innate feeling, that everything I see has a meaning, if I could but understand it. And this feeling of being surrounded with truths which I cannot grasp amounts to indescribable awe sometimes! [. . .] All day, glimpses from the other world-floating motes from that inner transcendental life, have been flitting across me, just as they used in childhood, when the seen and the unseen were one, an undistinguishable twin mystery; the one not yet forgotten, the other not yet learnt so perfectly as to dazzle, by its coarse glare, the spirit perceptions which the soul learnt to feel in another world.[16]

The echoes of Wordsworth's "Immortality Ode" are clear, as are the parallels between such intuitions of *meaning* in nature and the more clearly defined Platonism of George MacDonald, but it is worth noticing that such feelings are quite a common feature of the religious revival of the 1830s and 1840s. Many members of the Oxford Movement, for instance, like Keble, for whom neither Kingsley nor MacDonald had any great sympathy, found in nature a pattern of correspondences with the spiritual state of man, which, though they were sometimes schematized and elaborated to a degree quite unacceptable to the followers of Frederick Denison Maurice, nevertheless bore witness to a similar climate of feeling.[17] A tendency to give weight to such feelings was a feature of the time, rather than of any particular religious movement or philosophy, but it suggests that when he was writing *The Water Babies* Kingsley was able to appeal to certain contemporary ways of feeling about nature that made his parable instantly comprehensible. So far from producing a freak of fantasy, idiosyncratic and personal in its assumptions, he is writing within a familiar tradition.

It is a tradition of feeling much less familiar today. C. N. Manlove, for instance, in the course of one of the most interesting (if one of the most misguided) studies of Kingsley in recent years,[18] discovers what he believes to be a fundamental flaw in his attitude to nature: "The basic difficulty," he claims, "is that Kingsley is both a naturalist and a 'Platonist'; a man committed both to things considered by themselves and to the meaning or deeper Being behind them."[19] "As a scientist," he is committed "to the faithful record and minute delineation" of nature, "as a Christian to the demonstration of God's presence and the working of his spiritual laws."[20] The philosophical opposition between these two positions admittedly appears absolute. The former, or *Naturalist* position, claims to find values inherent in nature itself; while the latter purports to discover in the shifting ephemera of the natural world evidence, or symbols, of a hidden and unchanging reality of absolute forms *behind* the mere appearances of things. But the charge itself is not, of course, a new one. We find it, for instance, leveled by Blake against Wordsworth in 1826 when he first read his 1815 *Poems*. "Wordsworth must know," Blake scribbled in the margin of his edition, "that what he Writes Valuable is Not to be found in Nature."[21] It was a charge that was to be flung repeatedly at Wordsworthians by empiricists and transcendentalists alike throughout the nineteenth century, when they were not, like Kingsley himself, making the opposite charge: "Deep as was his conviction that nature bore upon her simplest forms the finger mark of God, he did not always dare simply to describe her as she was, and leave her to reveal her own mystery."[22] At the heart of the attitude to nature that Wordsworth bequeathed to the nineteenth century there was a fundamental ambiguity that puzzled and disturbed sometimes even his closest admirers.[23] Even from the days of Tintern Abbey in 1798 the two conflicting elements of Naturalism and Platonism had both been present in his work, not merely together, but as seemingly inseparable qualities:

> And I have felt
> A presence that disturbs me with the joy
> Of elevated thoughts; a sense sublime
> Of something far more deeply interfused,
> Whose dwelling is the light of setting suns,
> And the round ocean and the living air,
> And the blue sky, and in the mind of man:
> A motion and a spirit, that impels
> All thinking things, all objects of all thought,
> And rolls through all things. Therefore am I still
> A lover of the meadows and the woods,
> And mountains; and of all that we behold
> From this green earth; of all the mighty world
> Of eye, and ear—both what they half create,
> And what perceive; well pleased to recognize
> In nature and the language of the sense
> The anchor of my purest thoughts, the nurse,
> The guide, the guardian of my heart, and soul
> Of all my moral being.
>
> (*Tintern Abbey*, lines 93–111)

This is a good example of the kind of fusion of Naturalistic and Platonic sentiments that was to baffle Blake, and, at times, even Coleridge. For some it has always been merely irrefutable evidence of muddle or self-contradiction in Wordsworth; others have noted the degree of philosophical sophistication that accompanied his use of Berkeley, Isaac Newton, Shaftsbury, and even Spinoza in the course of the poem, and been less sure.[24] Wordsworth, for instance, did not fall into the naïve assumptions about describing nature "as she was" that entrap both Kingsley and Ruskin. The alternative is to believe that it was this very ambiguity that so interested Wordsworth: that he was consciously looking for a poetic resolution to the paradox that he himself had felt at the heart of his love for nature.

One critic who saw this paradox at the very center of Wordsworth's poetry was MacDonald. He was perhaps the first Victorian critic to point out that this contradiction in Wordsworth mirrored the classic Christian paradox of God as *both* immanent in Nature and transcendent over and beyond it. It was felt not as an escape into neat verbal formulae, but as an acute existential tension. "The very element in which the mind of Wordsworth lived and moved," writes MacDonald, "was a Christian pantheism. [. . .] This world is not merely a thing which God hath made, subjecting it to laws; but is an expression of the thought, the feeling, the heart of God himself."[25] This is a way of thinking easily neglected by the modern reader, often unprepared for the existential tone of much Victorian criticism, yet without it we can fail to understand why, for so many Wordsworthians of the day, this dichotomy in Wordsworth seemed to be of profound religious significance. It is central to the thought of Maurice, for example, who was probably a greater influence on Kingsley and MacDonald than any other single person. Wordsworth showed Maurice how thought could be inseparable from *feeling*—by which was meant not a passive emotionalism or sentimentality, but a dynamic quality of life and being that was capable of reconciling opposite or discordant qualities. For an age haunted by the pressures of Victorian materialism, nature seemed to offer another way: as the source of powerful feeling by which immanence spilled over into transcendence. As MacDonald put it:

[W]hatever we feel in the highest moments of truth shining through beauty, whatever comes to our souls as a power of life, is meant to be seen and felt by us, and to be regarded not as the work of his (God's) hand, but as the flowing forth of his heart, the flowing forth of his love of us, making us blessed in the union of his heart and ours.

Now Wordsworth is the high priest of nature thus regarded.[26]

What the Victorians discovered in Wordsworth was a view of Nature as a spontaneous overflow of Being—*natura naturans* rather than *natura naturata*. He seemed to give them an assurance of overriding unity and wholeness in God's creation that was manifestly lacking in a society passing through rapid social change. It was this sense of a fundamental unity, transcending contradictions and philosophical objections, that Kingsley, like MacDonald, felt he had found in Wordsworth.

But if Wordsworth underlay Kingsley's view of nature in a way that seemed to give sanction to the delight in paradox and contradiction that he had found in Rabelais and Sterne, he is also present in a different aspect of *The Water Babies*: the attitude to childhood. In Tom a number of strands of Victorian thought come together in microcosm. Kingsley was opposed not merely to the prevailing utilitarian and mechanistic views of man and society, but also to popular religious beliefs about Hell and divine retribution. As a chimney sweep, Tom had been denied his childhood; had been the slave of Grimes, and, in a wider sense, the slave of the whole oppressive economic system that Kingsley had been attacking ever since the days of *Alton Locke* and *Cheap Clothes and Nasty* in 1852. Child chimney sweepers had steadily increased in numbers since the days of the first reports on the subject in the 1780s that had moved Blake to write of the "little black thing amid the snow" in the *Songs of Experience*. Their death rate was appalling. Cancer of the scrotum was common in the boys—caused by crawling naked through the sooty flues. The mother of Anna Sewell, the author of *Black Beauty*, had gone from door to door collecting the £10 necessary to buy out one boy in the 1840s. Her brother had witnessed a master sweep choosing an apprentice at a workhouse, and selecting an orphan who had no one to protect him or inquire after him.[27] Kingsley was successful where other reformers had failed in finally getting the use of children for sweeping chimneys prohibited: the Chimney Sweepers Regulation Act became law within a year of the publication of *The Water Babies*.

As a water baby Tom had been literally given back his childhood, to live it again and grow healthily, not into the black and ragged urchin who throws stones at passing horses and wants to grow up to be a master sweep able to bully his boys like Grimes, but into a *real* man, endowed with all the vigor of Kingsley's ideal of "Christian manliness," who will be "a great man of science," who "can plan railroads, and steam engines, and electric telegraphs, and rifled guns, and so forth."[28] If, at one level, this substitution of healthy natural growth as a water baby for the diseased unnatural state of the chimney sweep is in essence a Wordsworthian one, it sits oddly with the aggressive industrialism—and implicit imperialism—of the consequences of science. In view of the fact that some of Kingsley's children later emigrated to both Australia and the U.S.A. with ideals of nation-building, one may well wonder about the degrees of irony here.

Moreover Kingsley has added two other important post-Romantic elements. The first is his rejection of the idea of eternal punishment. Byron had already called attention in stanza 14 of his (highly ironic) *Vision of Judgement* to the paradox that one might be damned for holding universalist views—here specifically for hoping that George III might escape Hell:

> I know this is unpopular; I know
>   'Tis blasphemous; I know one may be damn'd
> For hoping no one else may e'er be so.

But Byron was not an Anglican priest in charge of a parish. Kingsley's stand took him into conflict with Evangelicals and Tractarians alike. By the standards of many children's writers of the forties and fifties, Tom's early depravity,[29] however much it may have been a reflection of his poor environment, could only lead him to one end: Hell. This is the message of scores of children's books of an Evangelical slant throughout the middle years of the century. From anonymous tracts and short stories with titles like *Bob the Cabin Boy and his Captain*,[30] or *The Swearer's Prayer*,[31] or *The Death at School*,[32] through the works of Mrs. Trimmer, and later Mrs. Sherwood, we find children exhorted to goodness under the threat of God's judgment—often instantly at hand in the form of sudden death. Nor did such improving literature stop at death. The horrors of the Irish school mission sermon in James Joyce's *Portrait of the Artist* have exact counterparts in English Victorian tracts. Here, for instance, is an extract from the Reverend Joseph Furniss's *Sight of Hell*:

> The little child is in the red-hot oven. Hear how it screams to come out; see how it turns and twists itself about in the fire. It beats its head against the roof of the oven. It stamps its little feet upon the floor. [. . .] God was very good to this little child. Very likely God saw it would get worse and worse and never repent and so it would have been punished more severely in hell. So God in His mercy called it out of the world in early childhood.[33]

The appropriately named Furniss was not an Evangelical, but a Catholic Redemptionist Father. He was producing tracts of this kind for children from 1847 onwards, and the *Catholic Encyclopedia* estimates that of the order of four million copies of his works were sold in English-speaking countries throughout the world.[34]

The Tractarians took Hell no less seriously. In the same year that *The Water Babies* was published E. B. Pusey wrote to Henry Liddon that,

> I am sure that nothing will keep men from the present pleasures of sin, but the love of God and the fear of Hell: and that the fear of Hell drives people back to God, to seek [. . .] Him, and in seeking Him to love Him first because He delivered them from Hell, then for his own sake.[35]

This was likely to have been a view congenial to Liddon who, as Vice-Principal of Cuddeston, a leading Anglo-Catholic Theological College, had produced a series of meditations on death and hell of a quite macabre degree of gloom.

It was against this background that Maurice, in *The Kingdom of Christ*,[36] proclaimed a God who was a loving father to the "family" of his people. Even for the heathen, the unbaptized, and the unregenerate it seemed there was hope. Israel itself, he argued, had never been a gathered sect of believers, but first and foremost a family. You do not choose to belong to a particular family, you find yourself within it whether or not you come to reject it. The description of God as *father* arose from the experience of Israel in the Old Testament, and was confirmed and made central by the teachings of Jesus in the New. While not denying the freedom of man's will, Maurice asserted that all could be brought into the consciousness of belonging to the family of God—to which they already inescapably belonged simply by virtue of being human. To a generation reared within the gloomy strictness of Victorian Evangelicalism or its Tractarian reflection, this was a doctrine of liberation. At the end of the century Stuart Headlam, a leading light in the Christian Social Union, was to tell the fledgling Fabian Society that they probably did not know what it was "to have been delivered in the world of thought, emotion, imagination from the belief that a large proportion of the human race are doomed to endless misery."[37] To mid-Victorian children's writers, such as Annie Keary and Flora Shaw, Maurice's gospel meant that God was to be introduced into their books not to frighten children, but to reassure them. In a letter to Kingsley, Keary declared that though "almost all the orthodox held the opposite view," a cloud had been rolled "away from her vision of God."[38] As her letter to him shows, this was a theological tradition to which Kingsley had been committed long before Tom the chimney sweep was thought of. "The Evangelicals preach to sinners as if they were heathens," he complained in 1842, looking for a sudden conversion in a young man "as if he had not been all his life a member of the Church, a child of God, and an inheritor of the Kingdom of heaven!"[39] In the same year he read *The Kingdom of Christ* and, his wife recorded, "he always said that he owed more to that book than to any he had ever read, for by it his views were cleared and his faith established."[40] From thenceforth Maurice was to be his master: "the man who of all men whom I have seen, approached nearest to my conception of St. John, the Apostle of Love."[41] Little Tom owed his status as a child of God, an inheritor of the kingdom of heaven, to a tradition that went back through Maurice to Coleridge, and thence to an older, gentler, and more loving Christianity than that of the dominant Evangelicals and Tractarians. Not merely was there no Hell preached in Kingsley's parish church at Eversley, there was no corporal punishment in the Kingsley home.

Tom's life as a water baby is not only a chance to grow afresh, in a Wordsworthian sense, in a new childhood, it involves a discovery of what it means to belong to a family—something he had been denied as a sweep. At first he is a spectator of the strange sights and inhabitants of the river, though he is not really independent, since he is looked after invisibly by the fairies. Gradually he begins to learn his kinship with the other creatures, but it is only when he helps the lobster, a very alien form of life, that he is admitted into the society of his own kind, the other water babies, who have always been present, but were hitherto invisible to him. Similarly, as the story unfolds, we discover a curious identity between the poor Irish woman of the opening, who turns out to be "the Queen of the Fairies," Mrs. Bedonebyasyoudid *and* Mrs. Doasyouwouldbedoneby, *and* Mother Carey. Punishment itself, in the Mauricean scheme of things, is only another aspect of love—the love which, in turn underlies the *natura naturans*, the overflowing creativity of Mother Carey's dynamic life force that "rolls through all things." Finally, all is subsumed into the crowning vision of unity:

> "My name is written in my eyes, if you have eyes to see it there."
> And they looked into her great, deep, soft eyes, and they changed again and again into every hue, as the light changes in a diamond.
> "Now read my name," said she, at last.
> And her eyes flashed, for one moment, clear, white, blazing light; but the children could not read her name; for they were dazzled, and hid their faces in their hands.
> "Not yet, young things, not yet," said she, smiling.[42]

The reference is, of course, to the final canto of Dante's *Paradiso*, where in the climax of the "high fantasy" the Godhead is described as three inter-locking circles of different colors, each reflecting the other, dazzling the poet's vision as it draws up his will into "the Love that moves the sun and other stars."[43] But neither Tom nor Elie is yet ready for a vision of that uni-versal family of creation. They are still at an earlier stage of their evolution.

Evolution is, of course, the other major addition Kingsley has made to the Wordsworthian idea of nature. As a competent biologist he had under-stood and welcomed Darwin's *Origin of Species* when it was published in 1859, and he wrote to congratulate him on it. Unlike many literal-minded churchmen of the day, neither he nor Maurice felt their religious belief threatened by the evidence for mutation of species. Kingsley, however, went far beyond Maurice and even many agnostic Darwinians in his enthusiasm for the hypothesis and the ways in which it might be applied to man. For T. H. Huxley, possibly the greatest champion of Darwinian ideas (Professor Ptthmllnsprts in *The Water Babies*), evolution was a biological necessity but in its blind pressure towards the survival of the fittest, a moral evil. Its appli-cation in human society would involve unthinkable consequences—like infanticide for weak babies. Kingsley had a more mystical view of evolution, seeing it as a concrete expression of God's outpouring life force molding and re-creating nature. His reference to the notion "that people's souls make their bodies, just as a snail makes its shell," underlines this belief in nature as the manifestation of a dynamic spirit. It is reminiscent of Blake's belief that "man has no body as distinct from his soul." As early as 1850, in *Alton Locke*, Kingsley had written a fantasy of evolution in which the fevered poet dreams that he is a succession of creatures in the hierarchy of being, begin-ning "at the lowest point of created life" as a madrepore clinging to a rock without thought or individuality, then, successively, a crab, a remora, an ostrich, a mylodon, an ape, and finally a prehistoric man. He is told:

> He who falls from the golden ladder must climb through ages to its top.
> He who tears himself in pieces by his lusts, ages can make him one again.
> The madrepore shall become a shell, and the shell a fish, and the fish a
> bird, and the bird a beast; and then he shall become a man again, and see
> the glory of the latter days.[44]

Wordsworth had returned to his childhood to find the sources of new life and growth within him; Kingsley goes one better, returning to the cradles of life itself for renewal.

In *The Water Babies* evolution seems to be the natural process by which Maurice's conception of God's immanent shaping love in creation is given physical expression. It is, in Wordsworth's phrase, *the familial bond* itself. While one thought of the hierarchy of species in the terms of "All things bright and beautiful," as individual separate creations of the Almighty who "painted their glowing colors" and "made their tiny wings," species were not merely divided by immutability they also remained essentially *unrelated* to one another. What the French Revolution had done for France, and all Europe, Darwin now did for nature herself. With *The Origin of Species*, the family of nature was released, as if from an artificial caste system, into a consciousness of its own familyhood—perceiving for the first time its own essential unity and given a sense of belonging.

It is this family relationship of all things that Tom has painfully to learn afresh in his contacts with the insects, fish, crustacea, birds, then other water babies, and finally—the greatest test of all—even Grimes himself. Moreover, he can only reach Mother Carey beyond the Shiny Wall, and then the Other-end-of-Nowhere, by the help of his fellow creatures—muddled and confusing as their assistance often is, as in the case of the Gairfowl. The crowning paradox is that to reach Grimes Tom must walk *backwards* looking into his dog's eyes to find the way: a symbol that neatly sums up the whole journey backwards through life that he has had to make to discover himself, and to be "clean." It is only by so doing that he can discover the pity and forgiveness for Grimes, the person who has wronged him most. In the end, Tom can do for Grimes what even his own mother's tears cannot, for behind him lies experience of the divine love implicit in all creation. Yet

5.3 Percival Skelton: "Tom and the Gairfowl."
Illustration to Charles Kingsley's The Water Babies.

Tom's forgiveness is intensely personal; only *he* can release Grimes. The implicit love in creation can only become explicit in individuals:

> [B]elow all natural phenomena, we come to a transcendental—in plain English, a miraculous ground. . . . This belief was first forced on me by investigating the generation of certain polypes of a very low order. I found absolute Divine miracle at the bottom of all; and no *cause*, save that of a supremely *imaginative* (if I may so speak), as well as Almighty *mind*, carrying out its own ideas; but gravitation, or the simplest law, will show the same truth. What *efficient cause* is there that matter should attract matter? Why should it not repel matter? The only answer is, that God has so willed; and if we come to *final* causes, there is no better answer than the old mystic one, that God has imprest the law of *Love*, which is the law of his own being, on matter, that it may be a type of the spiritual world when healthy, and of the kingdom of heaven.[45]

It is clear already that the allegorical structure underlying the narrative of *The Water Babies* is extremely complex. Tom's immersion in the water in Vendale is "death" by drowning; it is also a baptism, and, as has been indicated, a rebirth (and the Pauline, New Testament, idea of baptism already implies this process of symbolic death and rebirth). But behind this is discernable a shadowy psychological schema of a return to the unconscious and a coming to terms with the lowest depths of the psyche before Tom's desire to be "clean" can become a reality. The moral education Tom undergoes at St. Brandan's Isle with Mrs. Doasyouwouldbedoneby and Mrs. Bedonebyasyoudid, with the stealing of the sweets and its prickly consequences, can be seen as both a necessary part of nature's teaching (and thus an expression of divine law), and, at the same time, a psychological discovery of sin and guilt. There is an ingenious Freudian interpretation of *The Water Babies* by Maureen Duffy, which claims Tom's coming down Elie's chimney as attempted rape, and his plunge beneath the water as a return to "the unborn foetus in its amniotic fluid"—as well as expressing "the questing penis."[46] Susan Chitty agrees with Miss Duffy that *The Water Babies* is a "fable about masturbation." Tom must be purged of his nasty habits before he is fit to enter heaven with Elie. The book's ethic "is concerned with how a boy may resist temptation and grow up pure to marry."[47] Neither author seems fully aware of the inherent contradictions that too detailed a schematization bring out. *Either* Tom is to grow up and marry Elie, *or* he is to enter heaven: does it really make sense to talk about him doing both? It would, indeed, be possible to produce a minute commentary on the various allegorical potentials of the story (both intended, and unintended) in this way, but in the end they run up against the fact that the fundamental inconsistencies of the book are not accidents, or mistakes, but part of its basic aesthetic structure. There *is* a great deal of consistent and carefully plotted allegory in *The Water Babies*, as we have seen, but to argue, as Manlove does from this, that these inconsistencies are flaws in the artistic workmanship is to misunderstand the kind of book Kingsley has written. It has the same unity as Harthover House: that unity of extravagant inconsistencies that he had found with such delight in Rabelais, and which reflected a quite other view of nature from that of the systematizers. Erich Auerbach says of Rabelais that his "entire effort is directed towards playing with things and with the multiplicity of their possible aspects; upon tempting the reader out of his customary and definite way of regarding things, by showing him phenomena in utter confusion; upon tempting him out into the great ocean of the world, in which he can swim freely, though it be at his own peril."[48] The very oceanic image that he finds himself using is significant when we think of how Kingsley has taken up the tradition. The renaissance feeling that "anything is possible" finds an echo in some of his own attitudes. Almost every event in *The Water Babies* carries with it a clear intimation of "inner meaning" and, at the same time, reinforces Kingsley's frequent warnings about taking the story too seriously. This mixture of the moralizing and the absurd is not an uneasy blend of two opposite traditions, but is entirely within the tradition of Rabelais. To quote Auerbach again:

> I consider it a mistake to probe Rabelais' hidden meaning—that is, the marrow of the bone—for some definite and clearly outlined doctrine; the thing which lies concealed in his work, yet which is conveyed in a thousand ways, is an intellectual attitude, which he himself calls Pantagruelism; a grasp of life which comprehends the spiritual and the sensual simultaneously, which allows none of life's possibilities to escape. To describe it in more detail is not a wise undertaking—for one would immediately find oneself forced into competition with Rabelais. He himself is constantly describing it, and he can do it better than we can.[49]

His constructs are never formless, he argues, "every line, every word, is strictly under control." It is a control that never deserts Kingsley either. A minute verisimilitude of detail is combined with an aesthetic architecture of pure fantasy—that flaunts its unreality and impossibility at every step.

Thus, the topography of the opening is localized and specific enough to be clearly recognizable—in spite of the typical disclaimer that accompanies it, shooting aside from the original point into apparent irrelevancy.

> The name of the place is Vendale; and if you want to see it for yourself, you must go up into the High Craven, and search from Bolland Forest north by Ingleborough, to the Nine Standards and Cross Fell; and if you have not found it, you must turn south, and search the Lake Mountains, down to Scaw Fell and the sea; and then if you have not found it, you must go northward again by merry Carlisle, and search the Cheviots all across, from Annan Water to Berwick Law; and then, whether you have found Vendale or not, you will have found such a country, and such a people, as ought to make you proud of being a British boy.[50]

The cliff, with its alternate layers of limestone and grass, rockrose, sax-ifrage, and thyme, is, of course, Malham Cove in Airedale—though the village has been moved slightly nearer the base of the crag. Tom follows the course of the Aire as it grows into a river, flows through a great industrial town (Leeds) and thence into the Humber, though the river itself more closely resembles, in flora and fauna, the Itchen in Hampshire where Kingsley in fact wrote much of the book.[51] The beach where Tom meets Elie again, with the Professor, is Scarborough. After that the geography becomes, of necessity, more vague, as we move from St. Brandan's Isle to the Shiny Wall (of the polar ice cap), but each individual scene is given a wealth of local detail—whether it be the birds he meets, or Tom's own exact length (3.87962 inches). Time runs fast or slow as the needs of the individual scene dictate: Elie grows into a beautiful woman waiting for Tom on the Isle for "many a hundred years" and when they finally meet again they fall so deeply in love that they stare at each other for "seven years more, and neither spoke nor stirred."

This mixture of verisimilitude in detail and total inconsistency on the grand scale is as true in the allegorical deep-level plot as it is in the surface narrative. If, for instance, we accept that Tom is drowned in Vendale in the first chapter, then what is he doing becoming a great engineer in the best tradition of Samuel Smiles at the end? We are never clear at *either* level if *The Water Babies* is about life, or life after death. If it is the latter, then what is Kingsley, the great anti-Catholic who regarded Romanism as heresy, doing with notions of purgatory? If the former, then what are we to make of Grimes's punishment? He may be rescued from Hell (or is it just a lower level of purgatory?), but he cannot be still alive in this world as Tom appears to be at the end. It is quite clear that these are questions we cannot ask, any more than we can question the variations in Pantagruel's size, according to the needs of Rabelais's particular episode.[52] The way in which Kingsley flaunts such massive structural inconsistencies at us is itself the best clue to the kind of story *The Water Babies* is.

We can perhaps see better what this new kind of allegorical fantasy is if we look for contrast at the other great Victorian fantasy writer (also a disciple of Maurice), George MacDonald.[53] By the time he wrote *Phantastes*, George MacDonald was, in effect, a defrocked Congregational minister—enjoying the rare distinction of having been driven out of his first church, at Arundel, in Sussex, for *heresy*. Given how far the Congregationalists lived up to their other name of *Independents* on matters of theology, this was a rare enough distinction. But the charges made against him were no less extraordinary. He had been arraigned by the elders of his Arundel congregation on two counts: firstly, that he had preached the possibility of life after death for the heathen, and, secondly, that he was tainted with what was sinisterly known as "German theology."[54] From then on he had been forced to earn his living and support a growing family purely by his writing. Hardly surprisingly he left the Congregationalists, and for some years had no connections with organized religion. It was only after meeting Maurice, who had helped him find a publisher for *Phantastes*, that he returned to the Church—this time the Church of England, as a member of Maurice's Vere Street congregation.

In a letter to Mrs. Scott, wife of A. J. Scott, the first principal of Owen's College, Manchester (later to become Manchester University), MacDonald writes of *Phantastes*, "I hope Mr. Scott will like my fairy-tale. I don't see what right the *Athenaeum* has to call it an allegory and judge or misjudge it accordingly—as if nothing but an allegory could have two meanings."[55] In an essay on "The Fantastic Imagination" he expands this point, "A fairy-tale is not an allegory. There may be allegory in it, but it is not an allegory. He must be an artist indeed who can, in any mode, produce a strict allegory that is not a weariness to the spirit."[56] The interest in exact definition of literary *kinds* is significant. With Kingsley and MacDonald we find the possibilities of fantasy as an art form consciously explored and openly discussed for the first time. MacDonald is not against allegory as such: he himself is one of the great allegorists of all time, and like Kingsley, he reserves a special admiration for Dante. What he wants to do is to differentiate between the mechanical rigidity of "strict allegory" and what he calls a "fairytale," which uses allegory as one of a number of modes of symbolic narration. He is determined to show how the form he has invented, or recreated, differs from allegory in a fundamental and theologically important way. An allegory can, by definition, have no more meaning than the author originally put into it. It is, in that sense, a medium entirely under his control. This, for MacDonald, denied it the status of a work of art. It was purely an artefact. In the same essay on "The Fantastic Imagination" he explains this

belief: "The fact that there is always more in a work of art—which is the
highest human result of the embodying imagination—than the producer
himself perceived while he produced it, seems to us a strong reason for
attributing to it a larger origin than the man alone—for saying at the last,
that the inspiration of the Almighty shaped its ends."[57]

Similarly, for MacDonald, *art* and *nature* seem to have been two parallel words, subject to the same laws and equally charged with the grandeur
of God. "Nature," he wrote, "is brimful of symbolic and analogical parallels
to the goings and comings, the growth and changes in the highest nature of
man."[58] "The Lord puts things in subdefined, suggestive shapes, yielding no
satisfactory meaning to the mere intellect. [. . .] According as the new creation, that of reality, advances in him, the man becomes able to understand
the words, the symbols, the parables of the Lord."[59] The synthesis of these
two worlds is man himself. The world around him "is but an outward figu-
ration of the condition of his mind; an inexhaustible storehouse of forms
whence he may choose exponents—the crystal pitchers that shall protest his
thought and not need to be broken that the light may break forth. The
meanings are in those forms already, else there could be no garment of
unveiling. [. . .] The man has but to light the lamp within the form: his
imagination is the light, it is not the form."[60] The mere use of language in
writing a story is thus in itself a theological activity. In *Lilith* Mr. Vane, the
narrator, tries to describe his "constant struggle to say what cannot be said
with even an approach to precision," and his consequent attempt to convey
"not the things themselves, but the feelings they wake in me."[61]

> A single thing would sometimes seem to be and mean many things, with
> an uncertain identity at the heart of them, which kept constantly altering
> their look. [. . .] While without a doubt, for instance, that I was actually
> regarding a scene of activity, I might be, at the same moment, in my con-
> sciousness aware that I was perusing a metaphysical argument.[62]

This, for George MacDonald, seems to have been at the heart of what he
means by a fairytale. Every "scene of activity" in it, and every event of the
narrative is simultaneously "a metaphysical argument, unlike our world,
whose symbols are partial and fragmentary." MacDonald's son and biographer described a conversation with his father on "the laws of symbolism"
like this:

> He would allow that the algebraic symbol, which concerns only the three
> dimensioned, has no *substantial* relation to the unknown quantity; nor
> the "tree where it falleth" to the man unredeemed, the comparison being

false. But the rose, when it gives some glimmer of the freedom for which a man hungers, does so because of its *substantial* unity with the man, each in degree being a signature of God's immanence. To a spiritual pilgrim the flower no longer seems a mere pretty design on the veil, "the cloak and cloud that shadows me from Thee"; for see! she opens her wicket into the land of poetic reality, and he, passing through and looking greatfully back, then knows her for his sister the Rose, of spiritual substance one with himself. So may even a gem, giving from its heart reflections of heavenly glory, awaken like memory in ourselves and send our eyes upwards. So also may we find co-substance between the stairs of a cathedral-spire and our own "secret stair" up to the wider vision—the faculty of defying the "plumbline of gravity" being the common and imaginative heritage.[63]

Behind such a comparison lies something very different from Kingsley's sense of a miraculous ground to nature, but no less meaningful: a Platonic mysticism that finds in the Rose a "signature of God's immanence," and in the gem an awakening and recognition of a truth once known, but now forgotten and overlaid. Thus Anodos, the hero of *Phantastes*, reading in the magic library of the mysterious palace, is like man scanning the "book of nature" for something deeper and more permanent that lay behind it:

I was trying to find the root of a manifestation, the spiritual truth whence a material vision sprang; or to combine two propositions, both apparently true, either at once or in different remembered moods, and to find the point in which their invisible converging lines would unite in one, revealing a truth higher than either, and differing from both.[64]

Here MacDonald's Platonism causes him to part company very sharply with Kingsley, for whom "novels and story books are scarcely worth your reading, as long as you can read the great green book, of which every bud is a letter, and every tree is a page."[65] Critics have been startled before by a bluff anti-intellectualism in Kingsley, and we need to beware of taking the writer decrying books too seriously; often, as here, it is the premise to a paradox. Fairytales are untrue, he begins by explaining, "because they are not strange and wonderful enough";

[T]ruth is as much larger than fiction, as God is greater than man; as much as the whole universe is larger than the little corner of it that any man, even the greatest poet or philosopher, can see; and as much grander, and as much more beautiful, and as much more strange. [. . .] Be sure that no man can ever fancy anything strange, unexpected, and curious, without finding, if he had eyes to see, a hundred things around his feet more strange, more unexpected, more curious, actually ready-made already by God.[66]

In telling us, therefore, of the extraordinary life of the river bed in *The Water Babies*, Kingsley is exhibiting natural theology in action, and revealing moral truth. For MacDonald, on the other hand, the truth is hidden *beneath* nature, rather than visible in the surface of things; it is the job of the artist to create the hidden pattern afresh in his own work. Whereas Kingsley's world is, and remains, *this* world, MacDonald's two adult fantasies depend on the interrelation and tension between two separate worlds. As MacDonald himself puts it:

> The natural world has its laws, and no man must interfere with them in the way of presentiment any more than in the way of use; but they may themselves suggest laws of other kinds, and a man may, if he pleases, invent a little world of his own, with its own laws.[67]

Perhaps the fullest exploration of the moral law in fantasy, however, comes in the story of Irene and Curdie, told in *The Princess and the Goblin* (1872) and *The Princess and Curdie* (1882). Here, in these earlier books, Mr. Raven's remark in *Lilith* that "[t]here is in your house a door, one step through which carries me into a world very much another than this," is given a wider currency with the medieval allegorized sense of

5.4 Arthur Hughes: "The Princess's Castle."
Illustration to George MacDonald's The Princess and the Goblin.

"house" standing for the human "body." By general agreement, *The Princess and the Goblin*, is MacDonald's most successful fairy story. For G. K. Chesterton it was his masterwork: all MacDonald's other fairy stories were "illustrations and even disguises of that one."[68] In the story of the princess Irene the coexistence of the two worlds is achieved by perhaps the cleverest device of all. Irene is sent away to the mountains, because her mother is not strong, and is brought up "in a large house, half castle, half farmhouse, on the side of a mountain, about half-way between its base and its peak."[69] These suggestions of an allegorical framework are rapidly, if unobtrusively, amplified as the story unfolds. Not merely is the castle halfway up a mountain, but Irene holds a halfway position in the house. In the attics, up a strangely elusive stairway, she finds a very old and beautiful lady, whose name is *also* Irene, and who tells her that she is in fact her great-great grandmother. Later we learn that she is getting on for two thousand years old. She lives off the eggs of white doves, and seems to spend most of her time sitting spinning in her room. Not surprisingly, the princess's nurse doesn't believe a word of the story when she is told about it, and Irene discovers that the old lady is not always so accessible. On her

5.5 Arthur Hughes: "The Winding Stair."
Illustration to George MacDonald's The Princess and the Goblin.

5.6 Arthur Hughes: "The Grandmother."
Illustration to George MacDonald's The Princess and the Goblin.

next trip up to the attics she is nowhere to be found. This elusiveness also extends to the grandmother's possessions. Irene is later taken into her grandmother's bedroom and shown an enormous moon like light that never goes out. Sometimes, especially in crises, this light can be seen outside the castle miles away; other times it seems to be invisible—one curious property is that it is often easier to see from a distance than close up. The old lady tells the Princess a "secret" that "if that light were to go out you would fancy yourself lying in a bare garret, on a heap of old straw."[70] This is subsequently confirmed by Curdie, the miner's son, who cannot at first see either the grandmother or her wonderful possessions: "I see a big, bare, garret room [. . .]" he says, "a tub, and a heap of musty straw, and a withered apple, and a ray of sunlight coming through a hole in the middle of the roof and shining on your head, and making all the place look a curious dusky brown."[71] Only after certain tests that involve trusting Irene's word is Curdie able (or permitted) to see the grandmother and her world.

In these books (especially *The Princess and the Goblin*) the two worlds appear to coexist perfectly within our own world. Though the transitions are often unexpected, they do not involve magical metamorphoses or mysterious entrances like cupboards or mirrors. All they demand is something that approximates very closely to *faith*: that is, not just belief, or even acceptance, but a very positive *moral* quality that involves, among other things, acting on trust. But though, like the grandmother's lamp, the main outlines of an allegorical structure are easy to see from a distance, close to, the details are much harder to piece together. For instance, some of the grandmother's attributes, such as her age ("getting on for two thousand years"), her name (Irene, meaning "peace"), and her sustenance from the doves, suggest an allegory of the Church—and her role as guardian and seer might seem to confirm this. But, on the other hand, she is apparently accessible to very few people, and even these have difficulty in finding her. Even more embarrassing, she is totally invisible to such servants as the nurse; her marked preference for royalty is only reinforced when much later we learn that even Curdie (whose father's name, significantly, is Peter) is really of royal lineage. Much of this apparent inaccessibility may reflect MacDonald's own experience with the Church in practice—especially his own virtual expulsion from the Arundel church for heresy. Something of this disillusion with the visible ecclesiastical organization may well appear in the grandmother's elusiveness, and it is possible to allegorize royalty just as Carroll did in *Through the Looking Glass* in the mystical communion where all are kings and queens. Nevertheless, there are problems. However this elitism is glossed, it still

5.7 Arthur Hughes: "Curdie and the Goblins."
Illustration to George MacDonald's The Princess and the Goblin.

smacks of MacDonald's rejected Calvinism, and is in fundamental opposition to the universal family of Maurice's vision that had been directly responsible for drawing him back into the church.

Just as the princess has her grandmother, and namesake, living above her in the house, so there are also things below her—goblins burrowing in the mountainside and eventually even into the cellars of the castle itself. As we saw in an earlier chapter, these goblins although they are horrible and misshapen and shun the light of day, were once "very like other people." Their ancestors had chosen to go underground because the king had imposed on them too many taxes, or had "required observances they did not like": they had been repressed and had become degenerate and foul, the more dangerous for not being normally visible.[72] Most dangerous of all is their queen, who has *stone* shoes. Clearly there is here the makings of a medieval three-story universe. The princess stands poised between heaven above her and hell beneath. The queen of the goblins is a foil to the grandmother herself. But there is a second possibility, more easily describable in Freudian terms of *superego*, *ego*, and *id*. The goblins have been surface-dwellers, and have chosen to go underground. They are *evil* primarily in their desire for their own way at all costs; they hate the people of the surface—and above all the miners, such as Curdie and his father—but they desire to capture the princess to be wife of their own hideous prince, Harelip. There are shades here of Pluto and Persephone, with similar psychological undertones. Above all, they cannot bear poetry, or to be laughed at. Curdie routs them on numerous occasions simply by mocking them with doggerel and insulting rhymes. Eventually they attempt to divert streams within the mountain to flood the castle and drown its inhabitants, but they are thwarted by Curdie who has been able to listen to their plans deep inside the mine, and nearly all of them are drowned in the inundation.

Much of this can be allegorized, sometimes into elaborate schemes. Irene becomes the *soul* or *psyche* and the rest are either aspects of her own personality, or metaphysical agents of various hues. The moment we have begun to articulate this schema, however, the problems once again come flooding in. If Irene is the soul, and her materialistic unbelieving nurse merely an attribute or aspect of herself, much of the personal tension of the story is lost. Irene's argument with the nurse over whether she should kiss Curdie, having promised to do so, is presented as a very personal clash of wills. Moreover, Irene herself, as a character, has senses, good and bad inclinations, and so on, with the result that we are simply caught up in the kind of infinite regress that always threatens this kind of literature. We are, in fact, caught by the very dangers of "strict allegory" that MacDonald warns is a "weariness of the spirit." Too strong an allegorical consistency is always in danger of threatening the reality of the surface narrative. If we are not careful, *good* will engage all our sympathies in the struggle with *evil*; *courage* will inevitably defeat all comers; and *beauty* will outshine all her peers. We can sympathize with the sulky irritation of King Padella in combat with Prince Giglio: "If you ride a fairy horse, and wear fairy armour, what on earth is the use of my hitting you?"[73]

It is this danger that Kingsley had averted by his use of Rabelais, and a technique of deliberate inconsistency. MacDonald has behind him a much more highly developed mysticism, and works with symbols of a very different kind, but the result is the same. "This world," for him, is not a consistent place, but is the meeting place of two very different kinds of reality, neither of which is fully capable of accounting for everyday experience. Materialism is forced to be reductionist with spiritual experiences; mysticism often fails to take account of material forces. We cannot fully reconcile the two realms. In *At the Back of the North Wind* the preternatural goodness of little Diamond, the hero, instead of arousing gratitude or admiration in those he has helped, merely produces contempt. Moreover, from a worldly point of view this attitude is, at least in part, justified. He *is* very much of a prig. There is nothing childlike about him. There is no easy

5.8 Arthur Hughes: "Diamond and the North Wind."
Illustration to George MacDonald's At the Back of the North Wind.

reconciliation of the two worlds: in human experience they remain, as they appear, polar opposites. Tragedy is a perpetual possibility; as the crucifixion must remind Christians, there is no easy reconciliation.

For MacDonald this was certainly true. Critics have noted the much darker mood of *The Princess and Curdie*, with its hints of evolution in reverse, as well as a feeling of widespread corruption insideously eating away the whole kingdom.[74] It is true that in many ways the book is not as well written as the first one, but to seek the reasons for this merely within MacDonald's state of mind in 1882 seems to me to ignore the tragic possibilities that were always inherent in the story from the first. The ending is startlingly bleak. Instead of the Princess and Curdie living vaguely but suitably "happy ever after," we have this:

> Irene and Curdie were married. The old king died, and they were king and queen. As long as they lived Gwyntystorm was a better city, and good people grew in it. But they had no children, and when they died the people chose a king. And the new king went mining and mining in the rock under the city, and grew more and more eager after the gold, and paid less and less heed to his people. Rapidly they sank towards their old wickedness. But still the king went on mining, and coining gold by the pailful, until the people were worse even than in the old time. And so greedy was the king after gold, that when at last the ore began to fail, he caused the miners to reduce the pillars which Peter and they that followed him had left standing to bear the city. And from the girth of an oak of a thousand years, they chipped them down to that of a fir tree of fifty.
>
> One day at noon, when life was at its highest, the whole city fell with a roaring crash. The cries of men and the shrieks of women went up with its dust, and then there was a great silence.
>
> Where the mighty rock once towered, crowded with homes and crowned with a palace, now rushes and raves a stone obstructed rapid of the river. All around spreads a wilderness of wild deer, and the very name of Gwyntystorm had ceased from the lips of men.[75]

At one level the moral is clear. Each advance, each moral achievement is only for those who have come by it the hard way—by their own labor. One does not inherit spiritual capital for long. No settlement lasts forever. Yet however acceptable this message may be as a generalized statement, at a personal level the reader is moved to protest. Why is childlessness to be the fate of the little boy and girl we have seen growing up in *The Princess and the Goblin*? Was it merely to cause a temporary pause in the wickedness of Gwyntystorm that they were for so long tested and trained? Is this to be the end of the family of the great-great-grandmother and, by implication, nearly two thousand years of history? The suggestion of the passing of Christendom in the self-destructive greed of nineteenth-century commercial society is unmistakable. "Riches," MacDonald commented elsewhere, "indubitably favour stupidity."[76] "One may readily conclude how poorly God thinks of riches," he once told a wealthy Glasgow congregation, "when we see the sort of people he sends them to."[77]

It is possible that Irene's childlessness follows the medieval tradition that we find in Dante among others where Rachel, Jacob's second and best-loved wife, is the *type* of the contemplative life: beautiful but barren. Childlessness, it is implied, is the price that must be paid for some kinds of spiritual insight.[78] Yet such an interpretation, with its undertones of monasticism and celibacy, is very far from the theological world of Maurice or Kingsley, and MacDonald's own more highly developed mysticism did not inhibit him from having eleven children of his own, and adopting two others. Moreover, such a lack of children would be a setback to the process of spiritual evolution that is so prominent in the *Princess* books. What Chesterton meant by "optimistic Calvinism" was MacDonald's belief that mystical insight and religious experience was *potentially* open to all, and one day would be the possession of all, however rare it might be at the present, just as Maurice's "family" of the Church was for all. Yet, as we can see here, MacDonald's Mauricean optimism is balanced by a no less thorough going pessimism. It is this acute tension between two very different spiritual viewpoints that is the key to the best of his fantasy.

J. R. R. Tolkien has remarked that "Death is the theme that most inspired George MacDonald."[79] As we have seen, Death is one of the central themes of Victorian literature as a whole: it is, for instance, equally one of the pivotal points of *The Water Babies*. But Tolkien, one of MacDonald's greatest admirers in the twentieth century, is being characteristically precise in his observation: what he means, I believe, is that instead of being drawn, like so many of his contemporaries, to deal with death as a problem, or a fear to be allayed or played upon, MacDonald actually finds the roots of his inspiration in the fact of death itself. *At the Back of the North Wind*, *The Golden Key*, and *Lilith,* all show this paradox clearly, and even in the early *Phantastes* death appears to be an essential element of Anodos's education. Little Diamond in *At the Back of the North Wind* is a child increasingly set aside from normal experiences by his contact with the North Wind, and his eventual death at the end of the book is seen more in terms of going home from an alien place, than with the pathos normally accompanying that ritual set-piece of Victorian fiction, the child deathbed scene. Similarly Mossy and Tangle in *The Golden Key*, a much simpler allegorical story, are seen throughout as pilgrims through life whose reason is only to be found in their destination. At the beginning of *Lilith* it is clear that this world is the normal and *real* one, the other world is dream-like with odd juxtapositions and transitions of space and time. Gradually as the story unfolds, and Vane becomes increasingly committed to trying to help the children, the other world assumes a greater and greater reality, and this world is experienced more and more as the dream. As a result, the actual significance of death has been subtly transformed. Whereas before it was a finality to be feared and avoided, now it is a barrier to be surmounted as quickly as possible, since it is what separates Vane from *reality*. As in a theatrical transformation scene, what was an apparently blank wall is discovered to be a gauze screen through which light is shining from the other side in such a way as to make this side seem in darkness—or a dream. The technique mirrors the meaning. We are shown death structurally transformed from darkness to light—but without any lessening of its strangeness and unfamiliarity. Something of the same kind happens with Kingsley—though the tone is utterly different. At first Tom's life as a water baby is presented as a magical escape from the reality of the chimney sweep's enslaved existence, but gradually we are made to feel that the moral and spiritual symbols of the underwater world are in some sense more real than the distinctions of our own—based on such irrelevancies as class and education. The difference from MacDonald, as I have said, is one of tone. For all their similarities, Kingsley and he belong to utterly different mental sets. To see their similarities in philosophy or literary theory is to understand something about their age and their culture; to see their differences is to guess at what made two very different kinds of men. Kingsley, the botanist, marine biologist, and historian is fascinated by every minute detail of this world; "other" worlds are constructs—telling us yet more about this. MacDonald is a temperamental Platonist, only interested in the surface of this world for the news it gives him of another, hidden reality, perceived, as it were, through a glass darkly. At the end of *Lilith* he links his fantasy with the much wider mysticism of Plato that has found echoes in the intuitions of a minority in every age of our literature.[80]

> Now and then, when I look round on my books, they seem to waver as if a wind rippled their solid mass, and another world were about to break through. Sometimes when I am abroad, a like thing takes place; the heavens and the earth, the trees and the grass appear for a moment to shake as if about to pass away; then, lo, they have settled again into the old familiar face! At times I seem to hear whisperings around me, as if some that

loved me were talking of me; but when I would distinguish the words they cease, and all is very still. I know not whether these things rise in my brain, or enter it from without. I do not seek them; they come, and I let them go.

Strange dim memories, which will not abide identification, often, through misty windows of the past, look out upon me in broad daylight, but I never dream now. It may be, notwithstanding, that, when most awake I am only dreaming the more! But when I wake at last into that life which, as a mother her child, carries this life in its bosom. I shall know that I wake, and shall doubt no more.

I wait; asleep or awake, I wait.

Novalis says, "Our, life is no dream, but it should and will perhaps become one."[81]

Chapter 6

From *Bildungsroman* to Death-Romance: *Phantastes*, *Lilith*, and German Romanticism

Ever since its publication, George MacDonald's *Phantastes* has baffled many readers, critics, and even many admirers. Nor is that bafflement easily assuaged by its subtitle, *A Faerie Romance for Men and Women*, and a string of prefatory quotations from the German Romantic poet, Novalis, which seem to imply that the story is modeled on German Märchen—folk, or fairy stories. They can be translated as follows:

> One can imagine stories which have no coherence, but only association of events, like dreams; poems, which simply sound lovely, and which are full of beautiful words, but which lack sense or coherence, or at most have single verses which can be understood, like fragments of the most varied objects. This true poetry can at most have a general allegorical meaning and an indirect effect like music. For that reason, nature is as purely poetic as a magician's room, or a physicist's, a children's nursery, a padded cell and a larder. [. . .]
>
> A fairy story is like a disjointed dream-vision, an ensemble of wonderful things and occurrences, for example, a musical fantasy, the harmonic sequences of an Aeolian harp, nature itself. [. . .]
>
> In a real fairy tale everything must be wonderful, secret and coherent; everything must be alive, each in a different way. The whole of nature must be marvellously mixed with the whole of the world of spirits; here the time of the anarchy, lawlessness, freedom of nature in its natural state, the time before the world, comes in. [. . .] The world of fairy-tale is a world which is the very opposite of the world of reality, and for that very reason is as thoroughly like it as chaos is to completed creation.[1]

Thus whether or not MacDonald was "tainted" by German *theology*—as the Elders of the Arundel Congregational Church had charged—German *literary* influence is thus clearly, if ambiguously, acknowledged at the outset of MacDonald's first novel. But what was it about Germany that was to prove so influential not merely on MacDonald, but on the whole development of English fantasy?

In the early nineteenth century Germany was immensely fashionable in Britain. The British royal family maintained strong links with its Hanoverian roots. Britain and Prussia enjoyed not merely close military, but ever closer cultural ties since their victory at Waterloo in 1815, culminating in Queen Victoria's marriage to her beloved Prince Albert of Saxe-Coburg-Gotha in 1840. The wedding had even been followed by a proposal for a joint Anglican-Lutheran bishopric of Jerusalem in 1841 (anticipating eventual union between the English and Prussian state churches). Nevertheless much of the popular picture of Germany was based on sheer ignorance. Though things had improved slightly since 1821 when Edward Bouverie Pusey, the future Regius Professor of Divinity at Oxford, on setting out to learn about new developments in German theology had discovered that only two people in the entire university knew any German at all, German was still not taught in British schools or universities. Those who, like Carlyle, Coleridge, De Quincey, or George Eliot, had attempted to create a wider awareness of German culture through translation and articles appealed only to a narrow section of the reading public.[2]

The revolutionary philosophy of Kant and Hegel, like the no less iconoclastic theology of Strauss and Feuerbach, was largely untranslated until mid-century, and much of the work of the German Romantics, including Novalis, the Schlegels, and Schleiermacher was not translated until the twentieth century.[3] For most people, Germany was not so much the land of advanced thought as one of dark forests, romantic castles, and musical boxes.[4]

That this image from German folklore, based not merely on the pioneering researches of the brothers Grimm but on the writings of Novalis and his fellow Romantics, not to mention Mme de Stael's propagandist French portrait of the country in her book *De l'Allemagne*,[5] was part of a cohesive national effort to reinvent a truly German culture that might effectively unify a country humiliated by the Napoleonic Wars and still divided politically into over three-hundred independent states was, of course, little understood by the British. Nor did they understand the degree to which this elevation of fairy stories was not only because they represented something truly German enough to satisfy an increasingly nationalistic readership, but because there was, in truth, very little else to work on.

For a variety of historical reasons, the novel as a form had never enjoyed the kind of prestige in eighteenth-century Germany that it had come to hold in England.[6] A reference book published in Leipzig in the 1770s, for instance, has no entry at all under *novel*, the noun, and under the adjective, *novelistic*, merely comments tartly:

> Thus one describes whatever in content, tone, or expression bears the characteristics which prevailed in earlier novels—such as fondness for adventures, stiltedness in actions, events, feelings. The natural is more or less the exact opposite of the novelistic.[7]

In Martin Swales's memorable phrase, the novel in Germany was born with "a bad conscience." It is hardly surprising, therefore, that the first German novels of note had the loose episodic structure and fantastic events more commonly associated with fairy stories than with the kind of closely plotted, realistic structures pioneered by Jane Austen in English and which had rapidly become the norm of the nineteenth-century novel. As we shall see, this is as true of Goethe's *Wilhelm Meister* by the self-styled leader of German "classicism" as it was of Novalis's ultra-Romantic (and romantically incomplete) novel, *Heinrich von Ofterdingen*—both of which were to prove hugely influential in the development of MacDonald's own work.

This problem of the relationship of the parts to the whole—central to all fantasy—has always been at its most acute in *Phantastes*. Despite its superficially fragmented construction, some readers have found an innate underlying unity in the whole work. Robert Lee Wolff, in his pioneering study of MacDonald,[8] was one of the first to discuss this tension between the apparently episodic and even picaresque arrangement of incidents and raise the possibility of an overall allegorical or symbolic structure. Like all his fellow German Romantics, Novalis had not been afraid of contradicting himself, but, as Wolff points out, the problem of intention here is compounded by the fact that in the passages by MacDonald quoted at the beginning of this chapter, Novalis had originally written not that "everything must be wonderful, mysterious and coherent" (thereby contradicting the first paragraph) but that it should be "incoherent" (*unzusammenhängend*). It was his friends and posthumous editors, Ludwig Tieck and August Schlegel, who made the alteration for purposes of their own. For Wolff's largely Freudian interpretation any sense of unity overriding the apparently fragmented construction can be attributed more to the degree to which its author reveals his own unconscious needs and fantasies than to any deliberate constructional subtlety,[9] but for others the novel's total coherence (however achieved) has been its essential feature. C. S. Lewis, for instance, records that a key step in his conversion to Christianity was triggered by the chance finding of a copy of *Phantastes* on a railway station bookstall in 1916.

The more one studies Lewis's account of this particular accident of fortune, indeed, the more bizarre does it become. Admittedly any "conversion" narrative is likely to be a more than usually edited and subjective version of the facts, but, if Lewis's telling of the story is to be even half believed, it makes the conversions of Augustine, Wesley, or Newman seem events of the severest necessitarian logic by comparison. Here is part of his account of that first reading of *Phantastes*:

> Turning to the bookstall, I picked out an Everyman in a dirty jacket, *Phantastes*, a faerie Romance, George MacDonald. [. . .] That evening I began to read my new book.
>
> The woodland journeyings in that story, the ghostly enemies, the ladies both good and evil, were close enough to my habitual imagery to lure me on without the perception of change. It is as if I were carried sleeping across the frontier, or as if I had died in the old country and could never remember how I came alive in the new. For in one sense the new country was exactly like the old. I met there all that had already charmed me in Malory, Spenser, Morris and Yeats. But in another sense all was changed. I did not yet know (and I was long in learning) the name of the new quality, the bright shadow, that rested on the travels of Anodos. I do now. It was Holiness. For the first time the song of the sirens sounded like the voice of my mother or my nurse. Here were old wives' tales; there was nothing to be proud of in enjoying them. It was as though the voice which had called to me from the world's end were now speaking at my side.[10]

Here certainly is that sense of wonderful and secret coherence that MacDonald had discovered (however illegitimately) in the Novalis quotations, but in recollecting that coherence Lewis immediately and naturally enters into the allegorical imagery of the story he is describing. It was as if, almost like Anodos, the hero of *Phantastes*, he had been "carried sleeping across a frontier" to somewhere where the allurements of the most exotic literary forms—which clearly included for him the Arthurian cycle and the *Faerie Queene*—were one and the same with the stories of his mother or nurse. Here Lewis slips easily into the imagery of the "grandmother" and "wise-woman" that pervades not just *Phantastes*, but so many of MacDonald's other stories. Yet the inversion of the sinister "dark shadow" of the novel into the "bright shadow" of holiness seems in context almost willful.

Take, for instance, the path of Anodos (whose name means "pathless") towards self-knowledge through disobedience in *Phantastes*. He enters a lonely cottage in the forest and finds a woman reading. Beyond her is a door, and he is seized at once by an irresistible desire to know what is beyond it. She warns him, but he persists and looks in through it. It is an ordinary broom cupboard but as his eyes get used to the darkness he realizes that it has no back:[11]

> All at once, with such a shiver as when one is suddenly conscious of the presence of another in a room where he has, for hours, considered himself alone, I saw that the seemingly luminous extremity was the sky, as of night, beheld through the long perspective of a narrow, dark passage, through what, or built of what, I could not tell. As I gazed, I clearly discerned two or three stars glimmering faintly in the distant blue. But, suddenly, as if it had been running fast from a far distance for this very point, and had turned the corner without abating its swiftness, a dark figure sped into and along the passage from the blue opening at the remote end. I started back and shuddered, but kept looking, for I could not help it. On and on it came, with a speedy approach but delayed arrival; till, at last [. . .] it [. . .] rushed up to me, and passed me into the cottage. [. . .]
>
> "Where is he?" I said, in some alarm, to the woman, who sat reading.
>
> "There, on the floor, behind you," she said, pointing with her arm half-outstretched, but not lifting her eyes. I turned and looked, but saw nothing. Then with a feeling that there was yet something behind me, I looked round over my shoulder; and there, on the ground, lay a black shadow the size of a man.[12]

Anodos's subsequent struggle to rid himself of his shadow illustrates MacDonald's theory of the fairytale perfectly. As we discover, the shadow cannot merely be read as "original sin," or the "unconscious," the Jungian "shadow," or even some prototype of the Freudian "id," for it operates at two levels in the story. At one level it may indeed stand for some, or indeed all, of these. Anodos is both frightened and disgusted by the dark menacing presence of the shadow, always with him: it insidiously destroys all sense of beauty and wonder in the world around him as he travels, imprisoning him into something like Blake's "cavern'd man" lit only by the fragmented evidence of the five senses as Locke imagined them to be. Simultaneously, however, the discovery of this dark shadow through the forbidden door illustrates the process by which this comes about. It is part of the psychodrama: forming a symbol of his own mental processes. The image itself enlarges our own self-understanding by illustrating its own function. There is, to put it simply, more than we intend in any allegorical image simply because behind it is the forbidden door and the shadow.

> Between the conception and the act
> Falls the shadow.[13]

Nevertheless, though it is one thing to read the novel as both a moral allegory and a psychodrama—as Lewis was well aware, the novel's name is lifted from Phineas Fletcher's *The Purple Island* (1633) where "Phantastes," or "Fancie," is the second of the three allegorical councillors who control the castle of the mind—it is surely quite another to find in it a gateway to the whole doctrinal panoply of institutional Christianity. Fairy stories, whether German or English, have played a significant underground role in European cultural history, but they have not been especially noted in either country for causing religious conversions. Indeed, they have more often been the object of gravest suspicion by guardians of culture and orthodoxy![14]

It may be that part of the clue to Lewis's reaction to *Phantastes* is to be found in the meaning he attached to that word *holiness*. Though at that stage he does not seem to have been particularly well read in German literature, by the early 1930s, when he came to reflect on what had happened to him, he was certainly enough of a classically trained philologist to know that *hagios*, the New Testament word most often translated into English as "holy," like its Hebrew Old Testament counterpart, *quadosh*, came from a root meaning "separate" or "set aside" for a deity or deities[15]—with suggestions of an even earlier meaning of "polluted" or "unclean."[16] Indeed, his final comments on the unexpected effects of his casual purchase seem to be an implicit reference to such connotations of the word:

> Up till now each visitation of Joy had left the common world momentarily a desert—"the first touch of the earth went nigh to kill." Even when real clouds or trees had been the material of the vision, they had been so only by reminding me of another world; and I did not like the return to ours. But now I saw the bright shadow coming out of the book into the real world and resting there, transforming all common things and yet itself unchanged. [. . .] That night my imagination was, in a certain sense, baptised; the rest of me, not unnaturally, took longer. I had not the faintest notion what I let myself in for by buying *Phantastes*.[17]

The language of the Wordsworthian visionary reaches back through a whole literary tradition to the classical world, both pagan and Christian. Thus for Lewis holiness is not so much an attribute of particular characters in the narrative, nor even of plot-structure, but rather the transformation of the mundane world into something new, set aside by divinity, and transcendent. Indeed, the transformation of the *shadow* from what was originally "polluted" and destructive into a source of inspiration and joy is precisely the kind of metaphor of redemption that would have appealed to his philological imagination. But, of course, as we have seen from the earlier quotation, Lewis's previous sense of the mundane world (even at the stage where he then was of what he was later to call "popular realism") was already essentially a *literary* one of a particular kind. As Lewis himself was to note afterwards, his road to conversion via Philosophical Idealism, Pantheism, and finally Theism, though it seemed a natural enough one to him at the time, was in fact a highly unusual one for the early twentieth century.[18] What he does not add, but seems clear in retrospect, is the degree to which his route was influenced by his literary taste. The world of his imagination was, we note, that of Malory, Spenser, Morris, and Yeats. None of them, it is true, were notably Christian writers (indeed, two of the four were distinctly hostile to the Christianity they knew) but all four were not merely writers of fantasy but also the creators and users of potent literary myths. All four were creators not just of fictions, but of complex metafictions—creating from the material of myth and legend highly self-conscious mythopoeic works of art. The "baptism" of Lewis's imagination was thus, it seems, a baptism and a sanctification not so much of literature per se as a means of approaching the transcendent (a view Lewis was both drawn by and, for that reason, highly sceptical of) but more specifically of the particular kind of literary synthesis such works implied.

What *Phantastes* seems to have given to Lewis above all was a glimpse of the possibility of a developing synthesis in which language, literature, and thus the entire record of human imaginative experience could be brought into a unified whole. It had showed him a way (or, at least, perhaps the possibility of a way) in which the literary or poetic transformation of sense-experience could be given some kind of objective meaning and validity. Thus Anodos awakes on the morning of his twenty-first birthday to find himself already, *literally*, in transition from one world to the other:

> While these strange events were passing through my mind, I suddenly [. . .] became aware of the sound of running water near me; and looking

out of bed, I saw that a large green marble basin, in which I was wont to wash, and which stood on a low pedestal of the same material in a corner of my room, was overflowing like a spring; and that a stream of clear water was running over the carpet, all the length of the room, finding its outlet I knew not where. And, stranger still, where this carpet, which I had myself designed to imitate a field of grass and daises, bordered the course of the little stream, the grass blades and daises seemed to wave in a tiny breeze that followed the water's flow; while under the rivulet they bent and swayed with every motion of the changeful current, as if they were about to dissolve with it, and, forsaking their fixed form, became as fluent as the waters.

My dressing table was an old fashioned piece of furniture of black oak, with drawers all down the front. These were elaborately carved in foliage, of which ivy formed the chief part. The nearer end of this table remained just as it had been, but on the further end a singular change had commenced. I happened to fix my eye on a little cluster of ivy leaves. The first of these was evidently the work of the carver; the next looked curious; the third was unmistakably ivy; and just beyond it a tendril of clematis had twined itself about the gilt handle of one of the drawers. Hearing a slight motion above me, I looked up, and saw that the branches and leaves designed upon the curtains of my bed were slightly in motion. Not knowing what change might follow next, I thought it high time to get up; and, springing from the bed, my bare feet alighted upon a cool green sward; and although I dressed in all haste, I found myself completing my toilet under the boughs of a great tree.[19]

This is MacDonald at his best. What in the hands of many writers would remain merely a set piece becomes in MacDonald's hands also a *symbolic* event. The flowering of the manmade decorations in the carpet and the carvings immediately suggests that this other world, Fairyland, is to be in some sense more *real* than the one Anodos is leaving. What with us is artificial, there is natural. The stream of water overflowing from the basin is literally the River of Life: as it flows across his carpet it brings to life everything it touches.[20] Imitation becomes what it imitates. Presumably, by inference, we are also meant to assume the same of Anodos himself—and the final chapter of the book suggests that this is so. It is the morning of his twenty-first birthday, and, appropriately, his first action in this new world is to stoop and wash himself in the stream. But this explicit archetypal symbolism has an unexpected side effect. We are suddenly enabled to see the old room as it vanishes with a new intensity of detail. The unexpected metamorphosis of the room from "art" to "life" shows us the clichéd luxuriance of flower and vegetation patterns dear to mid-Victorian bedroom taste with the shock of seeing the familiar for the first time. The juxtaposition with the "other" world shows us our own in a new way. And that, of course, is the purpose of MacDonald's whole technique. The deliberate aesthetic inversion provides an ironic second layer of meaning: in the story we are suddenly brought from art to life; in reality, since the story we are reading is itself a work of art, we are moving from life to art. The "new reality" is being created by MacDonald as author in order to reveal what is latent, but not explicit in the old.

In *Lilith*, MacDonald's last novel, in a parallel scene the hero, Mr. Vane, enters the other world by a device already made familiar to us by Lewis Carroll—a mirror:

> The small chamber was full of light. [. . .] A few rather dim sunrays, marking their track through the cloud of motes that had just been stirred up, fell upon a tall mirror with a dusty face, old fashioned and rather narrow—in appearance an ordinary glass. It had an ebony frame, on the top of which stood a black eagle with outstretched wings, in his beak a golden chain, from whose end hung a black ball.
>
> I had been looking at rather than into the mirror, when suddenly I became aware that it reflected neither the chamber nor my own person. I have an impression of having seen the wall melt away, but what followed is enough to account for any uncertainty:—could I have mistaken for a mirror the glass that protected a wonderful picture?
>
> I saw before me a wild country, broken and heathy. Desolate hills of no great height, but somehow of strange appearance, occupied the middle distance; along the horizon stretched the tops of a far off mountain range; nearest me lay a tract of moorland, flat and melancholy.
>
> Being short sighted, I stepped closer to examine the texture of a stone in the immediate foreground, and in the act espied, hopping toward me with solemnity, a large and ancient raven, whose purply black was here and there softened with gray. [. . .] Nowise astonished at the appearance of a live creature in a picture, I took another step forward to see him better, stumbled over something—doubtless the frame of the mirror—and stood nose to beak with the bird: I was in the open air, on a houseless heath![21]

These are just two of a series of images of the relation of art to life in the course of the stories—as we shall see, another example in *Lilith* is a book in the library which is half in the other world, half in this. Here, however, the other world literally holds up a mirror to our own. The symbolic significance is obvious: the work of art, in this case *Lilith* itself, reveals to us our own world in a new light. Many of Mr. Raven's speeches are designed to ram this point home. This is as much the proper function of fantasy as it is of any realistic novel, but whereas the events of the realistic novel must perforce work at one remove from spiritual realities, fantasy can show them in a much more direct (though still symbolic) manner simply by the kinds of event it can portray. Abstractions can thus be shown as concrete entities.

Though this may seem at first sight a very far cry from Novalis's idea of a fairy story, it may nevertheless serve to illuminate certain elements in what MacDonald was attempting with his new and highly potent fictional form. In any case there were other elements from German Romanticism besides Novalis at work on MacDonald's imagination.

Among the epigraphs in *Phantastes* are quotations not merely from Lewis's favorites, the Arthurian legends and Spenser, but also Shakespeare, the Metaphysical poets, Coleridge, Wordsworth, and Shelley; and from the Germans: Heinrich Heine, Jean Paul (Richter), Fredrich Schiller, Schleiermacher, and Goethe. Though such a heterogeneous selection of writers could hardly be accused of any kind of religious orthodoxy, what they do have in common is that they are all creators of "Romances" of one kind or another. Whatever MacDonald was attempting to do in creating his adult fairy story, Lewis was clearly right in detecting in him an eclectic literary taste in many ways akin to his own: in its mode of operation at once metafictional and intertextual.

Notably absent from this list, interestingly enough, is E. T. A. Hoffmann, whose novella, *The Golden Pot*, has, following Greville MacDonald's suggestion in his biography of his father, regularly been cited as being the probable model for *Phantastes*.[22] Yet, despite MacDonald's clear appreciation of Hoffmann, such a statement is, in fact, highly misleading. Though certain incidents in *Phantastes*, such as the whispering voices in the tree that begin Hoffmann's story and end MacDonald's, are clear examples of the latter's borrowing (be it said, to good advantage), any structural resemblance between *The Golden Pot* and *Phantastes* is in fact very slight. Hoffmann's story, with its tightly constructed sequential narrative and plethora of irrelevant magical wonders offers no suggestion of hidden allegory nor even development of character. In no way does it offer the kind of model for a sustained full-length allegorical Romance that MacDonald by his network of epigraphs and quotations seems to be so self-consciously striving to recreate in his new form.

For this the influence of Goethe was much more important. Goethe was still little more than a name to the British public—known chiefly through a bad translation of Werther—even after the appearance of Carlyle's classic translation of *Wilhelm Meister* in 1824, the year of

MacDonald's birth. Though Carlyle had previously contributed translations for serialization in the *London Magazine* (including a *Life of Schiller*) and was later to translate *The Golden Pot* in 1827, *Wilhelm Meister* was his first independently published literary work and, as such, it was undoubtedly chosen with the aim of furthering the reputation of its twenty-nine-year-old translator as well as its original author. In this he was at least partially successful: if the initial public response was not overwhelming, demand was strong enough for a second edition in 1839. As Carlyle was well aware, nothing quite like it had appeared in English before.

From its first publication in 1796, *Wilhelm Meisters Lehrjahre* had attracted controversy. Goethe had begun his loose and episodic novel as early as 1777, when he was both a Minister of State in Weimar and director of the Court Theatre, and he worked on it spasmodically until 1785, by which time he had completed the fifth book. He did not resume writing until 1794, in very different circumstances, when he rapidly completed the remaining three books.[23] By that stage what had seemingly begun as an autobiographical novel of theatrical life had turned into the first (and arguably the greatest) example of the genre later to be known as a *Bildungsroman*.

The degree to which the novel reflects this checkered writing-history is a matter of controversy. The earlier books tell the story of how young Wilhelm rejects the middle-class commercial world in which he was brought up, and, under the guise of a business trip financed by his father, joins and eventually runs a troupe of itinerant actors. While on this extended period of absence from home he has a series of more or less disastrous and unsuitable love affairs with women ranging from two actresses to a countess, in the process acquiring a number of dependents including a small child which, as he afterwards learns, is his own—borne by Marianne, his first love who has subsequently died. In the midst of these adventures he learns that his father has also died. The loosely strung episodes of this narrative are given further shape by a second, metafictional plot based on Shakespeare's *Hamlet*. On first being introduced to the play by the mysterious Jarno, Wilhelm takes the play to himself, undertaking not merely to rewrite it in accordance with the needs of the time, but also to direct it, and even to act the part of the prince himself. The parallels with his own life are carefully highlighted. He is haunted by guilt over the neglect of his father (significantly, less so over Marianne—a not-so-innocent but equally misused Ophelia). His closest friend and confidant is even known as "Horatio" (though we are told that is not his real name). In the later sections of the book direct references to the players in *Hamlet* and his own troupe are stressed: culminating in a scene where Jarno points out, in a passage reminiscent of Act. II, Sc. 2, the symbolic parallels between the playhouse and the world.[24]

In the final books of the *Apprenticeship* and in its sequel, the *Travels*, all semblance of conventional naturalism is set aside. Jarno, along with several other equally enigmatic figures, turns out to belong to a secret society, the Society of the Tower, which takes its name from the tower of the mysterious rambling castle of a nobleman called Lothario. This organization, it transpires, has been keeping a beneficent watch over Wilhelm almost from the start, limiting the potentially disastrous consequences of his mistakes, and eventually, in a scene echoing the initiation of Tamino in *The Magic Flute*, admitting him to the mysteries of their Order. At the end of the novel, he is finally rewarded with the hand of the beautiful lady, the Amazon, with whose image he has been in love (when he remembers) for most of the novel, and who conveniently turns out to be the sister of the Countess for whom he has long also nourished a hopeless passion.

He is not to be allowed to enjoy his lady at this stage, however. Once safely betrothed, he is immediately sent off again on his travels—the subject of the next volume. For its metafictional structure this sequel, the *Travels*, relies less on Shakespeare than on the work of another, no less metafictional English writer: Sterne's *Sentimental Journey*—at one point Wilhelm is even casually referred to as "Yorrick," Sterne's mouthpiece and protagonist as well as the one-time owner of the skull in *Hamlet*'s graveyard scene. Throughout the narrative level there are a good many "shandian" interludes; at a philosophical level the emphasis is less on the gaining of worldly experience than on the stages of religious awareness.[25]

Any reader of MacDonald is immediately struck by the startlingly familiar imagery from which these complex allegories are created. We have already mentioned the rambling castle, with the secret in the tower (and even, at one point, hobgoblins!)—so central to *The Princess and the Goblin*—but these borrowed elements of the *Apprenticeship* pale into insignificance with the flood of ingredients MacDonald has culled from the *Travels*. Miners "allured by the metallic veins," boring through the rock, are held up by Jarno as types or exempla of the "enquiring thinker" "in a thousand ways endeavouring to solve the hardest problems";[26] there is a golden casket with a (missing) golden key—in connection with which a character even has, in the words of Carlyle's translation, to toil "through moss and tangle";[27] the protagonists are at another point led on a preordained route by mysterious arrows; there are even, for those who like to mix

MacDonald with Tolkien, dwarves (who, like MacDonald's goblins, have chosen to go underground and shun the light), and dragons.

Such elements, however, are less significant for our understanding of MacDonald than the way in which the episodic plots of both novels are constructed around a sense of the larger whole in which it is suggested that there is a hidden order permeating all existence, and that the growth of the youthful but symbolically named "Meister" is achieved both through its guidance and, eventually, by discovery of it. That this discovery is at the same time a *self*-discovery is made clear in the ceremony of Wilhelm's admission to the Society of the Tower when he is presented with an already printed book of his own life. The constant cross-reference to other works of literature, moreover, serves to create the impression that there is, similarly, a hidden meaning and order to be discovered through literature, and that there, too, understanding and self-discovery are but twin aspects of the same process. As a spiritual advisor to the "fair saint," a noblewoman who comes under the influence of Count Zinzendorf's Moravian sect, says:

> Life lies before us, as a huge quarry lies before the architect: he deserves not the name of architect, except when, out of this fortuitous mass, he can combine, with the greatest economy, and fitness, and durability, some form, the pattern of which originated in his spirit. All things without us, nay, I may add, all things on us, are mere elements: but deep within us lies the creative force, which out of these can produce what they were meant to be; and which leaves us neither sleep nor rest, till in one way or another, without us or on us, that same has been produced.[28]

In effect, what Lewis was to find with such astonishment in MacDonald was a redeployment not just of individual motifs and elements culled from Goethe, but a whole way of structuring experience, part-fantasy, part-realism, which go to make up the origins of the German *Bildungsroman*.

The German word *Bildung* is almost untranslatable in English. The most literal meaning would be that of "formation" or "growth" with the implication of internal organic self-development rather than merely the acquiring of a skill or training (as in the parallel word, *Ausbildung*). Thus Goethe's contemporary, the philologist Wilhelm von Humboldt, wishing, as he put it, to study "the faculty of speech in its inward aspect, as a human faculty" insisted that it must be understood in the context of a "philosophical survey of humanity's capacity for formation (*Bildung*) and with history."[29] Such connotations of "inwardness," "culture," and even introspectiveness have sometimes led to the word *Bildungsroman* being rendered in English as "the novel of self-cultivation"—a genre which no less a literary figure than Thomas Mann saw as being Germany's most distinctive cultural form.[30]

Though the term seems to have been coined in the early 1820s by Karl Morgenstern[31] it did not achieve wide currency until the end of the nineteenth century when it was taken up by Wilhelm Dilthey, who at first simply defined it in terms of what he saw as the first example: "I propose to call those novels which make up the school of *Wilhelm Meister* [. . .] *Bildungsromane*."[32] This he later summarized as:

> A regulated development within the life of the individual [. . .] each of its stages has its own intrinsic value and is at the same time the basis for a higher stage. The dissonances and conflicts of life appear as the necessary growth points through which the individual must pass on his way to maturity and harmony.[33]

Morgenstern's original definition, however, had been more subtly reflexive. For him the term should apply not merely to the *Bildung* of the hero, but also to that of the reader, whose own personal formation and self-development is fostered through involvement with the text.[34] Without plunging into the interesting question of his anticipation of later reader-response theories, it is worth noticing how closely such an idea of the *Bildungsroman* foreshadows the effect of *Phantastes* at least on a reader such as Lewis—not to mention his friend Arthur Greeves with whom he corresponded at length about his discovery.[35]

But Dilthey's concentration on the character of the hero should not allow us to lose sight of the degree to which such novels were always self-conscious literary artefacts. In an echo of Morgenstern's idea of the self-conscious reflexiveness inherent in the genre, one modern critic, Michael Beddow claims:

> We are invited to view the entire narrative as a piece of fiction which requires of us a response that includes an awareness of reading an imaginative construction, rather than an empirically accurate representation. At this level of reading, the mimetic claim to be "about" the hero's development is relativised by the wider claim that the narrative of the hero's experiences, precisely insofar as we perceive it to be a piece of fiction, offers insights into human nature which could not be adequately conveyed either in the form of discursive arguments or through a rigorously mimetic, non-self-conscious fictional work.[36]

Such an inherently metafictional description applies not merely to Goethe's *Wilhelm Meister*–still for Beddow, as for Dilthey, the supreme example of the genre–but also with extraordinary accuracy to *Phantastes*, and to the new form of "Faerie Romance" in English that we would now see as probably MacDonald's most significant stylistic achievement. It also suggests the degree of MacDonald's debt to Goethe.

But so what? What difference does it make to our reading of *Phantastes* if we see it in terms of the organic unity of a *Bildungsroman* rather than the a-logical fragmentation of a fairy story? Do we really need to refer to German literary theory to discover that Anodos's spiritual growth and development is a central theme of the story? Are there in fact any elements that we might be led to look for in the story by such a reclassification that we might otherwise be inclined to miss?

The most obvious answer is irony–especially irony in that peculiar new sense that we find with Goethe and the German Romantics.[37] Though we are familiar enough with it in Augustine, Dante, the metaphysical poets, and even in Bunyan, irony is not a quality that we are necessarily quick to associate with Victorian religious writing. Yet the moment we formulate the question it is clear that *Phantastes* is in fact a pervasively ironic work– at many levels. Most obvious is the constant disconfirmation of Anodos's expectations–from his first meeting with his variable-sized grandmother in the bureau to his mistakes over the various "white" and "marble" ladies he pursues with such energy throughout the narrative. It is clear throughout that this "fairy land" in fact corresponds neither to his wishes nor his expectations–derived mostly from other literature on the subject. This brings us at the metafictional level to the truly Goethean irony in the use of other parallel literary texts–not least, of which, as we have seen, is the one from Novalis stressing the fragmentary and elliptical nature of fairy stories. Not merely are we to bear Novalis in mind when reading *Phantastes*, we need also to read the Novalis in the light of *Phantastes*.

This pervasive sense of irony is also the clue to so much of the relationship between MacDonald's novel and the other literature on which it draws.[38] As we have seen, there was a very real sense in which the folktale or fairy story occupied in Germany the same cultural niche as the novel had come to do in Britain, but as a result it was normal for prose narrative to be judged not in its own terms, or in terms of prose realism, but rather for its *poetic* content. Thus Friedrich Schlegel, reviewing the first part of *Wilhelm Meister* in 1798, eulogizes it as "all poetry–high pure poetry. Everything has been thought and uttered as though by one who is both a divine poet and a perfect artist; and even the most delicate secondary features seem to exist in their own right and to rejoice in their own independent life, even against the laws of petty, inauthentic probability."[39] Sadly, Schlegel's own novel, *Lucinde*, whose vagueness and abstraction might well pass for poetic, proved so lacking in either plot or narrative as to be largely incomprehensible to the reader, then—or subsequently. Similarly, Tieck, comparing Cervantes with Shakespeare, takes it for granted that both are poets, working in a common medium.[40] In this connection it is revealing, for instance, that, in MacDonald's quotation from Novalis with which we began, the fairy story is discussed not as narrative (which it is taken for granted will have "no coherence") but as *poetry*—and the word used in the German is not *dichterish*, which would be employed in connection with actual verse and imaginative writing, but *poetisch*, which has a much more theoretical, abstract, and spiritualized flavor to it.[41]

Thus *Wilhelm Meister*'s enormous popularity and prestige in early nineteenth-century Germany stemmed not least from the fact that it seemed to rehabilitate what had hitherto seemed to many critics as a dubious and even illegitimate fictional form. In his introduction to the first edition of his English translation Carlyle quotes Schlegel on the contrast between it and its predecessors.

> To judge of this book,—new and peculiar as it is, and only to be understood and learned from itself, by our common notion of the novel, a notion pieced together and produced out of custom and belief, out of accidental and arbitrary requisitions,— is as if a child should grasp at the moon and stars, and insist on packing them into its toy-box.[42]

What was felt to be the inwardness and dignity of the way in which Goethe handled the new medium gave the lie to the eighteenth-century English stereotype of German literature summed up by Wordsworth in 1798 in his attack on "frantic novels, sickly and stupid German Tragedies."[43] This perception helped to pave the way for the great reappraisal that, helped by Carlyle's influence, was to fire the next generation of young Scots (in particular)[44] such as MacDonald with an enthusiasm for German literature, culture, and theology.

Yet the general improvement in status of the German novel with Goethe's great *Bildungsroman* served only to highlight a paradox that had always been latent in any literary expression of "self-development" as an aesthetic form. In his comments on the novel in his *Aesthetics*, Hegel puts in general terms what is, in effect, the central problem of *Wilhelm Meister*. The heroes of such novels, he writes, stand as individuals with their subjective goals of love, honour, ambition, or with their ideals of improving the world, over against the existing order and prose of reality which from all sides places obstacles in their path. [. . .] These struggles are, however, in the modern world nothing but the apprenticeship, the education of the individual at the hands of the given reality. [. . .] For the conclusion of such an apprenticeship usually amounts to the hero getting the corners knocked off him. [. . .] In the last analysis he usually gets his girl and some kind of job, marries and becomes a philistine just like the others.[45]

In other words, the very process of self-formation and the gaining of worldly wisdom, essential as it is to growth and maturity, is actually toward a goal that is fundamentally less interesting and less morally worthy than the raw immature idealism that preceded it![46] Certainly the ending of *Wilhelm Meister*, where our hero is paired with a beautiful aristocrat and given the job of managing a large estate purchased as an investment by a business syndicate, is highly ambiguous.

It is part of the ironic literary structure of MacDonald's *Bildungsroman* that the ending of *Phantastes* can be read not merely in relation to the narrative that precedes it, but also in relation to this problem in its progenitor: *Wilhelm Meister*. Thus Anodos, at the end of his experiences, so far from being better fitted for accommodation with the real world (in a question, that, as we have seen, was to be echoed by Arthur Machen fifty years later[47]) is left wondering how far he is now actually *unfitted* for it.

I began the duties of my new position, somewhat instructed, I hoped, by the adventures that had befallen me in Fairy Land. Could I translate the experience of my travels there, into common life? This was the question. Or must I live it all over again, and learn it all over again, in other forms that belong to the world of men, whose experience yet runs parallel to that of Fairy Land? I cannot yet answer. But I fear. [. . .]

I have a strange feeling sometimes, that I am a ghost, sent into the world to minister to my fellow-men, or, rather to repair the wrongs I have already done. [. . .]

Thus I, who set out to find my Ideal, came back rejoicing that I had lost my Shadow. [. . .]

What we call evil, is the only and best shape, which, for the person and his condition at the time, could be assumed by the best good. And so, Farewell.[48]

Whereas *Wilhelm Meister*, at the end of the Apprenticeship, is compared with Saul, the son of Kish, "who went out to seek his father's asses, and

found a kingdom,"[49] Anodos, can be certain not of present happiness, like
Goethe's hero, but only of future good. Though he is in some ways a sad-
der and a wiser man, there is no suggestion that his final condition involves
any kind of moral compromise with the values of the world. His "formation" has, on the contrary, given him a stronger sense of his own ideals—
even if he is also correspondingly more humble both about their value and
of his capacity to attain them. Notably, he does not get any of the women
he has been pursuing so earnestly. This strangely hesitant agnosticism of
MacDonald, the religious believer, similarly loses something of its quiet
irony if we fail to set it alongside the formulaic certainties of the agnostic
religious instruction of Goethe's ideal community at the end of the
Travels:

> Two duties we have most rigorously undertaken: first, to honour every
> species of religious worship, for all of them are comprehended more or
> less directly in the Creed: secondly, in like manner to respect all forms of
> government; and since every one of them induces and promotes a calcu-
> lated activity, to labour according to the wish and will of constituted
> authority, in whatever place it may be our lot to sojourn, and for whatever
> time. Finally, we reckon it our duty, without pedantry or rigour, to prac-
> tise and forward decorum of manners and morals, as required by that
> Reverence for Ourselves. [. . .] All this, in the solemn hour of parting, we
> have thought good once more to recount, to unfold, to hear and acknowl-
> edge, as also to seal with a trustful Farewell.[50]

Though one might wish for a little more of Novalis's incoherence at points
like this, nevertheless, if the striking parallels between *Phantastes* and
Wilhelm Meister suggest that MacDonald in creating his "fairy romance
for men and women" was in fact transplanting Goethe's *Bildungsroman*
into the alien but highly fertile context of English literature, we need to recognize first of all the inevitable and ironic transformation wrought by that
subtle change of air. Whereas, the prose romance in German was scarcely
recognized, in England it had a lineage reaching back to Malory; while
the indigenous German theater was of little account, England had
Shakespeare. In this sense the context of metafictional reference available
to MacDonald was far richer and more evocative than was possible for
Goethe in his own literature. It is highly significant that when Goethe,
comparing the demands on the hero of the drama (Hamlet, naturally!) with
the hero of the novel, needed to evoke a string of protagonists from novels,
his entire selection was from England: "Grandison, Clarissa, Pamela, the
Vicar of Wakefield, Tom Jones. [. . .]"[51] Contrarywise, in returning the com-

pliment, MacDonald by his references to Novalis, Hoffmann, Jean Paul, Schleiermacher, Heine, Schiller, and Goethe, is in fact doing something very different: whereas Shakespeare and the English eighteenth-century novelists were comparatively familiar in Germany, German writers of the late eighteenth-century literary renaissance, were, in contrast, little known, and even exotic figures to the more insular British readership of the 1850s. Goethe's literary references had the effect of placing his novel in relation to what he saw as the mainstream development of prose realism; MacDonald contrives to suggest that behind the veil of normality in that tradition was something marvelous and magical that could not be wholly eradicated from everyday life. In the very literature where Goethe had assiduously sought bourgeois reality, MacDonald discovers romance—awaiting only the mysticism of Novalis and his fellow Germans to be awakened into new life.

But the ironies of the change in referential context are minor compared with the consequences of the shift in medium from realism to fantasy. Though *Wilhelm Meister* is hardly realistic by the later standards of the nineteenth century, it is certainly no fairy story either. MacDonald was one of the few nineteenth-century writers to recognize that realism and fantasy are two sides of the same coin: that realism is as much an arbitrary and literary convention as fantasy, and that fantasy is as dependent on mundane experience as realism.[52] By invoking Novalis as his mentor, and moving his own *Bildingsroman* overtly into the realm of the fantastic, MacDonald was able to bring out latent resources of irony in the genre that were unavailable even to Goethe himself in his more overtly naturalistic mode. Anodos's adventures in Fairy Land, after all, conclude with his account of his own death—the acceptance of which, as we know from *Lilith*, MacDonald saw as being an essential factor in any kind of spiritual maturity. The irony of Christ's maxim "He that would save his life, must lose it" is always present in MacDonald's imagination. Moreover, the structural technique of placing the process of self-formation not in this world but in a fantastic other world immediately circumvents what we have seen is the major thematic problem of Goethe's *Bildungsroman*. If there is, as I believe, a sense in which *Phantastes* is the most satisfactory English adaptation of the *Bildungsroman*—much more so than, say, Dickens's *Great Expectations* or George Meredith's *Ordeal of Richard Feverel*, which have been commonly advanced as examples of the genre[53]—it is not so much because it is the most faithful replica of its outward characteristics, but because (to use a very German argument) it is the truest expression of its spirit. In adapting and radically changing the original form to suit his particular needs,

MacDonald in fact solved the problem that had dogged Goethe and his successors working, however loosely, within the tradition of realism. The contradiction between moral idealism and worldly accommodation that worried Hegel is ultimately, of course, a theological one, and can in the end only be solved in theological terms. But theological solutions do not necessarily make good novels. To find through Goethe's irony an appropriate literary and aesthetic form for such an abstraction is an extraordinary achievement—perhaps in its own way one of the greatest achievements of Victorian fiction.

But important as this metaphysical transformation of the *Bildungsroman* undoubtedly is in terms of literary history, it would still hardly explain the impact that *Phantastes* had on the eighteen-year-old Lewis, who, at that stage of his life and in the middle of the First World War, was most unlikely to have known or cared about the problems of the German novel. What seems to have excited Lewis is the manner in which MacDonald had managed to give a new relevance and meaning to the fantastic romances of Malory, Spenser, Morris, and his other heroes. By showing the limitations of conventional realism to portray vital aspects of human growth and development, MacDonald had not merely helped to legitimize Lewis's own literary taste, he had also obliquely and ironically suggested a profound critique of genre and, incidentally, of contemporary assumptions about realism. To suggest that, for Lewis, *Phantastes* served as an introduction to what we would now, with rather a parochial sense of history, call "postmodernism" seems at first sight an unlikely perspective, yet, as we have seen, there is a good argument for such a case. It should also make us look more carefully at our own conventional assumptions about postmodernism.

But if *Phantastes* was generally received with somewhat mystified praise, *Lilith* has had no such luck. The usual critical reaction has been that though it contains poetic or, more often, *mystical* insights, it is at best a severely flawed work, and, at worst, a failure. Rolland Hein allows it "a vivid sense of place" and that it has an "aura of the dream, with the startling immediacy of its scenes and the peculiar force of its logic, is maintained with admirable consistency" but nevertheless judges that "the weight of the idea [. . .] is not integrated with the symbolism," and that it is generally weak on dramatic quality. Overall it is "an uneven performance [. . .] somewhat inferior to *Phantastes*."[54] Though Colin Manlove, like Robert Lee Wolff, has modified his opinion of MacDonald quite sharply over time, he is only marginally more complimentary to *Lilith*. He recognizes much more clearly than Hein the mythopoeic force of the book, but continues to feel that MacDonald, "a rather nervous seer,"[55] has attempted to graft onto a kind of residual mystical Calvinism a belief in free will which it will not take.[56]

Probably the best, as well as the most generous, twentieth-century appreciation of *Lilith* comes, once again, from C. S. Lewis. In a letter to his friend Arthur Greeves, of September 1, 1933, he writes:

> I have just re-read *Lilith* and am much clearer about the meaning. The first thing to get out of the way is all Greville Macdonald's (sic) nonsense about "dimensions" and "elements." [. . .] That is just the sort of *mechanical* "mysticism" which is worlds away from Geo. MacDonald. The main lesson of the book is against secular philanthropy—against the belief that you can effectively obey the 2nd. command about loving your neighbour without first trying to love God.
>
> The story runs like this. The human soul exploring its own house (the Mind) finds itself on the verge of unexpected worlds which at first dismay it (Chap. 1–V). The first utterance of these worlds is an unconditional demand for absolute surrender of the Soul to the will of God, or, if you like, for Death (Chap. VI). To this demand the soul cannot at first face up (VI). But attempting to return to normal consciousness finds by education that its experiences are not abnormal or trivial but are vouched for by all the great poets and philosophers (VII *My Father's MS*). It now repents and tries to face the demand, but its original refusal has now rendered real submission temporarily impossible (IX). It has to face instead the impulses of the subconscious (X) and the slightly spurious loyalties to purely human "causes"—political, theological etc. (XI). It now becomes conscious of its fellow men: and finds them divided into "Lovers" [. . .] and "Bags" or "Giants." [. . .] But because it is an unconverted soul, has not yet died, it cannot really help the Lovers and becomes the slave of the Bags. In other words the young man, however amiably disposed towards the sweet and simple people of the world, gets a job, or draws a dividend, and becomes in fact the servant of the economic machine (XII–XIII). But he is too good to go on like this, and so becomes a "Reformer," a "friend of humanity"—a Shelley, Ruskin, Lenin (XIV). Here follows a digression on Purgatory (XV–XVII).
>
> With the next section we enter on the deepest part of the book which I still only v. dimly understand. Why do so many purely secular reformers and philanthropists fail and in the end leave men more wretched and wicked than they found them? Apparently the unconverted soul, doing its very best for the Lovers, only succeeds first in *waking* (at the price of its own blood) and then in becoming the tool of, *Lilith*. Lilith is still quite beyond me. One can trace in her specially the Will to Power—which here fits in quite well—but there is a great deal more than that. She

is also the real ideal somehow spoiled: she is not primarily a sexual symbol, but includes the characteristic *female* abuse of sex, which is love of Power, as the characteristic male abuse is sensuality (XVIII–XXIX). After a long and stormy attempt to do God's work in Lilith's way or Lilith's work in God's way, the soul comes to itself again, realises that its previous proceedings are "cracked absolutely" and in fact has a sort of half-conversion. But the new powers of will and imagination which even this half-conversion inspires (symbolised in the horse) are so exhilarating that the soul thinks these will do instead of "death" and again shoots off on its own. This passage is v. true and important. MacDonald is aware of how *religion itself* supplies new temptations (XXX–XXXI). This again leads to another attempt to help the Lovers in his own way, with consequent partial disaster in the death of Lona (XXXII–XXXVII). He finds himself the *jailer* of Lilith: i.e. he is now living in the state of tension with the evil thing inside him only just held down, and at a terrible cost—until he (or Lilith—the Lilith part of him) at last repents (Mara) and consents to die (XXXVIII–end). [. . .]

I have emphasised the external side too much. Correct everything above by remembering that it is not only the Lovers outside against the Bags, but equally the Lover in himself against the Bag in himself.[57]

I have quoted Lewis at some length here because he enunciates two very important principles of interpretation which few, if any, other modern critics seem to have grasped. The first is that every event in the other world of *Lilith* is purely spiritual. It is interesting that, though Lewis is well aware of MacDonald's own strictures against allegory "as everywhere a weariness to the spirit," he reads the narrative of *Lilith* as a systematic allegory rather than simply a loose assemblage of symbols. In support of this reading it is worth noting that events in what one might call the *internal* narrative are blatantly nonrealistic. Not merely is it populated by monsters, shape-changers, and skeletons, but in spite of apparently ferocious violence, few are ever killed—not just Lona, but even, it seems, those trampled by elephants in Bulika!

The second principle follows directly from this: all events in the book are therefore to be read as internal and taking place *within* the individual psyche. Thus, according to this reading, the children, or Lovers, are not to be seen as *immature* (as Hein suggests) but rather as *childlike* (as in the Sermon on the Mount). As his final paragraph suggests, Lewis is not altogether certain about the consistency of his own argument here, especially whether Vane's attempts to help the children are futile gestures towards external philanthropy, or attempts to develop certain qualities within himself—or even both. But such a separation is in any case impossible: one cannot consider many so-called "internal" qualities such as generosity, and helpfulness to others, without also taking into account the corresponding "external" actions. The psyche does not free-float in a vacuum. What is clear is that, according to Lewis, *Lilith* is to be read primarily as a narrative of *self*-exploration and *self*-discovery.

In this connection we should note the role played by books, and therefore the library, in the plot. One book in particular—which refers specifically to Lilith—actually spans the two worlds. For MacDonald self-knowledge is not simply a matter of introspection, as it were, of internal trial-and-error, but draws also on a huge body of inherited wisdom far greater than any individual can hope to acquire by direct experience. This in turn may give us a further clue as to how we are to understand *Lilith* itself, as a book, and the metafictional freight which it carries. One obvious example for later critics might be the presence of what we would now call "Jungian" archetypes in the shape of the "wise woman" (Mara), the "old man" (Mr. Raven), etc.—raising the obvious question of how far Lilith herself might correspond to the Jungian *anima*.

Certainly the character or function of Lilith herself requires, as he says, further elucidation. As Lewis admits to Greeves, she remains the most significant gap in his argument and, indeed, is "quite beyond" him. Perhaps one way of trying to take this analysis a step further, therefore, might be to take up the hint about the significance of books given above and look first for other *literary* antecedents for Lilith. One immediately comes to mind: Geraldine in Coleridge's *Christabel*. She, too, has on her side some mysterious and terrible mark:

> Like one that shuddered, she unbound
> The cincture from beneath her breast:
> Her silken robe, and inner vest,
> Dropt to her feet, and full in view,
> Behold! her bosom and half her side—
> A sight to dream of, not to tell!
> O shield her! Shield sweet Christabel!
>
> (248–54)

Though she seems more to be a usurper of the mother's role than natural mother (who we are told is dead), there is in her attitude to Christabel more than a hint of the Lilith/Lona relationship. Like Lilith also, Geraldine appears to be some kind of vampire who is first rescued by Christabel and then has to be carried by her over the threshold of the castle. Similarly Geraldine's fatal attraction for Sir Leoline is repeated in Lilith's powerful erotic appeal to Vane. Because Coleridge's poem was unfinished, we cannot be sure of the mysterious Geraldine's role—though most early readers assumed that she was clearly up to no good. More recently, Karen Swann, for instance, sees her as in some sense Christabel's "double," and cites a wealth of contemporary material on hysteria.[58] But the degree of moral uncertainty surrounding her is disturbingly similar to that surrounding Lilith. Even the fact that Coleridge's poem is unfinished can be paralleled by the "unfinished" ending of *Lilith* itself, where, with Novalis, or Keats death-haunted "Ode to a Nightingale," the narrator has to ask "Do I wake or sleep?"

What we do know for certain, however, is that Coleridge's poem had already been the origin of some of the most powerful myths of the nineteenth century. It was Byron's manuscript copy of *Christabel* that, we recall, was the inspiration behind the writing of Mary Shelley's *Frankenstein* that fateful evening in Geneva when Shelley's party met with Byron. Less well known is that Byron's personal physician, a Dr. Polidori, also produced a novella as a result of that meeting: *The Vampyre*. There seems little doubt that just as C. S. Lewis was later to appropriate Lilith as Jadis, the Queen and White Witch in his *Chronicles of Narnia*, so MacDonald, a long-time admirer of Coleridge,[59] had appropriated the figure of Geraldine for his own uses in *Lilith*.

Perhaps the strangest confirmation of Lilith's essentially literary origins, however, is the fact that she *herself* is apparently the author of the mysterious book in the library alluded to above, one end of which lies in the real world of the novel, the other end of which only exists in the spiritual/internal one. There is a hint here, of course, that it is in the nature of all books to span this gap between external and internal worlds—we recall that MacDonald's first publication, in 1855, was a poem entitled *Within and Without*. But that hardly prepares us for one of the strangest features of this particular book: that the passage read aloud by Mr. Raven is in the form of an autobiographical and confessional poem by Lilith herself. That it is actually *by* her and not the kind of conventional artistic projection we see, for instance, in Milton's first-person portrayal of Satan, is made more probable by the fact that we are told that the book is handwritten on parchment,[60] and is in a language which Vane had never before heard, but which he nevertheless understood perfectly.[61] In other words, it is not a published aesthetic construct at all, but written in some universal language of the soul. What Mr. Raven reads, therefore, is not about Lilith, it *is* in some sense Lilith—and what we learn about her is very curious indeed:

> But if I found a man that could believe
> In what he saw not, felt not, and yet knew,
> From him I should take substance, and receive
> Firmness and form relate to touch and view;
> Then should I clothe me in the likeness true
> Of that idea where his soul did cleave![62]

According to this, not merely is she in a very real sense Vane's creation—or even, more accurately, his *projection*—she is a projection not of his worst desires, but of his highest aspirations. Not for nothing does this passage provide strong verbal echoes of the definition of "faith" in Hebrews: "the substance of things hoped for, the evidence of things not seen" (11:1). Moreover, his initial attraction for Lilith is part of a Romantic hungering for something transcendent and beyond himself:

> For by his side I lay, a bodiless thing;
> I breathed not, saw not, felt not, only thought,
> And made him love me—with a hungering
> After he knew not what—if it was aught
> Of but a nameless something that was wrought
> By him, out of himself; for I did sing
>
> A song that had no sound into his soul;
> I lay a heartless thing against his heart,
> Giving him nothing where he gave his whole
> Being to clothe me human, every part;
> That I at last into his sense my dart,
> Thus first into his living mind I stole.

She is indeed a vampire, but one who sucks not the blood but the soul of her victims. Her appeal is the more subtle and dangerous in that she takes the form of her victim's most cherished and noblest desires. Yet in the end she stands for Death.

This is a second problem which Lewis scarcely deals with. The all-pervading sense of Death in *Lilith* is brushed aside in his bracketed reference to chapters "XXXVIII–end"—not, as one might think, simply a brief coda, but a full eight chapters in all which return to what is in effect the central theme of the book, Mr. Raven's repeated invitation to come into his house to die as a prelude to action:

> Do not be a coward, Mr. Vane. Turn your back on fear, and your face to whatever may come. Give yourself up to the night, and you will rest indeed. Harm will not come to you, but a good you cannot foreknow.[63]

At the center of this argument is a complete inversion of life and death:

> "None of those you see," he answered, "are in truth quite dead yet, and some have but just begun to come alive and die. Others had begun to die, that is to come alive, long before they came to us; and when such are indeed dead, that instant they will wake and leave us. Almost every night some rise and go. [. . .] This is the couch that has been waiting for you."[64]

Finally, in these last chapters, Vane accepts this daunting offer, and in that sleep of death he learns what dreams may come—cycles of previous life in a manner reminiscent of the ending of Kingsley's *Alton Locke*.

> Then the dreams began to arrive—and came crowding.—I lay naked on a snowy peak. The white mist heaved below me like a billowy sea. The cold moon was in the air with me, and above the moon and me the colder sky, in which the moon and I dwelt. I was Adam, waiting for God to breathe into my nostrils the breath of life.—I was not Adam, but a child in the bosom of a mother white with radiant whiteness. I was a youth on a white horse, leaping from cloud to cloud of a blue heaven, hasting calmly to some blessed goal. For centuries I dreamed—or was it chiliads? or only one long night?—But why ask? for time had nothing to do with me; I was in the land of thought—farther in, higher up than the seven dimensions, the ten senses: I think I was where I am—in the heart of God.—I dreamed away dim cycles in the centre of a melting glacier, the spectral moon drawing nearer and nearer, the wind and the welter of a torrent growing in my ears. I lay and heard them: the wind and the water and the moon sang a peaceful waiting for a redemption drawing nigh. I dreamed cycles, I say, but for aught I knew or can tell, they were the solemn aeonian march of a second, pregnant with eternity.[65]

But here we encounter a strange ambiguity. Mr. Raven (or Adam, as he turns out to be) tells Vane that he is dreaming, and that, as in our world, one of the conditions of dreaming is that you cannot necessarily tell if you are awake or asleep—whereas, of course, if you really are awake, you can be sure you are not dreaming. It is a fairly safe rule: if you do not know whether you are dreaming or not, you are. Thus, we discover, the whole book is built upon the paradox that to be "alive" is but to "dream," but to be "dead" is to be "awake." Recalling the quotation from Novalis with which MacDonald prefaced the last chapter of *Phantastes*: "Our life is no dream; but it ought to become one, and perhaps will," we are suddenly confronted with a new, existential gloss on the traditional Platonic belief that human life is but a dream of a greater reality. The mere fact that such a suspicion has frequently been held—and may have crossed the minds of many of us at some point in our lives—is powerful evidence that it is true. If we were truly awake, we would be in no doubt about our state. In his dream Vane now longs to be awake:

> I was about to rise and resume my journey, when I discovered that I lay beside a pit in the rock, whose mouth was like that of a grave. It was deep and dark; I could see no bottom.
>
> Now in the dreams of childhood I had found that a fall invariably woke me, and would, therefore, when desiring to discontinue a dream, seek some eminence whence to cast myself down that I might wake: with one glance at the peaceful heavens, and one at the rushing waters, I rolled myself over the edge of the pit.
>
> For a moment consciousness left me. When it returned, I stood in the garret of my own house, in the little wooden chamber of the cowl and the mirror.
>
> Unspeakable despair, hopelessness blank and dreary invaded me.[66]

Yet even this is not the end. He returns to that other world yet again, when he is asleep in this; he awakes in that world, and is finally once more returned to this in such a way as to leave it still uncertain what was dream and what reality.

Such is the high seriousness of tone in *Lilith* that it is with something of a shock we realize that it has left us in the end with precisely that same ambiguity between life and death that we discovered built into the "Tomfooleries" of *The Water Babies*. Like little Tom, who has left the "shell" of his body behind in Vendale, but will grow up to be a great engineer, Vane appears to be both alive and dead. It is not clear if he has at last awoken from death in that other world, only to be returned to this, or if he has merely *dreamed* that he has awoken—so that his existence in this world is only part of the dream until he finally awakes. What began as two very separate worlds, though coexisting in the same space, have now combined in a single unity very similar to Kingsley's single inconsistent universe. Mr. Raven explains much the same point to Vane, and points out the corollary:

> "There is in your house a door, one step through which carries me into a world very much another than this."

"A better?"

"Not throughout; but so much another that most of its physical, and many of its mental laws are different from those of this world. As for moral laws, they must everywhere be fundamentally the same."[67]

This insistence on the uniformity of the moral law, whose claims "must everywhere be fundamentally the same," might become in the hands of a lesser Victorian moralist a kiss of death. By a paradox MacDonald himself would have appreciated, it is in fact the kiss of life: it is what prevents his "other worlds" from ever seeming arbitrary or frivolous. His characters never lose the feeling that, whatever the circumstances, their behavior towards others matters. His worlds are never private fantasies in which the other people encountered have no real existence of their own. As a result, what Chesterton called MacDonald's "optimistic Calvinism"[68] can include and contain a tragic vision that is unlike any other writer of the period. Free will exists; choice is important, and has necessary, if unpredictable, consequences. In *Lilith*, for instance, the highest virtue is consistently presented as obedience. Hence the allegorically named Mr. Vane's instructions that in order to help the innocent children find water (the water of "life," without which their land is parched and they are in constant danger)[69] he must first sleep in Mr. Raven's house—as we have seen, an invitation, in short, to death. Only those who have already thus died, it is implied, will be proof against the temptations of idealism embodied in *Lilith*.

This brings us back to the initial comparison between MacDonald's two great adult romances. If *Phantastes* is essentially a *Bildungsroman*, *Lilith* is something for which the English cannot even borrow a word from German, for it is such a rare phenomenon that there is no such thing in either language. If it existed, or we were to coin such a term, it would be *Todsroman*: a "death-romance."

Here we confront what is for me by far the most difficult problem in *Lilith*: the centrality, even the celebration, of Death. We have already quoted Tolkien's remark: "Death is the theme that most inspired MacDonald."[70] Yet the treatment of death here is not quite what we might expect from an old man who knows that he is within a few years—or perhaps even months—of his own death. It is, for instance, strikingly unlike that other great English *Todsroman*, Dickens's *Mystery of Edwin Drood*, which reeks of physical decay and death and was left tantalizingly unfinished by its author's actual death in 1870. Death for MacDonald here is not the end of things, but, as it were, a misplaced beginning. It is the alternative to that subtlest and most insidiously attractive of all corruptions: the human idealism from which Lilith herself feeds. If what we have said so far in support of Lewis's allegorical and internalized interpretation of *Lilith* is correct, then Mr. Raven's "house of death" is primarily a symbolic expression of the spiritual reality of man's absolute dependence on God.

If that sounds more like something out of Schleiermacher than MacDonald we should not be surprised. We recall that the original charge made against MacDonald when he was compelled to resign his ministry in Arundel was that he was "tainted with German theology." There are direct quotations from Schleiermacher in MacDonald's work as early as *Phantastes*. Equally to the point here is Schleiermacher's proclamation of the essentially personal and firsthand nature of all religion:

> What one commonly calls belief, accepting what another person has done, wanting to ponder and empathise with what someone else has thought and felt, is a hard and unworthy service, and instead of being the highest in religion, as one supposes, it is exactly what must be renounced by those who would penetrate into its sanctuary. To want to have and retain belief in this sense proves that one is incapable of religion; to require this kind of faith from others shows that one does not understand it.[71]

To "die" in Mr. Raven's sense is something you *yourself* must do. It is not a secondhand experience. But not merely must Vane learn to move from secondhand to firsthand religious experience, so, I suspect, must the reader of *Lilith*. MacDonald has as it were turned Schleiermacher's dictum on personal knowledge into an aesthetic principle of originality. In true Romantic style, originality in experience begets originality in expression.

In this sense death in *Lilith* is perhaps best seen a reversed sacrament. A *sacrament* is commonly defined as "the outward and visible expression of an inner spiritual event." It is a symbolic act. In our world death is not a symbol, but the final event of life. Here, in *Lilith*'s other world what is in our world the physical reality of death becomes the symbol for the greater reality of human dependence on God. As if this were not difficult enough, MacDonald compounds our problems by giving this new meaning of death an almost erotic attraction. Just as the intellectual attraction of what Lilith stands for is transmuted into a strong sexual attraction for Lilith herself, so now the attraction of Mr. Raven's house of death carries an almost equivalent erotic charge. It is this, presumably, that gave the first Victorian readers of the novel such problems with it. We know, for instance, that MacDonald's wife was severely "troubled by the book's strange imagery" and was never really reconciled to it.[72] But there are other allied elements that have proved equally difficult for later readers to cope with.

A similar reversal of inner and outer states makes dreams acquire a greater reality than waking states. *Lilith* ends with the same transvaluation of consciousness from Novalis that, as we have seen, prefaces the concluding chapter of *Phantastes*: "Our life is no dream, but it should and will perhaps become one." But here, with the extraordinary ending of *Lilith*, MacDonald's *Todsroman*, the uncompromising nature of this vision is brought home to the reader as perhaps nowhere else in Romantic fiction. The discovery that the first "waking" is itself only a dream is unsettling enough in itself, but it also gives the second "waking," where Vane is unceremoniously pushed back into his own library, an even greater ambiguity. If, for instance, the events of the previous chapters were a dream in the above sense, given, as he puts it, "by Another,"[73] are we to conclude that he is at the moment of writing still dreaming (as in the first waking)? or that he is at present waking, and awaiting the return of the dream? This is not an accidental uncertainty, for, as Roderick McGillis has convincingly shown, the uncertainty and ambiguity of the ending is not the result of confusion or sloppy writing but the product of careful and deliberate revisions.[74] We are *meant* to be left in uncertainty.

But is this not what we might have expected from Lewis's exposition of the book to Greeves? If the events of the other world are to be interpreted as a purely internal and spiritual allegory, then by dreaming in the sleep of death in Mr. Raven's house, Vane is actually wider awake than in his original state. Moreover, he is not returned to his attic mirror, with its suggestions of self-contemplation, and from where he entered the other world, but to his library—to the world of books where the collective learning and spiritual experience of others is assembled. That is where this journey into self-exploration must now continue.

His task is not to inhabit one world or the other, but rather constantly to straddle the two and to insist (despite appearances) on their ultimate congruity. This visionary state, like the vision of ordinary sense-perception, requires not one point of reference, but two. Only when we see with both eyes do we have the stereoscopic vision that enables us to place ourselves in the material world. Similarly, MacDonald implies, only by a correspondingly stereoscopic perspective can we place ourselves in the moral and spiritual world. Thus Mr. Raven is, and is not, a Raven/a Librarian/a Sexton/ and Adam. Mara is both woman and cat. And Lilith? Woman/leopard/ leech/vampire; she is surely the hidden pride that masquerades behind the self-sufficiency of fallen human ideals. She is, for MacDonald, the greatest temptation of all, and the last to be relinquished, for she is herself the embodiment of Death. She is, by a clear piece of symbolism, the last to enter Mr. Raven's house, for only then shall Death die.

Chapter 7

Worlds within Worlds:
Kipling and Nesbit

In his earliest time I thought he perhaps contained the seeds of an English Balzac; but I have given that up in proportion as he has come down steadily from the simple in subject to the more simple—from the Anglo-Indians to the natives, from the natives to the Tommies, from the Tommies to the quadrupeds, from the quadrupeds to the fish, and from the fish to the engines and screws.

Henry James[1]

One of the reasons why Rudyard Kipling's reputation has always been so controversial is the difficulty of classifying him. Was his the voice of the arch-imperialist? Or the cool headed and pessimistic critic of imperialism? Or simply that of the hooligan?[2] Was he a natural short story writer, or a novelist manqué? Was he primarily a realist or a creator of fables? Was there, as James implies in his letter of 1897 quoted above, a progressive and alarming dehumanizing in his writing? Into such discussions, sometimes almost by accident, we find still more elusive "hints of yet another Kipling," as C. S. Lewis puts it:

There are moments of an almost quivering tenderness—he himself had been badly hurt—when he writes of children or for them. And there are the "queer" or "rum" stories—*At the End of the Passage, The Mark of the Beast, They, Wireless.* These may be his best work, but they are not his most characteristic.[3]

It is that last throwaway sentence that gives us pause: "his best work, but . . . not his most characteristic." Even Lewis, who was one of Kipling's most perceptive critics, has a clear preconception of his characteristics that, somehow, excludes his best work, which is simply if quaintly described as "queer" or "rum."

Another formidable critic, Bonamy Dobrée, sees much of Kipling's work in terms of *fables*—but has some difficulty in defining what, in Kipling's case, the word means.

> All stories worthy of the name are partly fables, in that they contain an idea—otherwise they are no more than anecdotes. The "point" of a story is its revelation of, or singling out of, some characteristic of human nature or behaviour; its moral is applicable to our daily doings. The "idea" of a fable goes beyond the local or immediate; its theme is universal. But it is impossible to draw a clear line between the two. In any event, the word "fable" is very vague, more so than "parable" or "allegory," in themselves constituting elements in a fable, which, according to common usage, is an impossible, or at least highly unlikely story, though improbability is not in itself a criterion.[4]

Kipling himself offers us a definition in a somewhat different key. It is clear enough, up to a point.

> When all the world would keep a matter hid,
> Since truth is seldom friend to any crowd,
> Men write in fable, as old Aesop did,
> Jesting at that which none will name aloud.
> And this they needs must do, or it will fall
> Unless they please they are not heard at all.
> (The Fabulists, 1917)

Fables are for the "inner ring" of those few who can understand. As Kipling tells us, *Puck of Pook's Hill* was intended to come into this category of stories with a secret meaning, but this, I suspect, has little to do with the qualities that Lewis valued in his children's books, nor does it entirely satisfy Dobrée's meaning of a *fable*. For almost all his readers, what is best about *Puck of Pook's Hill* or the other fables is not a hidden allegorical meaning—though that may contribute to it—but a sense of extra meaning in the events because they suggest a universe that is richer and fuller of possibilities than had hitherto been dreamed of. For those of us familiar with the tradition of Victorian fantasy that lay behind him, this difficulty of exact definition is a familiar one. Kipling is a natural fantasist, in the sense that he is always trying, in even his most realistic stories, to cram more into reality than it can possibly hold. The reasons that led him in middle life to turn increasingly away from the realism of his early Indian stories towards the worlds of Mowgli, Puck, and the *Just-So Stories*, were in essence the same as those which had made George MacDonald before him repudiate the charge of being an "allegorist" and insist that he was a writer of "fairy stories." The turning to fantasy was neither a degeneration "from the simple to the still more simple" as James had supposed, nor a psychic retreat from the complexities of the adult world, as others have suggested, but the logical next step in Kipling's development as a writer. The fact that they were "children's fantasies" was irrelevant. Of *Rewards and Fairies*, he commented, "the tales had to be read by children, before people realized that they were meant for grown ups."[5] From the first, Kipling was a man haunted by other worlds, and as his art developed he became progressively more skillful in suggesting the intersection of different plains of reality.

At its simplest we can see this in his fascination with the world of work. The mysteries of a man's profession make one kind of inner ring of knowledge about people, and what they are. In his autobiographical sketch, *Something of Myself*, he describes how at the age of seventeen he became a member of the Punjab Club at Lahore.

> And in that Club and elsewhere I met none except picked men at their definite work—Civilians, Army, Education, Canals, Forestry, Engineering, Irrigation, Railways, Doctors, and Lawyers—samples of each branch and each talking his own shop. It follows then that that "show of technical knowledge" for which I was blamed later came to me from the horse's mouth, even to boredom.[6]

Other more esoteric worlds were opened for him by the Freemasons, which he was able to join under age "because the Lodge hoped for a good secretary." "Here I met Muslims, Hindus, Sikhs, members of the Arya and Brahmo Samaj, and a Jew tyler, who was priest and butcher to his little community in the city. So yet another world opened to me which I needed."[7] Lewis, like other critics since, has observed how "Kipling is first and foremost the poet of work," showing in detail men in their professional skills almost for the first time in fiction. But even he does not see how this delight of Kipling's with the closed worlds of particular professions is only a part of a still wider fascination with the possibilities of yet other closed worlds lost to us through time, or the limitations of sense and mortality. For Lewis it is only an extension of the thrills of the secret society:

In the last resort I do not think he loves professional brotherhood for the sake of the work; I think he loves work for the sake of professional brotherhood. [. . .] To belong, to be inside, to be in the know, to be snugly together against the outsiders—that is what really matters.[8]

But Kipling wants to be in the know about things at a much more profound level than either the professionals of the Punjab Club or the Freemasons could offer. He wants to be in the know about the universe.

In *The Bridge Builders*, one of the best of his early fantasies, the dazzling display of intricate technical knowledge of bridge construction is set within a story of Hindu gods that is only incidentally a fable. The bridge in question is an enormous railway bridge across the Ganges.

With its approaches, his work was one mile and three-quarters in length; a lattice-girder bridge, trussed with the Findlayson truss, standing on seven-and-twenty brick piers. Each of those piers was twenty- four feet in diameter, capped with red Agra stone and sunk eighty feet below the shifting sand of the Ganges' bed. Above them ran the railway-line fifteen feet broad; above that, again, a cart road of eighteen feet, flanked with footpaths. At either end rose towers of red brick, loopholed for musketry and pierced for big guns, and the ramp of the road was being pushed forward to their haunches. The raw earth-ends were crawling and alive with hundreds upon hundreds of tiny asses climbing out of the yawning borrow-pit below with sackfuls of stuff; and the hot afternoon air was filled with the noise of hooves, the rattle of the driver's sticks, and the swish and roll down of the dirt. The river was very low, and on the dazzling white sand between the three centre piers stood squat cribs of railway-sleepers, filled within and daubed without with mud, to support the last of the girders as these were riveted up. In the little deep water left by the drought, an overhead-crane travelled to and fro along its spile-pier, jerking sections of iron into place, snorting and backing and grunting as an elephant grunts in the timber-yard. Riveters by the hundred swarmed about the lattice side-work and the iron roof of the railway-line, hung from invisible staging under the bellies of the girders, clustered round the throats of the piers, and rode on the overhang of the footpath-stanchions; their firepots and the spurts of flame that answered each hammer stroke showing no more than pale yellow in the sun's glare. East and west and north and south the construction-trains rattled and shrieked up and down the embankments, the piled trucks of brown and white stone banging behind them till the side-boards were unpinned, and with a roar and a grumble a few thousand tons more material were thrown out to hold the river in place.[9]

In charge of the works are two British engineers, Findlayson and his assistant Hitchcock, and their lascar foreman, Peroo. The first part of the story is entirely taken up with the excitement of watching the bridge grow: the skill and patience required of the engineers, and their hopes and frustrations: "the months of office work destroyed at a blow when the Government of India, at the last moment, added two feet to the width of the bridge, under the impression that bridges were cut out of paper, and so brought ruin to at least half an acre of calculations—and Hitchcock, new to disappointment, buried his head in his arms and wept." As the bridge nears completion, there is a sudden flood, and the exhausted Findlayson, partly under the influence of opium pep-pills taken to keep himself going, is swept away down river in a small boat with Peroo. Uncertain whether the bridge is holding in the floodwaters, or already collapsing, they are washed up on a tiny island in the river. On it is a tiny Hindu shrine surrounded by animals which have also apparently fled there to escape the rising waters. The animals however can speak. They are witnessing a council of the gods: Kali, Shiv, Hanuman, Ganesh, Krishna, and the rest. The river, in the form of a crocodile, complains bitterly of the bridge by which men have tried to bind her, and still more bitterly of her failure to destroy it with the flood. There follows a debate among the gods on the bridge's significance. At first the implication seems to be that it is of no importance at all in the vast time scale of India. People are only *dirt* after all. "It is but the shifting of a little dirt. Let the dirt dig in the dirt if it pleases the dirt," says Ganesh, the elephant. But, it is then hinted, even the gods themselves are fated to fade and decay before this immense time span. The bridge is meaningless in itself—yet it is also a portent of changes that are more than meaningless cycles of events.

There is much in the story that smacks of fable, yet an account of it purely in those terms is inadequate. It seems to have not one, but many morals, according to the point of view. Is the white man's engineering no more than scratching the surface of the dirt, or does it portend the beginning of enormous changes that will affect the whole subcontinent, including, eventually, the worship of the old gods themselves? Are men before the gods no more than "flies, to wanton boys," or are they, in spite of appearances, masters of their fate? The story looks at the act of bridge-building at a number of simultaneous levels: at what it means in terms of the sheer technology (the "Findlayson truss" is a new invention); what it means for the men who have given years of their lives on the project; what it means for India, materially and spiritually; and, finally, at what is the ultimate meaning of such a vast undertaking? The worlds can be seen separately, yet

they interconnect. In order to be realistic in the widest sense Kipling has, as
it were, been forced into fantasy for a technique that will encompass his
theme.

Yet it would be a mistake to regard Kipling's growing use of fantasy
merely as an extension of the techniques of the short story. What links him
with the other writers we have been looking at is his fascination with the
way in which fantasy allows him to write of the fringe areas of human consciousness inaccessible to realism. In *The Brushwood Boy*, for instance, we
have what could be taken as a fable about the nature of fantasy itself as an
artistic medium. The hero, George Cottar, is a man of almost mechanical
perfection. His name even suggests the "cotter pin" in a machine: the pin
or wedge which fits into a hole to fasten an object in place. As the son of a
wealthy landowner, the head boy of his public school, at Sandhurst, and as
an officer in India he is a model of all that is expected of him. Yet beneath
the totally conventional and correct exterior he is possessed by dreams of a
strange country beyond a pile of brushwood on a mysterious seashore. The
total exclusion of fantasy from his waking life is matched by the peculiar
vividness and richness of his dream-world. Eventually, and by accident, he
meets in "real life" the girl who is, literally, "the girl of his dreams." As a
story it is not wholly successful: though the dream-world is vivid and con-
vincing, the waking reality is much less so. George is just too perfect. As a
symbol of the fantasy writer, however, whose dreams offer another parallel
inner world which he both wants and fears to share, the story has a power
which overrides the weakness of characterization. More successful is *The
Finest Story in the World* (1893) about a young bank clerk with literary
aspirations. What he wants to write is "high art"—which, unfortunately in
his case, means bad pastiches of popular poets. He has little or no originality or real literary talent. Yet there is another side to Charlie Mears. He tells
the author (who, it is implied, is Kipling himself) of a story he wants to
write about a galley slave. As he describes his "story" it is clear that he is not
inventing so much as remembering what he has once seen.

> The long oars on the upper deck are managed by four men to each bench,
> the lower ones by three, and the lowest of all by two. Remember it's quite
> dark on the lowest deck and all the men there go mad. When a man dies
> at his oar on that deck he isn't thrown overboard, but cut up in his chains
> and stuffed through the oar-hole in little pieces.
>
> "Why?" I demanded amazed, not to much at the information as the
> tone of command in which it was flung out.
>
> "To save trouble and to frighten the others. It needs two overseers to
> drag a man's body up to the top deck; and if the men at the lower deck

oars were left alone, of course they'd stop rowing and try to pull up the benches by all standing up together in their chains."[10]

Charlie is, it seems, able to recall fleetingly and fragmentedly episodes from previous existences with a wealth of detail unknown even to scholars of the period. The raw material of what would be the "finest story in the world" is dangled temptingly before the author—if only he can draw it out from Charlie without leading him to suspect that he is recalling previous incarnations. "The Lords of Life and Death would never allow Charlie Mears to speak with full knowledge of his pasts," as an Indian friend, Grish Chunder, explains when the author consults him. His prophesies come tragically true, as Charlie Mears falls in love and his "memories" are erased for ever.

> I understood why the Lords of Life and Death shut the doors so carefully behind us. It is that we may not remember our first and most beautiful wooings.[11]

At its simplest, *The Finest Story in the World* is an excellent short story—but it also introduces us to another much more odd and disturbing characteristic of Kipling's fantasy: its habit of coming true. The recently published "Bloxham Tapes" are the accounts of what purport to be previous existences of various people who, under hypnosis, can recall vivid details of the past of which their conscious minds knew nothing.[12] One man has recalled a naval battle from the Napoleonic Wars including circumstantial details unknown to naval historians in a weird parallel to Charlie Mears's story. Nor is this an isolated example. It is difficult to know how to phrase it without implying an explanation, but the fact remains that Kipling frequently appears to be in possession of information that he has no business to have. In *Puck of Pook's Hill*, for instance, he brings in a well in the wall of Pevensey Castle that was not in fact discovered until the year 1935. Other examples are even more dramatic.

> I quartered the Seventh Cohort of the Thirtieth (Ulpia Victrix) Legion on the Wall, and asserted that there Roman troops used arrows against the Picts. [. . .] Years after the tale was told, a digging party on the Wall sent me some heavy four-sided, Roman-made, "killing" arrows found *in situ* and—most marvellously—a rubbing of a memorial tablet to the Seventh Cohort of the Thirtieth Legion![13]

Such uncanny prescience makes one wonder if other stories of an apparently fanciful or speculative nature may not turn out similarly to be based on "inside knowledge." In *Proofs of Holy Writ* certain passages of the King James Bible of 1611 are attributed to Shakespeare. "Unprofessional" is a story about a doctor who cures a dying woman by the discovery that there are tidal actions in the body related to astrological influences. A critic of the 1960s objected that "There is surely something inartistic in the triumph within the fable of a therapy we know to have no existence outside it."[14] Recent research has suggested that the planets do indeed have a measurable effect on living tissue, and modern medical opinion would be much more cautious about dismissing Kipling's idea.[15]

Other stories, including some of Kipling's best fantasies such as *Wireless*, *They*, and *The Wish House*, show a similar psychic streak, although they do not depend on ideas or facts not generally known. Yet it would be wrong to assume that Kipling believed in the occult. Through his sister, Trix, who was a medium of sorts and practiced such phenomena as automatic writing, producing "messages" from the dead, he knew a good deal about spiritualism, and resolutely set his face against it, even after the death of his only son during the First World War. His best comment on it is in his poem "Endor":

> The road to En-dor is easy to tread
> For Mother or yearning Wife.
> There, it is sure, we shall meet our Dead
> As they were even in life.
> Earth has not dreamed of the blessing in store
> For desolate hearts on the road to En-dor.
>
> Whispers shall comfort us out of the dark—
> Hands—ah God!—that we knew!
> Visions and voices—look and hark!—
> Shall prove that the tale is true,
> And that those who have passed to the farther shore
> May be hailed—at a price—on the road to En-dor . . .
>
> Oh the road to En-dor is the oldest road
> And the craziest road of all!
> Straight it runs to the Witch's abode,
> As it did in the days of Saul,
> And nothing has changed of the sorrow in store
> For such as go down the road to En-dor![16]

In *Something of Myself* he observes that "there is a kind of mind that dives after what it calls 'psychical experiences.' And I am in no way 'psychic' [. . .] I have seen too much evil and sorrow and wreck of good minds on the road to Endor to take one step along that perilous road."[17] Though at least once in his life he seems to have had a clairvoyant experience, he suspected and feared the obsessional triviality of spiritualism as a system, and saw clearly enough how the misery of many of the people who resorted to mediums made them blind to the manipulation and fraud that so often goes along with psychical experience. But the interest in psychic phenomena was genuine, and clearly to some degree personal, providing much of the raw material of the other worlds on which his fantasy depends.

We have already seen in *The Finest Story in the World* how Charlie Mears's mind contained layer upon layer of previous memories. Such an idea, used in a quite different way, was to form the basis of one of his most sustained and complex works: the *Puck* books. Here the "mind" in question is not that of the individual children, Dan and Una, but of the English as a whole—made to come alive in the stories of the people of Sussex where Kipling had come to live. "England," he wrote in delight from his house at Burwash, "is a wonderful land. It is the most marvellous of all foreign countries I have ever been in."[18] To be English (and here he means "English" rather than "British") means to have assimilated and grown up with the experiences of Parnesius, Sir Richard Dalyngridge, De Aquila and Hugh the Saxon, Hal Dane, and the rest. They have become part of a collective unconscious, part racial, part cultural. The familiar hills and woods of the Weald are simultaneously parts of Merlin's Isle of Gramarye, where every name and landmark is charged with historical meaning. Puck's song sets the theme:

> See you the dimpled track that runs,
> All hollow through the wheat?
> O that was where they hauled the guns
> That smote King Philip's fleet.
>
> See you our little mill that clacks,
> So busy by the brook?
> She has ground her corn and paid her tax
> Ever since Doomsday Book.
>
> See you our stilly woods of oak,
> And the dread ditch beside?

> O that was where the Saxons broke,
> On the day that Harold died [. . .]
>
> She is not any common Earth,
> Water or wood or air,
> But Merlin's Isle of Gramarye,
> Where you and I will fare.

Kipling wrote here of what he knew. In digging a well on his land his work-men found "a Jacobean tobacco pipe, a worn Cromwellian latten spoon and, at the bottom of all, the bronze cheek of a Roman horse-bit."

> In cleaning out an old pond which might have been an ancient marl-pit or mine-head, we dredged two intact Elizabethan "sealed quarts" that Christopher Sly affected, all pearly with the patina of centuries. Its deep-est mud yielded us a perfectly polished Neolithic axe head with but one chip on its still venomous edge.[19]

With the *Puck* stories, Kipling could truly be said, as he claimed, to be play-ing his cards as he had been dealt them. The stories wrote themselves.

But if these objects and their stories are part of what it means to be English, it does not follow that one must be conscious of that heritage. Stories in which children are taught their history by magic trips into the past are not a new idea: *The Story of the Amulet* was published the same year as *Puck of Pook's Hill*, but the two stories are entirely different in technique. In *Puck of Pook's Hill* the children *stay* in their own time, and the people they meet come to them, under Puck's aegis, from out of their own. In a rather poignant story from *Rewards and Fairies*, the girl from the eighteenth century who tells her tale to the children is clearly (to an adult reader) dying of T.B., but she is unaware of the fact—in other words, she is *still* living in her own time, and has been conjured from it, not from any place after death. The magic of the story, made by the children acting scenes from *A Midsummer Night's Dream* three times on Midsummer Eve in the middle of a fairy ring under Pook's hill, brings all history to a time-less point—the present. Even more interesting, by Puck's magic of "oak, and ash, and thorn" the children are made to forget each story almost as soon as they have heard it. There are no doubt deliberate echoes here of *The Finest Story in the World,* where the "Lords of Life and Death" shut the doors so carefully on our memories of other ages that we shall not go mad, but there is no suggestion here that the children's knowledge is dangerous; simply that one does not need to be conscious of what one knows in order to know it. Puck is in himself a kind of collective unconscious. His stories do not need to be recalled, but recognized when they are met with—just as the children recognize and remember Puck, Parnesius, or Sir Richard when they meet them in the woods. Dan and Una are England's future, and they inherit the past as they grow up within the common culture. Though they originated in Kipling's own children—who, incidentally, did act a version of *A Midsummer Night's Dream* at that very spot near Batemans in Burwash—Dan and Una are also very obvious symbolic children. Their very names suggest the masculine and feminine virtues of courage and unity England needs.

7.1 H. R. Millar: "Puck." Illustration to Rudyard Kipling's Puck of Pook's Hill.

The second story of the group, *Young Men at the Manor*, shows how the two are connected. There is no suggestion that the Norman Sir Richard's vow never to enter the Hall of his newly won Manor until he is invited by the bitter and resentful Saxon Lady Aelueva is anything but exceptional and extraordinary. De Aquila's attitude to Richard is like that

of Maximus to Parnesius: impressed by his sense of honor, but contemptu-
ous of someone so politically naïve that he cannot see his own advantage:

> "You'll never be an Emperor," he said. "Not even a General will
> you be."
> I was silent, but my father seemed pleased.
> "I came here to see the last of you," he said.
> "You have seen it," said Maximus. "I shall never need your son any
> more. He will live and he will die an officer of a Legion—and he might
> have been Prefect of one of my Provinces."[20]

Maximus, like De Aquila, is apparently taken at his own valuation, and it is
only slowly in the course of the stories that we discover how utterly wrong
they both were about their young subordinates. Maximus has to depend on
Parnesius's loyalty to hold the Wall under conditions that a more politically
minded officer would have refused or evaded. Richard gains the friendship
of Hugh, the loyalty of the Saxons—who would otherwise have murdered
them all (including probably De Aquila)—and finally marries Aeluva. The
moral courage to resist short-term expediency eventually brings much bigger rewards. Such courage is not typical, but it is of exceptional deeds that
history is composed. "In God's good time," says De Aquila, "which because
of my sins I shall not live to see, there will be neither Saxon nor Norman in
England."[21] In *Rewards and Fairies* this theme is extended in stories like
Brother Square Toes to include the Americans, whom Kipling sees as sharing a common history and destiny. It is left to Puck to point the final
moral: "Weyland gave the Sword! The Sword gave the Treasure, and the
Treasure gave the Law. It's as natural as an oak growing."[22] We are almost
convinced, and yet . . . Puck's confident political wisdom seems to echo the
voices of Maximus and De Aquila, not of Parnesius and Richard. Not for
the first time we are aware of two voices in Kipling that seem to be saying
very different things.

Perhaps because of their moral complexity, the *Puck* stories held a special place in Kipling's affections. In *Something of Myself* he tells us more
about their creation than he does about any of the rest of his work:

> [S]ince the tales had to be read by children, before people realized that
> they were meant for grown ups; and since they had to be a sort of balance
> to, as well as seal upon, some aspects of my "Imperialistic" output in the
> past, I worked the material in three or four overlaid tints and textures,
> which might or might not reveal themselves according to the shifting
> light of sex, youth, and experience. [. . .] So I loaded the book up with

allegories and allusions, and verified references [. . .] put in three of four really good sets of verses; the bones of one entire historical novel for any to clothe who cared; and even slipped in a cryptogram, whose key I regret I must have utterly forgotten.[23]

The combination of particular events, like the finding of the Roman horse-bit or the neolithic axe, and the allegorical framework of the whole gives us a clear lead as to the way Kipling constructs his fantasy. Alternative worlds are built upon each other like the layers of a cake: the worlds of child and adult, fairy and familiar each enrich and provide comment on the others.

Though the style is unique to Kipling, it is not difficult to see how this method of construction has been evolved from his earlier Victorian fore-runners. He was brought up in a world of myth, poetry, and fantasy. Staying with his cousins, the Burne Jones, during his brief holidays from the dreadful "house of Desolation" where his parents had left him in Southsea when they went back to India, the young Kipling was exposed to a world in which the exotic was normal. In addition to his uncle, Sir Edward Burne-Jones the painter, who would play elaborate games of make-believe with the children, there was "the beloved Aunt herself reading us *The Pirate* or *The Arabian Nights* of evenings, when one lay out on the big sofa sucking toffee, and calling our cousins 'Ho Son,' or 'Daughter of my Uncle' or 'O True Believer.' "[24] Among the visitors to the house were "an elderly person called 'Browning' who took no proper interest in the skir-mishes which happened to be raging on his entry,"[25] and William Morris, who did. On one occasion he recalled Morris, or "Uncle Topsy" as he was known, sitting on the rocking horse in the nursery "slowly surging back and forth while the poor beast creaked" telling "a tale full of fascinating horrors, about a man who was condemned to bad dreams."[26] Much later he was to recognize this story in *The Saga of Burnt Njal.* The child Kipling's own secret reading of adventure and poetry at Southsea, and later at the United Services College at Westward Ho!, where he was allowed the run of the Head's private library, reinforced this delight in mystery and romance.

His fantasy is the culmination of one strand in the Victorian sensibil-ity. The problems of an extended plot always inherent in the Gothic tradi-tion are solved by the medium of the short story—where Kipling's greatest skills lay. His one full-length novel, *The Light that Failed,* was itself a fail-ure. The brilliant and haunting images that give the fantasies of Dickens, Kingsley, MacDonald, or Morris their power are made even more striking by the concentration and compression of Kipling's plots, which work pre-cisely through such images. One revealing use of reference illustrates the point. In *At the Back of the North Wind* MacDonald tells us of two people who had returned before little Diamond to give accounts of what it was like "at the back of the North Wind." One was Dante; the other was Kilmeny, the peasant girl from the Thirteenth Bard's Song in James Hogg's *The Queen's Wake* (1813). According to the legend she went up the glen to listen to the birds and pick berries, and when she did not come back, she was given up for dead. Eventually she returned with the story that she had been carried away to the land of spirits, of glory and light, from where she had had a vision of the world below, with its war and sin. She had asked to be allowed to return and tell her friends, and she came both transformed and sanctified. After a month she returned from whence she had come, and was never seen again. MacDonald quotes some fourteen lines of Hogg, which clearly for him sum up the essence of visionary fantasy:

> Kilmeny had been she knew not where,
> And Kilmeny had seen what she could not declare;
> Kilmeny had been where the cock never crew,
> Where the rain never fell, and the wind never blew;
> But it seemed as the harp of the sky had rung,
> And the airs of heaven played round her tongue,
> When she spoke of the lovely forms she had seen,
> And a land where sin had never been;
> A land of love and a land of light,
> Withouten sun, or moon, or night;
> Where the river swayed a living stream,
> And the light a pure and cloudless beam:
> The land of vision it would seem,
> And still an everlasting dream.[27]

The parallels with Novalis and his emphasis on the greater reality of the "dream world" are striking enough to account for MacDonald's interest in Hogg's poem. Kipling's use of this, however, is even more interesting. As Dan and Una return after their first meeting with Puck their father asks them how their play had gone, and it turns out that neither can remember what had happened afterwards. Apparently amused, father echoes MacDonald's quotation:

> Late—late in the evening Kilmeny came home,
> For Kilmeny had been she could not tell where,
> And Kilmeny had seen what she could not declare.[28]

It is not until we remember that the children's father is, of course, Kipling himself that we begin to realize with what economy he has packed the brief reference. By the magic of "oak, and ash, and thorn" the children cannot declare where they have been or what they have seen in their timeless vision of history. Kipling, however, the creator, can do, and has done so—in the process establishing Puck's link with the visionary worlds of Hogg and MacDonald. For those privileged to see, the magic world is all around us, in every mark in the corn or name of a hill. The initiation of Dan and Una, so far from being a unique event is part of a tradition of visionary experiences—and it is essentially a *literary* tradition. What Dante, Hogg, MacDonald, and Kipling are all doing is describing publicly, to you, the reader, secret and private experiences in such a way that you can continue to feel their privacy. It is a paradox at the heart of literature.

But not all the influences on Kipling's fantasy were from the past. Among the most immediate stimuli for the *Puck* stories had been Edith Nesbit's *The Phoenix and the Carpet*, published in 1904. As was her habit with authors she admired, Nesbit had sent Kipling a copy on publication and it had been received with delight by the children at Bateman's.[29] His influence is no less marked on her. As early as *The Wouldbegoods* in 1901 she had made the Bastable children act out stories from *The Jungle Books* and even try to talk in the language of Kipling's characters. The parallels and contrasts between the two writers show us the final flowering of the Victorian tradition of fantasy—even though the best work of both falls strictly into the Edwardian period. In spite of the fact that she was seven years older than Kipling, Nesbit had shown none of his precocious development, and she did not begin to write any of the books she is now remembered by until the early years of the twentieth century, when she was over forty. Like Kipling, she was a natural fantasy writer, and her late start was due as much as anything to her difficulty in discovering her true bent in face of the overwhelmingly realistic conventions of the Victorian novel. Her now forgotten novels for adults failed partly because of their tendency towards the fantastic.

Like Kipling, Nesbit had had a disturbed and somewhat insecure childhood. Her mother was widowed when she was four, and thereafter they moved frequently, and seemingly at random. She was sent to a variety of more or less unsatisfactory schools in England and France. Her career as a professional writer was more or less forced upon her by circumstances. A hurried marriage at the age of twenty-one when she was seven months pregnant had left her as the breadwinner for a family when, within a few months, her husband, Hubert Bland, contracted smallpox. While he was ill his partner in business made off with the funds.[30] This shaky start to the marriage set the pattern that was to continue. In contrast with the order and stability of the Kipling household under the beneficent dictatorship of Mrs. Kipling (who held the purse strings and even gave Rudyard his "pocket money"), the Nesbit/Bland household, even in its later years of prosperity, was disorganized, unstable, and bohemian. Hubert Bland's two great hobbies were socialism and womanizing. To H. G. Wells, whose tastes were much too similar for friendship, he boasted that he was "a student, and experimentalist . . . in illicit love."[31] Like many compulsive seducers, he combined promiscuity with a strong sense of the conventions he defied. He was a staunch, if not strict Roman Catholic, and relations within the Fabian society were severely strained when he found Wells making advances to his daughter Rosamund while she was still a teenager. All Bernard Shaw's acid but calculated tact was needed to heal the breach.[32] The quarrel was the more ironic since Rosamund was not Nesbit's child at all, but one of Bland's by Alice Hoatson, her companion-cum-housekeeper—and Bland's mistress. It says much for Edith Nesbit's character that she adopted both the illegitimate children of this union, and brought them up with her own. It was many years before they found out the truth. Commenting on this often strained *ménage à-trois*, Wells observed "all this E. Nesbit not only detested and mitigated and tolerated, but presided over and I think found exceedingly interesting." Moore agrees, but adds that "It had taken her many years to reach that comparative detachment."[33] In the meantime, Nesbit herself indulged in a number of love affairs, perhaps partly compensatory, with (among others) Shaw, Richard le Galienne, and even Dr. Wallis Budge of the Egyptian section of the British Museum. Yet the marriage endured, and in a strange way Nesbit and Bland were deeply dependent on each other. When he died in 1914, she was heartbroken.

If the nonsense fantasies of the mid-Victorians, Lear and Carroll, had been the product of inhibition, it would scarcely be possible to argue the same of Nesbit, who made a point of matching the unconventional state of her private life with equally unconventional public behavior. Noel Coward described her as "the most genuine Bohemian I ever met."[34] She dressed in long, loose-fitting, flowing dresses, very far removed from the elaborate tightly corseted costumes of late-Victorian and Edwardian fashions, and smoked heavily, even in public—a habit which almost certainly contributed to her death of lung and heart disease in 1924. Moreover, she had begun her scandalous ways early—long before she met Bland. When she was removed from a French convent school at the age of eleven, she left behind her, for the nuns to discover, two empty wine bottles of which she had pre-

sumably drunk the contents, and in middle age she persuaded officials at
the Paris Opera to open all the windows (an unheard of thing) by pretend-
ing to faint and gasping for air at various strategic points in the building. As
she herself seems to have recognized by her frequent references to him, if
she had an affinity with any of the earlier fantasy writers it would be with
Kingsley. To some child fans she wrote:

> I am very pleased to have your letters, and to know that you like my
> books. You are quite right to like Kingsley and Dickens and George
> MacDonald better than you like me.[35]

The modesty was not assumed. Nesbit always thought of herself primarily
as a poet, even after the great financial success of her children's books.
While her serious poetry is scarcely remembered, it is the poetic sensibility
in her prose that links her with Kipling, and makes her, with him, one of
the great fantasists.

It is this quality too that marks off so unmistakably the great writers
like Nesbit and Kipling from other late-Victorian fantasists, such as F.
Anstey,[36] probably best known today as the author of *Vice Versa* (1882).
Anstey's novel *The Brass Bottle* was published in 1900, and several critics
have noted the similarities between it and *The Phoenix and the Carpet*.
The brass bottle of the title contains an Arabian Jinn which had been
imprisoned there thousands of years before by Solomon for various mis-
deeds. His effusive gratitude to his rescuer in modern London is, of course,
a menace, and provides the setting for a series of comic magical disasters.
As do so many of the nineteenth-century fantasies, the story draws heavily
and in some detail on *The Arabian Nights*. Nevertheless, clever as much of
it is, it remains at the level of situation-comedy, lacking the sharpness or
depth of character to be found in either Nesbit or Kipling, or any of the
wider social and philosophical concerns. As in most light comedy, Anstey's
world is a thinner simpler place than the one we all know.

The sense of an extra poetic richness and depth in the worlds of both
Nesbit and Kipling was helped by a common illustrator of remarkable talent, H. R. Millar. He worked closely with both authors, and with Nesbit in
particular he became adept at translating her slightest hints into substantial
visual images—sometimes a matter of necessity when she was so late with
her copy that he had to work from scrawled chapter précis rather than the
finished text. Nevertheless his results so delighted her that she used to
insist there was telepathy between them. His picture of the Psammead, was,

she declared, "exactly like the creature she had in her own imagination."[37] Certainly it was Millar who gave form to so many of her most dramatic images. We have already seen what he did with her prehistoric monsters, the Great Sloth and the Dinosaurus. He captures no less successfully the tabletop architecture of the Magic City, at once grandiose and exotic in design, yet familiar and domestic in detail and materials. As with all the great illustrators of fantasy, Cruikshank, Doyle, Lear, or Tenniel, it is the meticulous attention to details where every article tells a story that brings the pictures to life. Behind that ability to add "something more" to a scene than we might perceive in real life lay a visual tradition stretching back to Hogarth, and beyond. Millar was to Nesbit's fantasy what Tenniel was to Carroll's.[38]

As both Nesbit and Kipling developed as writers it is clear that it is this "poetic" element, the desire always for something *more*, that made the confines of conventional realism increasingly unsatisfactory. Dobrée writes of how Kipling's "broodings on life," his family disasters, and his own ill-health led him more and more toward "adding a fourth dimension to the pictures he presented of human beings, their actions and reactions."[39] Nesbit's work in the early 1900s shows a remarkably similar tendency. The world of *The Wouldbegoods* and *The Treasure Seekers* gives way to that of the Phoenix and the Psammead and the Three Mouldiwarps, and the more complex supernatural of *The Magic City* and *The Enchanted Castle*. Like Kipling, Nesbit came to need a larger stage for her realism than reality permitted. Just as Dan and Una, growing up in a Sussex village, could only come to understand the complex tapestry of their cultural inheritance through the "magic" of Puck, so Nesbit's children needed magic to see their suburban London society in perspective.

The Story of the Amulet, for instance, is built around a series of visits to the remote past, or, in one dramatic case, the future. But given the superficial framework, the resemblance to *Puck of Pook's Hill* is slight. As has been pointed out, Kipling's children themselves stay in the present. As a result their view of history is personal: it is essentially a series of deeds, great or small, performed by unsung heroes. There is cumulative progress, but it is made up of the actions of brave individuals who played their cards as they had been dealt them. "What else could I have done?" is the refrain of *Rewards and Fairies*. Nesbit, the socialist, is less concerned with individuals than with societies. She wants to show not the similarities with our own time, but the enormous differences between the outlook of other ages and our own. C. S. Lewis records how, as a child, *The Story of the Amulet* was his favorite Nesbit novel for this reason. "It first opened my eyes to antiquity, the dark backward and abysm of time."[40] But the resulting picture, as it is slowly built up, incident by incident, is a devastating critique of her own society. We have already had hints of this from the Phoenix, but his open disapproval of the drab dreariness of Edwardian London might well be dismissed as the natural nostalgia of a creature more accustomed to an Egyptian temple of its own than the modern, Fire Assurance Office. But *The Story of the Amulet*'s message is more insistent. The children find a dirty little girl crying in St. James's Park. Her parents are dead, and she is about to be taken into the Workhouse. With an ironic echo of Shakespeare's *Cymbeline*—shortly to be explained—she is called Imogen. The children take her to see their lodger, the "learned gentleman" from the British Museum,[41] who wishes sadly that they "could find a home where they would be glad to have her"—and the Psammead, being present, is at once forced to grant his request. They find themselves in ancient Britain. The children are amazed. "But why *here*?" says Anthea in astonishment, "Why *now*?"

> "You don't suppose anyone would want a child like that in *your* times—in *your* towns?" said the Psammead in irritated tones. "You've got your country into such a mess that there's no room for half your children—and no one to want them."[42]

Then the little girl meets a woman who resembles her mother, and who has lost a child just like her—and there is a joyful reunion. As in Kipling, there are hints here either of reincarnation, or of the recurrence of certain types in every generation—but the Psammead refuses to be drawn. "Who knows? but each one fills the empty place in the other's heart. It is enough."[43]

Twentieth-century progress is such that it no longer has a place in anyone's heart for the unwanted child. But this is in turn symptomatic of a much wider inhumanity. By means of another unguarded wish in the Psammead's presence, the Queen of Babylon is enabled to visit London. The children proudly show her the sights.

> And now from the window of a four-wheeled cab the Queen of Babylon beheld the wonders of London. Buckingham Palace she thought uninteresting; Westminster Abbey and the Houses of Parliament little better. But she liked the Tower, and the River, and the ships filled her with wonder and delight.
>
> "But how badly you keep your slaves. How wretched and poor and neglected they seem," she said, as the cab rattled along the Mile End Road.

"They aren't slaves; they're working people," said Jane.

"Of course they're working. That's what slaves are. Don't you tell me. Do you suppose I don't know a slave's face when I see it? Why don't their masters see they're better fed and better clothed? Tell me in three words."

No one answered. The wage system of modern England is a little difficult to explain in three words even if you understand it—which the children didn't.

"You'll have a revolt of your slaves if you're not careful," said the Queen.

"Oh, no," said Cyril; "you see they have votes—that makes them safe not to revolt. It makes all the difference. Father told me so."

"What is this vote?" asked the Queen. "Is it a charm? What do they do with it?"

"I don't know," said the harassed Cyril. "it's just a vote, that's all! They don't do anything particular with it."

"I see," said the Queen; "a sort of plaything."[44]

In a society brought up on the Bible, Babylon has always had a bad press. To compare twentieth-century London, with all its tourist attractions, unfavorably with Babylon, not merely in terms of architecture, but even in morals and general humanity, was a final calculated insult. The condemnation of the present is rounded off by a visit to the future. The first thing they notice in comparison with the "sorry-present" is the cleanliness and lack of pollution.

> As they came through the doors of the (British) Museum they blinked at the sudden glory of sunlight and blue sky. The houses opposite the Museum were gone. Instead there was a big garden, with trees and flowers and smooth green lawns, and not a single notice to tell you not to walk on the grass and not to destroy the trees and shrubs and not to pick the flowers. There were comfortable seats all about, and arbours covered with roses, and long trellised walks, also rose-covered.[45]

In view of the 1970s' fight by conservationists to preserve the buildings opposite the British Museum, the passage has an unintentionally ironic ring today. The general picture of a clean London with gardens and flowers everywhere inhabited by people with long flowing clothes and happy faces is an amalgam of the vague Fabian daydreams of the time about the coming socialist paradise. Though there are sharper typical Nesbit touches, such as men being in charge of babies, and playing with them, the overall picture is similar to the sort of optimistic view of the future being painted by H. G. Wells. The similarity is deliberate: the children meet a small boy named

Wells, after the "great reformer." The real parallel, however, is with Imogen. This boy too is crying in the park, but, it turns out, this is because he has been punished for the dreadful crime of dropping litter by being expelled from school for the day–"for a whole day!" Having explained the joys of his project-centered curriculum to the children, he takes them home. His house has no need of ornaments because every single thing in it is beautiful. For safety, it is centrally heated, and the furniture in the nursery is padded to prevent children hurting themselves. To show their gratitude for the hospitality they have received, the children offer to take his mother with them through the amulet to see their London.

> The lady went, laughing. But she did not laugh when she found herself, suddenly, in the dining room at Fitzroy Street.
> "Oh, what a *horrible* trick!" she cried. "What a hateful, dark, ugly place!"
> She ran to the window and looked out. The sky was grey, the street was foggy, a dismal organ grinder was standing opposite the door, a beggar and a man who sold matches were quarrelling at the edge of the pavement on whose greasy black surface people hurried along, hastening to get to the shelter of their houses.
> "Oh, look at their faces, their horrible faces!" she cried. "What's the matter with them all?"
> "They're poor people, that's all," said Robert.
> "But it's *not* all! They're ill, they're unhappy, they're wicked."[46]

The parallel with the Queen of Babylon is complete.

Nesbit's hatred of the sorry-present is taken to its logical conclusion in one of her last books, *Harding's Luck* (1909). Dickie Harding, a little lame orphan boy from the slums of Deptford, acquires by magic another "self" as his own ancestor, Richard Arden, in James I's reign. No longer a cripple, in this other life he lives in a great house with servants and friends among the green fields and orchards of Deptford. As always, Nesbit is not above loading the dice: just as it was sunny in the future and wet in the present (not *all* fog and rain is due to pollution!), so it helps to be rich and an aristocrat if you are to live happily in the early seventeenth century. Nevertheless, the comparison is a serious one. The "welfare state" of the great Jacobean house, where everyone has his place but all are looked after, is contrasted with the misery of laissez-faire Edwardian England with its ugliness and unemployment and neglect of its children. The men of the twentieth century seem to be all manipulators of people or money: con-men or pawnbrokers; the men of the seventeenth century (who closely resemble some of the twentieth-century characters in looks) are craftsmen of skill and integrity.

The possibilities of time travel are exploited for their own dramatic value, however, and not merely for social comment. One of the most effective scenes is where Dickie's cousins, Edred and Elfrida, who are the central characters in an earlier Nesbit story, *The House of Arden*, nearly get the whole family executed for High Treason by singing "Please to remember the Fifth of November/Gunpowder treason and plot . . ." *before* the Gunpowder Plot has happened. But even here the opportunities for social comment are not altogether wasted. Dickie's nurse, who mysteriously seems to understand about time travel, warns him to be very careful what he says, or she will be "burned as a witch." He urges her to come back with him to the twentieth century—for "they don't burn people for witches there."

> "No," said the nurse, "but they let them live such lives in their ugly towns that my life here with all its risks is far better worth living. Thou knowest how folk live in Deptford in thy time—how all the green trees are gone, and good work is gone, and people do bad work for just so much as will keep together their worn bodies and desolate souls. And sometimes they starve to death."[47]

Eventually Dickie makes the choice to return forever to the seventeenth century, where he is not crippled (both literally and, we presume, metaphorically) and can be happier than he ever will in the present. Though it is done partly as a sacrifice, to allow the other Arden children to inherit, it is the most complete rejection of the present in any fantasy of the period.

In an argument with Edred and Elfrida in *The House of Arden*, Richard makes use of the nurse's argument himself for rejecting the twentieth century.

> "Why don't you want to come with us to our times?"
> "I hate your times. They're ugly, they're cruel," said Richard.
> "They don't cut your head off for nothing anyhow in our times," said Edred, "and shut you up in the Tower."
> "They do worse things," Richard said. "I know. They make people work fourteen hours a day for nine shillings a week, so that they never have enough to eat or wear, and no time to sleep or be happy in. They won't give people food or clothes, or let them work to get them; and then they put the people in prison if they take enough to keep them alive. They

let people get horrid diseases, till their jaws drop off, so as to have a particular kind of china. Women have to go out to work instead of looking after their babies, and the little girl that's left in charge drops the baby and it's crippled for life. Oh! I know. I won't go back with you. You might keep me there for ever." He shuddered.[48]

As a book *Harding's Luck* is uneven. With its companion volume, *The House of Arden*, it forms a separate group from either Nesbit's earlier fantasies, which, like *The Phoenix and the Carpet*, or the *Psammead* books, center on Edwardian London and are fairly episodic in structure, or the late ones which involve totally "other" worlds. They are in some ways her most ambitious experiment in that they tell essentially the same story from two points of view, and involve some of the basic problems of science fiction: time travel, for instance.

This was one of the questions that always puzzled the children—and they used to talk it over together till their heads seemed to be spinning round. The question of course was: Did their being in past times make any difference to the other people in past times? In other words, when you were taking part in historical scenes, did it matter what you said or did? Of course it seemed to matter extremely—at the time.[49]

They are told by the nurse that they can, in fact, leave no trace on times past—from which we, if not the children, may be intended to glean some theory (Hegelian or Marxist?) of the inevitability of history.[50] But the difference between Dickie's journeys into the past and those of the children in *The Story of the Amulet* is that they always remained physically themselves—visibly visitors to another time or place—whereas Dickie is somebody else. In Jacobean England he is not lame, for example. He is a different physical person, Richard Arden. This raises an even more puzzling problem—which Nesbit herself is aware of—that if Dickie has "become" young Richard Arden of 1606, what has happened to the boy who was previously "Richard Arden"? Indeed, if we read the text closely it is not clear that the "Richard" who refuses to come to the twentieth century with Edred and Elfrida is in fact Dickie. His comment that "in your time nobody cares" is, to say the least, ambiguous. The nurse in *Harding's Luck* suggests that the "missing" Edred and Elfrida from 1606 are "somewhere else—in Julius Caesar's time, to be exact—but they don't know it, and never will know it. They haven't the charm. To them it will be like a dream that they have forgotten."[51] But this system of interchanging personalities has to be endless, if it is to work at all. Moreover, the more people that are doing it, the less remarkable it becomes—unless we are to assume that, as in *The Finest Story in the World*, we all carry within us the memories of every life that we have "lived." The very strengths of fantasy are in danger of becoming weaknesses—the "rules" are in danger of being lost.

Nevertheless *Harding's Luck* has some of the best descriptions to be found anywhere in Nesbit, such as the opening passages which set the tone of the whole book.

> Dickie lived at New Cross. At least the address was New Cross, but really the house where he lived was one of a row of horrid little houses built on the slope where once green fields ran down the hill to the river, and the old houses of the Deptford merchants stood stately in their pleasant gardens and fruitful orchards. All those good fields and happy gardens are built over now. It is as though some wicked giant had taken a big brush full of yellow ochre paint, and another full of mud colour, and had painted out the green in streaks of dull yellow and filthy brown; and the brown is the roads and the yellow is the houses. Miles and miles and miles of them, and not a green thing to be seen except the cabbages in the greengrocers' shops, and here and there some poor trails of creeping-jenny drooping from a dirty window-sill. There is a little yard at the back of each house; this is called "the garden," and some of these show green— but they only show it to the houses' back windows. You cannot see it from the street [. . .] there were no green things growing in the garden at the back of the house where Dickie lived with his aunt. There were stones and bones, and bits of brick, and dirty old dish cloths matted together with grease and mud, worn out broom heads and broken shovels, a bottomless pail, and the mouldy remains of a hutch where once rabbits had lived. But that was a very long time ago, and Dickie had never seen the rabbits. A boy had brought a brown rabbit to school once, buttoned up inside his jacket. [. . .] So Dickie knew what rabbits were like. And he was fond of the hutch for the sake of what had once lived there.
>
> And when his aunt sold the poor remains of the hutch to a man with a barrow who was ready to buy anything, and who took also the pail and the shovels, giving threepence for the lot, Dickie was almost as unhappy as though the hutch has really held a furry friend. And he hated the man who took the hutch away, all the more because there were empty rabbit skins hanging sadly from the back of the barrow.[52]

As a child's view of the world, this movement from the general to the particular, with its trains of association about the rabbits, is among the best things she ever wrote. But alongside this kind of acute observation are passages of slack writing and hackneyed themes. The nurse wavers between "Odds Bodikins!" and modern English—not wholly to be accounted for by her time changes! For many modern readers the discovery that little lame Dickie of Deptford is really the rightful Lord Arden in the twentieth century does not give quite the thrill that this unwearied theme, with its echoes of Curdie's hidden royalty and *Little Lord Fauntleroy*, clearly gave Nesbit's contemporaries. Yet, this said, *Harding's Luck* does display at its best a quality that gave Nesbit's fantasy its enduring greatness, and sets her beside Kipling as one of the giants of the genre.

This is the underlying sense of a stable and ordered moral world. Her magic is often mysterious, and occasionally perfunctory, but it never gives the impression of being arbitrary or meaningless. In part, this is achieved by a network of literary cross-references to other writers—particularly, as we have seen, to fellow writers of fantasy. Just as Kipling's Puck knows his *Midsummer Night's Dream* and is steeped in English literature, so we get the impression from Nesbit that her magic is not her creation, but belongs to a much deeper and older world than can be conjured up by any single writer alone. Her work is studded with allusions of this kind. Dickie Harding reads Kingsley when he gets the chance. The children in *Wet Magic* are reading from *The Water Babies* at the beginning, and when the mermaid wishes to convince them that they really will be able to come under the water with her, she too makes reference to it.

> "Someone once told me a story about Water Babies. Did you never hear of that?"
>
> "Yes, but that was a made-up story," said Bernard stolidly.
>
> "Yes, of course," she agreed, "but a great deal of it's quite true, all the same."[53]

On the page before there had been casual references both to Heine and Matthew Arnold. Even the invocation that summons up the mermaids is a quotation from a master of fantasy on a cosmic scale: Milton himself.

> Sabrina fair,
> Listen where thou art sitting,
> Under the glassy green, translucent wave
> (*Comus*, 859-61)

More delightfully zany is the parrot in *The Magic City* who is disinclined to "ordinary conversation" (p. 171), and will only quote from Dryden's translation of the *Aeneid*, which sends everyone to sleep. In both *The Magic*

7.2 H. R. Millar: "Lucy, Philip and the Parrot Leave the City 'on the Top of a Very Large and Wobbly Camel.'" Illustration to E. Nesbit's The Magic City.

City and *Wet Magic* buildings or caves are actually made of books, and characters, both pleasant and unpleasant, are constantly leaking out of them into the respective magic worlds. The symbolism of literature as itself constituting a magic world is obvious. All literature is a way of enriching our reality and enabling us to discover in it more than we knew.[54] Fantasy is the extreme example by which we understand how the rest works.

Yet mere references alone are not sufficient to establish continuity with the tradition. As MacDonald had clearly seen, an invented world may have any set of rules the writer chooses, provided they are consistent with each other, but the moral law "remains everywhere the same." There is no hint of Nesbit's own unconventional lifestyle in her writings: indeed, her stories may be seen as a tribute to the order that she personally so much lacked.

7.3 H. R. Millar: "'The Gigantic Porch'—Building with Books."
Illustration to E. Nesbit's The Magic City.

But, if so, the "order" is not that of the Victorian conventions. Like her
predecessors, and like Kipling, she lays stress on the permanent values of
honor, truthfulness, fair-mindedness, loyalty, love, and self-sacrifice. At their
most limited these need be no more than the virtues of the tribe or in group
against the rest, but, as with Kipling at his best, Nesbit is also aware of the
limitations of the tribal code. Beyond what Kipling called "the Law," but not
superseding it, are other qualities of reconciliation and forgiveness whose
roots are religious. This is a fact that it is easy to overlook. It is only when we
meet their contemporaries like R. M. Ballantyne or Rider Haggard who lack
this other dimension that we begin to see what differentiates the fantasy of a
Kipling or a Nesbit from mere adventure stories or excursions into the
exotic. In the twentieth century it marks the difference between the great

fantasy writers, such as Tolkien or Lewis, and a host of science-fiction writers who, however good they may be as storytellers, seem in the end to inhabit an arbitrary and simplified world rather than one richer and more complex than our own. Writers will often show more of themselves in their books than to their friends, and it would have come to less of a surprise to many of her readers than to her circle of Fabian friends when, in 1906, just after she had begun her great series of magical fantasies, she was received into the Roman Catholic Church. It was a quest of a different kind for another world that would enrich her own. Though she later became sceptical about the exclusive claims of Catholicism.[55] Nesbit never lost her religious faith. From her letters, and from accounts of close friends it seems clear that toward the end of her life it grew increasingly important to her.

From her books we have a surprising amount of evidence of a philosophical kind. It has often been noticed that Plato and the Bible are the two greatest philosophical influences on English literature; it has less often been observed how great their influence has been specifically in the direction of fantasy. Nevertheless, their pull is obvious. Both suggest the existence of other worlds impinging on this, but of a greater reality, as part of a greater metaphysical and moral whole that is ultimately beyond man's understanding. We have already seen something of the biblical influence. The writers Nesbit seems to mention most often, Kingsley, MacDonald, and among her contemporaries, Kipling, all owe much to the Christian Platonic tradition, but in many ways Nesbit was possibly the greatest Platonist of them all. It is the side of her work most frequently misunderstood even now. Ever since her biographer, Doris Langley Moore, placed *The Magic City* and *The Enchanted Castle* among her least successful books, they have been largely ignored or dismissed by critics. She herself finds the construction of the former "loose and rambling,"[56] and another writer on children's books, Anthea Bell, is even more forthright. "Not much need be said of *The Magic City*," she declares, "For once, she had an excellent idea and never rose to it; she develops it in rather a prosaic, plodding manner foreign to the other fantasies."[57] Nor has *The Enchanted Castle* fared any better, being "not quite in the same rank with the works which preceded it."[58] The problem with any writer who worked as quickly and, often, as carelessly as Nesbit did is that peculiarities in her work can be plausibly dismissed as bad workmanship. In fact, Nesbit is very rarely a bad workman in her children's books. *The Magic City* and *The Enchanted Castle* present us with a very different kind of fantasy from stories like the *The Phoenix and the Carpet* and the *The Story of the Amulet* which, for all their serious social awareness, are essentially humorous and episodic.

Both have quite a complicated cumulative philosophical structure. They involve the discovery not so much of magic creatures in this world, as of the existence of other worlds alongside this one.

The Magic City is in a world of art—in its widest sense. It is only entered by an act of creativity of some kind. Not merely is Philip's tabletop city there and all his other models, but so is Mr. Perrin, the carpenter who made his first set of bricks "true to the thousandth of an inch"—and so is every other person who helped to make any part of the materials. "D'you see," asks Perrin, "*Making*'s the thing. If it was no more than the lad that turned the handle of the grindstone to sharp the knife that carved a bit of a cabinet or what not, or a child that picked a teazie to finish a bit of the cloth that's glued on to the bottom of a chessman—they're all here."[59] Even the evil "Pretenderette," the steely eyed nurse, is there, who absentmindedly rebuilt a few bricks of Philip's city she had knocked over with her sleeve. Through Mr. Noah, Nesbit goes to unusual trouble to explain the rules of her universe.

7.4 *H. R. Millar: "'He Walked On and On. . . .' Philip Lost in His Own Creation."*
Illustration to E. Nesbit's The Magic City.

[Y]ou see, you built those cities in two worlds. It's pulled down in *this* world. But in the other world it's still going on. [. . .]
Everything people make in that world goes on forever.[60]

If we had met this in a serious adult novel we would most probably recognize it at once. The underlying Platonism is obvious. Moreover, the idea that our created works of art have a timeless existence in an ideal order is a common twentieth-century critical notion[61] with roots in the nineteenth century as far back as Coleridge[62] and Nesbit goes out of her way specifically to include literature in the artistic forms of her magic world. People and animals are constantly escaping from books. We have already mentioned the Great Sloth in an earlier chapter. Others include the Hippogriff, or flying horse, and even finally Barbarians and a Roman army under Julius Caesar. Though Plato, of course, denied works of art as having a place in his world of ideal forms,[63] the appeal of his ideas has, paradoxically, always been greatest among artists—who have traditionally emphasized that his was primarily a mystical vision rather than a carefully worked-out system.

As always, Nesbit is inclined to present her beliefs in the form of parody—often, even, as self-mockery. Her obsessional and quite irrational belief that Bacon wrote Shakespeare's plays makes its appearance in the form of the jailer, Mr. Bacon Shakespeare, who has written twenty-seven volumes all in cipher on the subject of a crocheted mat that no one can unravel, but unfortunately forgotten the key. The structure of her ideas, however, is significant: though the construction of the book is complicated, it is the very antithesis of "loose and rambling." Philip's *official* task is to perform a series of heroic deeds to prove himself the "Deliverer" and not the "Destroyer" (the only two options open to him). Each is presented as a further stage of initiation and is marked by an ascending order of chivalry. When the Pretenderette, mounted on the winged Hippogriff, kidnaps Philip and flies away with him Lucy protests that Mr. Noah had told her that "the Hippogriff could only carry one." "One ordinary human being," said Mr. Noah gently, "you forget that dear Philip is now an earl."[64] In fact, of course, Philip's *real* task is to learn to love Lucy, the daughter of the man his sister has just married, and whom he deeply resents. The tasks are an opportunity for them to work together. In the first, Philip has to rescue Lucy from a dragon. In the second they have to unravel a carpet which is not woven, but crocheted—a fact which Philip cannot see until Lucy points it out to him. As they proceed, the tasks become progressively more psychologically "unraveling" as they deal with personal renunciation, self-sacrifice, and finally the Great Sloth and the Pretenderette herself—who had become unlovable from being unloved. By a device faintly reminiscent of *The Brushwood Boy*, Philip's sister Helen, who has created with him as a game a secret and forbidden island, is found to be on the island—because it is part of her dream as well as his. In giving the island away, Philip has to renounce her, since that is her only route into the magic world. Again, the symbolism of their changing relationship is obvious. Later, in real life when she has returned from her honeymoon she admits to remembering dimly her dream.

In both *The Magic City* and *The Enchanted Castle* there are repeated hints that all knowledge is but a recognition of what we have known all along. This Platonic recognition theme[65] is central to the growing maturity of the children. Many of Philip's deeds are in fact performed first, as the thing which needed to be done, and then discovered to be the next stage afterwards. The giving of the forbidden island to the homeless islanders is done simply because they *are* homeless, and must be found somewhere to live. It is immediately after this act that the reconciliation of Philip and Lucy takes place. Similarly, in *Harding's Luck*, long before Dickie has first been into the past, he finds that he recognizes the interior layout of Arden Castle when he helps to burgle it, although he has never been there before. Being a burglar in what is, unknown to you, your own "home" is a typical Nesbit twist of irony—but as a symbol it can be seen at a number of levels. Much of the story can in fact be taken as an experiment in *déjà vue*: the feeling of having "been here before." Sometimes, as in Kipling, this is specifically linked with notions of reincarnation. Dickie, for instance, meets people in Jacobean England who are apparently "the same" as people he knew in the slums of Deptford, but the way in which the device is used suggests that Nesbit is more interested in the way the same people will behave under different circumstances, than she is in actual reincarnation—although this, too, of course is a Platonic theme.[66] Much more specifically Platonic is the nurse's question to Dickie, when, in trying to explain what has been happening she seems to be quoting Novalis: "Dids't never hear that all life is dream?"

Nesbit certainly had, and it is in her treatment of this central notion of so much Victorian fantasy that she stands most clearly in the Platonic Christian tradition of Hogg, Novalis, MacDonald, and Kingsley. The unreal or illusory nature of time, which comes in almost every one of these later fantasies, is part of a wider feeling that life itself is but a dream into which we bring reports, like the poor shepherd girl Kilmeny, of a greater reality beyond. In *The Enchanted Castle* there is a magic ring that—discon-certingly—is just what its possessor says it is. Much of the story is taken up with a series of comic misadventures similar in kind to those with the Psammead in *Five Children and It*. The ring can be used to create things, to become rich, to become invisible, and even to grow—all with equally confusing and disastrous consequences. At the same time, however, the ring also initiates its wearers into another world where statues become alive and monsters roam the grounds of Yalding Castle. The statues of Greek gods scattered around the grounds become the real Greek pantheon, and the children join them in a feast—a literal symposium. In the final chapter the children with Lord Yalding and his fiancée are present at a vast mystical vision of the great dance of creation:

> The moonbeam slants more and more; now it touches the far end of the stone, now it draws nearer and nearer the middle of it, now at last it touches the very heart and centre of that central stone. And then it is as though a spring were touched, a fountain of light released. Everything changes. Or, rather, everything is revealed. There are no more secrets. The plan of the world seems plain, like an easy sum that one writes in big figures on a child's slate. One wonders how one can ever have wondered about anything. Space is not; every place that one has seen or dreamed of is here. Time is not; into this instant is crowded all that one has ever done

7.5 H. R. Millar: "The Monster Lizard Slipped Heavily into the Water."
Illustration to E. Nesbit's The Enchanted Castle *(1907).*

or dreamed of doing. It is a moment, and it is eternity. It is the centre of the universe and it is the universe itself. The eternal light rests on and illuminates the eternal heart of things. [. . .]

Afterwards none of them could ever remember at all what had happened. But they never forgot that they had been somewhere where everything was easy and beautiful. And people who can remember even that much are never quite the same again. And when they came to talk of it next day they found that to each some little part of that night's great enlightenment was left. [. . .]

Then a wave of intention swept over the mighty crowd. All the faces, bird, beast, Greek statue, Babylonian monsters, human child and human lover, turned upward, the radiant light illumined them and one word broke from all.

"The light!" they cried, and the sound of their voice was like the sound of a great wave; "the light! the light—"[67]

There is an extraordinary, yet significant, parallel to this scene in a minor key at the end of *The Magic City*. To rid the city of Barbarians who have escaped from Caesar's *Gallic War*, Caesar himself is summoned from

7.6 H. R. Millar: "Caesar Drives the Barbarians Back into History."
Illustration to E. Nesbit's The Magic City.

the same book. He and his legions are clearly meant to stand for order and civilization against chaos and barbarism. After a night of fighting the barbarians are safely driven back between hard covers, and as dawn breaks Caesar passes judgment on the Pretenderette. Though he had been called up originally for a limited military objective, he now seems to have taken over the role of lawgiver. But the "Law" is that of love. In a "Last Judgment" scene the loveless Pretenderette is condemned to serve the people of Briskford, newly released from the Great Sloth, until they love her so much they cannot bear to part with her—at which point, of course, her "punishment" ceases to be one. Any possible theological implications of this judgment of Caesar are rapidly passed over because as he speaks both children now see an extraordinary resemblance between him and Lucy's father (now to be Philip's also). At the same moment the sun rises and they are dazzled by the light on his armor. When they open their eyes he is gone. The justice transmuted into love, the glimpse of a father in this (for Philip a new discovery), and the dazzling light are all familiar images. The whole incident is important in that it is not necessary in any way to the plot, but presents a sudden, and slightly incomprehensible twist to the story. Though we can recognize in the "light" echoes of Plato's sun myth in *The Republic*, there are also nearer and more immediate references here to the European mystical tradition. As Kingsley did at the end of *The Water Babies*, Nesbit is harking back here (and even more in the passage from *The Enchanted Castle*) to the consummation of space and time in the contemplation of the "Light Eternal" at the end of Dante's *Paradiso*.

Finally, in such scenes as these there is the hint (it is no more) of that odd metaphysical frisson that links Dante with this minority tradition of Victorian children's writers, and that transforms fantasy from simple escapism into something much more enduringly rooted in the human psyche. It is present in canto III of the *Paradiso* when Dante suddenly discovers that the faces he thought were either reflections or figments of his own mind were, in fact, more real and alive than he could easily comprehend. It is present (as Keats saw) in Adam's dream in *Paradise Lost*, where he awakens and finds his dream is truth. It is present, as we have seen, tantalizingly and fleetingly in Carroll, Kingsley, MacDonald, and Kipling—and again here with Nesbit as Philip discovers that what he has glimpsed for a moment, after so much moral struggle, within the "magic city" has become part of the reality of his everyday life. The uncompromising Platonism of Anselm's ontological proof of God owes something of its curious magnificence to this same basic human desire for the dream that comes true. Keats had boldly attributed this power to the imagination, but by mid-century the all important shock of this transformational view of the imagination had been lost—and largely replaced by theories of aesthetics. In "Art" the mystery and urgency of other worlds had largely faded or become dissipated. It was left to children's writers such as Nesbit to create anew, and at a different level of experience, the "high fantasy" of a world too rich and complex to be contained by the conventions of Victorian naturalism.

Notes

Notes to Introduction

1 C. S. Lewis, *Out of the Silent Planet* (London: Macmillan, 1952), 170–71.
2 George Eliot, *Middlemarch* (Edinburgh: W. Blackwood, 1871–1872), book III, ch. 27.
3 Arthur Machen, *Hieroglyphics: A Note Upon Ecstasy in Literature*, rev. ed. (London: M. Secker, 1912), 64.
4 Arthur Machen, "A Fragment of Life," in *The House of Souls* (London: Grant Richards, 1906), 34–35.
5 Ibid., 84.

Notes to Chapter 1

1 Longinus was rediscovered in the sixteenth century, and his treatise only really became popular in England during the course of the eighteenth. Something of the problem of translators since 1800 can be seen by the fact that several versions feel obliged to translate *phantasia* as "imagination," and one recent version (that of D. A. Russell) actually renders it as "visualization" in a declared effort to overcome the problem of choice between the post-Romantic meanings of imagination and fantasy. See A. O. Prickard, *Longinus on the Sublime* (New York: Oxford University Press, 1906), 32–33. Also W. Rhys Roberts's translation (Cambridge: Cambridge University Press, 1935) and D. A. Russell's translation (Oxford: Clarendon Press, 1974). See also Owen Barfield, *History in English Words* (London: Faber & Faber, 1962), 208.
2 William Shakespeare, *Hamlet*, Act I, Scene ii, line 29.
3 Samuel Coleridge, *Collected Letters*, ed. E. L. Griggs, 6 vols. (Oxford: Clarendon, 1956–1971), 1:208.

4   Ibid., I:210.
5   Iona and Peter Opie, *The Classic Fairy Tales* (New York: Oxford University Press, 1974), 25.
6   I am indebted for this reference to Sheila Haines, "Thoughts for the Labouring Classes," Master's Thesis, Sussex University, 1975.
7   Doris Langley Moore, *E. Nesbit, A Biography*, rev. ed. (London: Ernest Benn, 1967), 34.
8   John Clare, *Letters*, ed. J. W. & Anne Tibble (London: Routledge & Paul, 1951), 210.
9   Lona Mosk Packer, *Christina Rossetti* (Cambridge: Cambridge University Press, 1963), 13–14.
10   The utilitarian schoolmaster in Dickens's *Hard Times*, 1854.
11   Thomas Carlyle, "Signs of the Times," in *Selected Writings of Thomas Carlyle*, ed. Alan Shelston,
     (London: Penguin, 1971), 72.
12   Samual Coleridge, *Biographia Literaria*, ed. J. Shawcross, 2 vols. (London: Oxford University Press, 1907), 1:202.
13   Ibid.
14   Ibid.
15   Thomas Carlyle, *Collected Works of Thomas Carlyle*, 16 vols. (London: Chapman & Hall, 1858), 1:3, ch. 3, p. 210.
16   Samuel Taylor Coleridge, *Lay Sermons*, ed. R. J. White (London: Routledge, 1972), 28–30.
17   Carlyle, *Collected Works*, 1:3, ch. 3, pp. 212–15.
18   Carlyle's description of Kant's "Reason" is significant in its antirational tone: "Not by logic or argument does it work; yet surely and clearly may it be taught to work; and its domain lies in that higher region whither logic and argument cannot reach; in that holier region where Poetry and Virtue and Divinity abide, in whose presence Understanding wavers and recoils, dazzled into utter darkness by that 'sea of light,' at once the fountain and the termination of true knowledge" ("The State of German Literature," *Critical and Miscellaneous Essays*, 4 vols. [London: Chapman & Hall, 1869], 1:96).
19   Thomas Balston, *Life of Jonathan Martin* (London: Macmillan, 1945).
20   Nikolaus Pevsner, *The Englishness of English Art* (London: Architectural Press, 1956), 61–72; It is difficult to say if the library of St. John's College, Cambridge, for instance, is the last example of "genuine" Gothic, or the first example of the Gothic "revival." Built in 1623, it was justified by the argument that "some men of judgment liked best the old fashion of church window, holding it most meet for such a building"; Pevsner, *Cambridgeshire* (Harmondsworth: Penguin, 1954), 124–25; R. W. Ketton Cremer, *Horace Walpole*, 3d ed. (London: Methuen, 1964), 135.
21   W. R. Ketton Cremer, *Horace Walpole: A Biography*, 3d ed. (London: Methuen, 1964), 136 (*The World*, March 22, 1753).

22 Ibid., 231–32.
23 Walpole to Mann, June 12, 1753; Ketton Cremer, *Horace Walpole*, 141–42. Horace Walpole, *The Yale Edition of Horace Walpole's Correspondence*, ed. W. S. Lewis, 43 vols. (New Haven: Yale University Press, 1961), 20:380.
24 Ketton Cremer, *Horace Walpole*, 179.
25 Ibid., 189.
26 H. A. N. Brockman, *The Caliph of Fonthill* (London: Werner Laurie, 1956), 38–39.
27 Ibid., Foreword by Nikolaus Pevsner, xii.
28 Boyd Alexander, *England's Wealthiest Son* (London: Centaur Press, 1962), 163.
29 Ketton Cremer, *Horace Walpole*, 192.
30 Nevertheless, Scott's own house, Abbotsford, was itself as much of a historical fantasy as Walpole's.
31 Brockman, *Caliph of Fonthill*, 69.
32 Susan Chitty, *The Beast and the Monk: A Life of Charles Kingsley* (London: Hodder & Stoughton, 1974), 65–86.
33 These are not listed by Harvey Darton in his near exhaustive *Children's Books in England*, 2d ed. (Cambridge: Cambridge University Press, 1958).
34 Horace Walpole, *Hieroglyphic Tales* (London: Elkin Mathews, 1926), 29.
35 See, for instance, Lady Craven's story, *Modern Anecdote of the Ancient Family of the Kinkvervankotsdarsprakengotchderns: A Tale for Christmas* (London, 1779). It was dedicated to Horace Walpole.
36 "Although the twenty-fifth century may find the *Tales* commonplace, they are too extravagant for us. It is a struggle to accept a pistachio nut drawn by an elephant and a ladybird, but a princess who speaks French in perfection and was never born is too much for us" (W. S. Lewis, *Horace Walpole*, The A. W. Mellon Lectures 1960 [London: Hart-Davis, 1961], 166). I quote the comment not because I agree with it, but as an illustration of the reaction of Walpole scholars to the kind of fantastic humor of the *Hieroglyphic Tales*.
37 Walpole, *Hieroglyphic Tales*, 81.
38 Ibid., 79.
39 Ibid.
40 Ketton Cremer claims that the number was six (*Horace Walpole*, 283).
41 They were republished by Elkin Mathews in 1926, the edition to which references here are given.
42 Ketton Cremer, *Horace Walpole*, 18.
43 Walpole, *Correspondence*, ed. Lewis, 20:165.
44   Ketton Cremer, *Horace Walpole*, 10.
45 The word certainly was in use in the later sense by Walpole's time. Abraham Tucker, in *The Light of Nature Pursued* (London, 1768), had compared the imagination to a rushing river which cannot be dammed (12). Alexander Gerard, in his "Essay on Genius," had given a similar active role to the

imagination. See Stephen Prickett, *Coleridge and Wordsworth: The Poetry of Growth* (Cambridge: Cambridge University Press, 1970), 81–82.

46 Laurence Sterne, "The Captive: Paris," *The Works of Laurence Sterne*, ed. J. P. Browne, 4 vols. (London: Bickers, 1885), 2:11.

47 Ibid., 11–12.

48 The phrase is as much Hartley's as Locke's, but both were of the common currency of contemporary psychology.

49 See A. D. Nuttall, *A Common Sky* (London: Chatto, 1974), ch. 1.

50 See, for instance, Coleridge's comment: "When a man refers to inward feelings and experiences, of which mankind at large are not conscious, as evidence of the truth of any opinion—such a Man I call A MYSTIC: and the grounding of any theory or belief on accidents and anomalies of individual sensations or fancies, and the use of peculiar terms invented or perverted from their ordinary signification, for the purposes of expressing those idiosyncracies, and pretended facts of interior consciousness, I name MYSTICISM [. . .] when with such views he asserts, that the same experiences would be vouchsafed, the same truths revealed, to every man but for his secret wickedness and unholy will—such a Mystic is a FANATIC" (*Aids to Reflection*, ed. T. Fenby [Edinburgh: J. Grant, 1905], 349).

The popular association between madness and mysticism is well illustrated by the title of an article that appeared in *Tilt's Monthly Magazine* for March 1833. It was headed "Bits of Biography. No. I: Blake the Vision Seer, and Martin, the York Minster Incendiary" (Balston, *Life of Jonathan Martin*, 98). See also Frederick Burwick, *Poetic Madness and the Romantic Imagination* (College Park: Pennsylvania State University Press, 1996).

51 William Gaunt, *Arrows of Desire* (London: Museum Press, 1956), 32.

52 Dante, *The Divine Comedy*, vol. 3: *Paradiso*, trans. John D. Sinclair (New York: Oxford University Press, 1969), canto 33, 484–85.

53 William Blake, *Complete Writings*, ed. Geoffrey Keynes (London: Oxford University Press, 1966), 149.

54 See Marcia Pointon, *Milton and English Art* (Manchester: Manchester University Press, 1970).

55 William Feaver, *The Art of John Martin* (Oxford: Clarendon, 1975), 11.

56 John Felham, *Picture of London for 1806* (London: Printed by W. Lewis for R. Phillips, 1806), 170; cited by Feaver, *Art of John Martin*, 12.

57 Feaver, *Art of John Martin*, 68–69.

58 Edward Bulwer Lytton, *The Last Days of Pompeii* (London: Routledge, 1903), 478, 482.

59 C. G. Jung, *The Archetypes and the Collective Unconscious,* in *Collected Works*, ed. H. Read, et al., trans. R. F. C. Hull (London: Routledge, 1959), 217.

60 E. Nesbit, *The Enchanted Castle* (London: Ernest Benn, 1956), 250.

Notes to Chapter 2

1   G. K. Chesterton, *The Victorian Age in Literature* (London: Williams & Norgate, 1925).

2   Jerome Buckley, *The Victorian Temper* (New York: Vintage Books, 1951), 12.

3   See, for instance, Ian Bradley, *The Call to Seriousness: The Evangelical Impact on the Victorians* (London: Cape, 1976), ch. 7.

4   Steven Marcus, *The Other Victorians: a Study of Sexuality and Pornography in Mid-nineteenth-century England* (London: Corgi Books, 1969).

5   The song from chapter 15 of MacDonald's *Phantastes*. See Robert Lee Wolff, *The Golden Key* (New Haven: Yale University Press, 1961).

6   F. E. Kingsley, *Charles Kingsley: His Letters and Memories of his Life*, 7th ed., 2 vols. (London: H. S. King, 1877), 1:475.

7   Ibid., 370.

8   See chapter 4 for a detailed comparison. Briefly, the difference lies in the way in which they handled forbidden or suppressed material. For Carroll there seems almost always the conscious elaboration of a game. It is only a shift in key from the complexities of the *Alice* books to two poems to the same baby: the first, the official variation for the parents, began:

> What hand may wreathe thy natal crown,
> Oh tiny tender spirit blossom,
> That out of Heaven has fluttered down
> Into this Earth's cold bosom?

The second, private poem starts:

> Oh pudgy podgy pup
> Why did they wake you up?
> Those crude nocturnal yells
> Are not like little bells.

9   See Patricia Allderidge, *The Late Richard Dadd 1817–1886* (London: Tate Gallery, 1974), 23.

10   Chesterton, *Victorian Age*, 245–46.

11   Richard H. Reis, *George MacDonald* (New York: Twayne Books, 1972), 41–42.

12   See above, ch. 5, p. 189; and ch. 7, p. 219.

13   William Thackeray, *Stray Papers by W. M. Thackeray 1821–1847*, ed. Lewis Melville (London: Hutchinson, 1901), 422.

14   Thomas Bewick, *Water Birds* (Newcastle: Edward Walker, 1816), 192–93.

15   Thackeray, *Stray Papers*, 396.

16   Blanchard Jerrold, *The Life of George Cruikshank* (London: Ward Lock Reprints, 1970), 9–12.

17   See William Feaver, *When We Were Young* (London: Thames & Hudson, 1977), 14.

18   William Empson, *Seven Types of Ambiguity*, 2d ed. (Harmondsworth: Penguin, 1961), 239–40.

19   John Ruskin, *Modern Painters*, 5 vols. (New York: Wiley, 1873), 5:379.

20   John Clubbe, *Victorian Forerunner: The Later Career of Thomas Hood* (Durham: Duke University Press, 1968), 16.

21   Thomas Hood, "Miss Kilmansegg and her Precious Leg," *Comic Annual* (1842), 14–15.

22   Ibid., 17.

23   Ibid., 19.

24   Ibid., 21.

25   Ibid., 38. Scander Beg (or Skanderbeg) was the national hero of Albania, who in the fifteenth century led the fight against the Turks. The member for the county was, of course, the Member of Parliament—whose "cost" could be measured in election bribes.

26   Ibid., 106.

27   Ibid., 69.

28   Cited by J. C. Reid, *Thomas Hood* (London: Routledge, 1963), 247.

29   Chesterton, *Victorian Age*, 131.

30   John Henry Newman, *Lectures on Certain Difficulties Felt by Anglicans in Submitting to the Catholic Church* (London: Burns & Lambert 1850), ch. 9.

31   Charles Dickens, *The Christmas Books*, vol. 1, ed. Michael Slater (Harmondsworth: Penguin, 1971), 33.

32   It is also, significantly, the theme of Charles Kingsley's *Hypatia* (London: Macmillian, 1853) and John Henry Newman's *Callista: A Sketch of the Third Century*, new ed. (New York/Boston: D & J Sadlier, 1856).

33   John Ruskin, *Unto this Last* (London: George Allen, 1901), 44–46.

34   *A Christmas Carol*, in *The Christmas Books*, 48.

35   Ibid., 49.

36   Ibid., 62.

37   J. S. Mill, *Autobiography of John Stuart Mills* (New York: Columbia University Press, 1924), 125.

38   *A Christmas Carol*, 128.

39   Ibid., 108.

40   Ibid., 151. Part of the greater slackness of construction in *The Chimes* can be seen in the fact that Doyle and Stanfield, the illustrators, presumably on Dickens's instructions, modeled their belfry on that of St. Dunstan in the West, Fleet Street, which had only been completed in 1830 (Ibid., 261).

41   Ibid., 152.

42   Thackeray, *Stray Papers*, 412.

43   Ibid., 404.

44   Ibid., 410.

45   Roger Lancelyn Green, *Tellers of Tales*, rev. ed. (New York: F. Watts, 1965), 24.

46   John Ruskin, *The King of the Golden River*, vol. 1 of *The Works of John Ruskin*, ed. T. Cook and A. Wedderburn, 39 vols. (London: George Allen, 1903), 1:316.

47 Ibid., 323.
48 W. M. Thackeray, "The Rose and the Ring," in *The Works of William Makepeace Thackeray* (London: Smith Elder 1891), 21:297-98.
49 Ibid., 373.
50 Ibid., 377.
51 Ibid., 396.

Notes to Chapter 3

1 Cited by Arthur Nethercot in *The Road to Tyermaine* (New York: Russell & Russell, 1962), 19-20.
2 After a wild and dissolute career, he committed suicide at the age of twenty-six.
3 See, for instance, Elizabeth MacAndrew, *The Gothic Tradition in Fiction* (New York: Columbia University Press, 1979); George Levine and U. C. Knoepflmacher, eds., *The Endurance of Frankenstein: Essays on Mary Shelley's Novel* (Berkeley: University of California Press, 1979); Anne K. Mellor, *Mary Shelley: Her Life, Her Fiction, Her Monsters* (New York: Methuen, 1988); Muriel Spark, *Mary Shelley* (New York: New American Library, 1988); James Heffernan, "Looking at the Monster: 'Frankenstein' and Film," *Critical Inquiry* 24.1 (Autumn 1997): 133-58.
4 George Levine, "Review of *Frankenstein*," *The Wordsworth Circle* 6.3 (Summer 1975), 208.
5 Mary Shelley, *Frankenstein* (London: Dent, 1912), 12-13.
6 Gideon Mantell, "Notice on the Iguanodon, a Newly Discovered Fossil Reptile, from the Sandstone of Tilgate Forest, in Sussex," *Philosophical Transactions of the Royal Society* 115 (1825): 179-86.
7 William Buckland, "Notice on the Megalosaurus or Great Fossil Lizard of Stonesfield," *Transactions of the Geological Society London*, series 2, vol. 1 (1824): 390-96.
8 W. H. Pinnock, *An Analysis of Scripture History* (Cambridge, 1848), 17 and 248.
9 See A. O. Lovejoy, *The Great Chain of Being* (Cambridge, Mass.: Harvard University Press, 1936), chs. 8 and 9.
10 Adrian J. Desmond, *The Hot-Blooded Dinosaurs* (London: Blond & Briggs, 1975), 14.
11 Edmund Gosse, *Father and Son* (London: Evergreen Books, 1941), ch. 5, p. 87.
12 Desmond, *Hot-Blooded Dinosaurs*, 15.
13 Gideon Mantell, *Journal*, ed. Cecil Curwen (London: Oxford University press, 1940), 125.
14 E. H. Gombrich, "Imagery and Art in the Romantic Period," in *Meditations on a Hobby Horse* (London: Phaidon, 1963), 124ff.

15 George MacDonald, *The Princess and the Goblin* (Harmondsworth: Puffin, 1964), 14.

16 Ibid., 92–93.

17 George MacDonald, *At The Back of the North Wind* (London: Strahan, 1871), 37.

18 George MacDonald, *The Princess and Curdie* (Harmondsworth: Puffin, 1966), 70.

19 Ibid., 91.

20 George MacDonald, *Phantastes, and Lilith*, Introduction by C. S. Lewis (Grand Rapids: Eerdmans, 1964), 210–11.

21 E. Nesbit, *Enchanted Castle*, 312.

22 Ibid., 347–48.

23 E. Nesbit, *The Magic City* (London: Ernest Benn, 1958), 258–59.

24 Ibid., 297.

25 Nesbit, *Enchanted Castle*, 176.

26 Ibid., 181–82, 185.

27 Lucy Clifford, "The New Mother," in *Anyhow Stories, Moral and Otherwise* (London: Macmillan, 1882). Reprinted in *Little Wide Awake: An Anthology from Victorian Children's Books and Periodicals*, ed. Leonard de Vries (London: Arthur Barker, 1967), 173–80.

28 William Morris, *The Early Romances of William Morris*, Introduction by Alfred Noyes (London: Dent, 1907), 154.

29 Ibid., 155.

30 Ibid., 156.

31 And closely parallel, too, to the fate of the House of Usher, in Edgar Allan Poe's *The Fall of the House of Usher* (Philadelphia: William E. Burton, 1839).

32 Edgar Allan Poe, *Tales of Mystery and Imagination* (London: Daily Express Publications, 1933), 128.

33 Ibid., 129.

34 Ibid., 130.

35 Robert Louis Stevenson, *Dr. Jekyll and Mr. Hyde* (London: Longmans, 1896), 26–27.

36 Oscar Wilde, *The Picture of Dorian Gray* (Harmondsworth: Penguin, 1949), 173–75.

37 Machen, *House of Souls*, 231.

38 Ibid., 231–32.

39 Ibid., 242.

40 Ibid., 433.

41 See Opie, *Classic Fairy Tales*, 81.

42 Ibid., 231.

43 Both examples are from many in the Print Room of the Victoria and Albert Museum; for the Lewis reference see *Surprised by Joy: The Shape of my Early Life* (London: Fontana, 1955; repr. 1959), 13.

44 Packer, *Christina Rossetti*, 150.

45 One such reconstruction of Aubrey Beardsley's *Under the Hill* has been attempted by John Glassco (Paris: Olympia, 1959; repr. London: New English Library, 1966).

46 Ibid., 50.

47 Ibid., 29–30.

48 Ibid., 61–62.

49 Beardsley was first of all at a prep school in Hurstpierpoint, and then at Brighton College.

50 It is quite possible that his attention had been drawn to it by Algernon Charles Swinburne's *"Laus Veneris." Poems and Ballads* (New York: Carleton, 1866). It had contributed to Swinburne's pagan and libertarian reputation.

Notes to Chapter 4

1 Vivien Noakes, *Edward Lear: The Life of a Wanderer* (London: Collins, 1968), 20.

2 Ibid., 35.

3 Letter to Chichester Fortescue, January 23, 1853, cited in Noakes, *Edward Lear*, 115.

4 Letter to Tennyson, June 9, 1855, cited in Noakes, *Edward Lear*, 127.

5 Angus Davidson, *Edward Lear: Landscape Painter and Nonsense Poet* (London: J. Murray, 1938), 15.

6 Letter to Chichester Fortescue, March 15, 1863, cited in Noakes, *Edward Lear*, 302.

7 His name, Prince William George of Schleswig Holstein Sonderburg Glucksburg, doubtless appealed to Lear.

8 Davidson, *Edward Lear*, 152–53.

9 Noakes, *Edward Lear*, 225.

10 There seems to me no foundation for Elizabeth Sewell's curious belief that "the Nonsense universe must be the sum of its parts and nothing more." Both Lear and Carroll invent worlds. (Elizabeth Sewell, *The Field of Nonsense* [London: Chatto, 1952], 98ff.).

11 Davidson, *Edward Lear*, 18–21.

12 Sewell, *Field of Nonsense*, 123.

13 Charles Kingsley, *Alton Locke, Tailor and Poet: an Autobiography* (London: Macmillan, 1890), 206.

14 Edmund Lushington, *Macmillan's Magazine* (April 1897); cited by Davidson, *Edward Lear*, 66–67.

15 Ibid., 59.

16 Davidson, *Edward Lear*, 21–23. Oddly enough, this kind of encounter was not uncommon. Both Rider Haggard and E. B. Pusey had similar experiences on public transport.

17 Ibid., 140–41.

18 Diary, November 1, 1862, cited in Noakes, *Edward Lear*, 227.

19 Davidson, *Edward Lear*, 186.

20 Alice's terror of the "enormous puppy" in Wonderland which "would be very likely to eat her up" reflects Carroll's own fears. Lear is even more dramatic:
    There was an Old Man of Leghorn
    The smallest that ever was born;
    But quickly snapped up he, was once by a puppy,
    Who devoured that Old Man of Leghorn.

21 For some close verbal parallels between Lear and Carroll see Sewell, *Field of Nonsense*, ch. 2.

22 Derek Hudson, *Lewis Carroll* (London: Constable, 1954), 24.

23 A. L. Taylor, *The White Knight* (Edinburgh: Oliver & Boyd, 1952), 6.

24 Ibid., 7.

25 Lewis Carroll, *Alice's Adventures in Wonderland* (London: Macmillan, 1887), 89.

26 Here, as elsewhere, I am heavily indebted to Taylor, *White Knight*.

27 William Wordsworth, *Prelude*, 1805 ed., Book X, lines 902–905.

28 *Alice's Adventures in Wonderland*, 17.

29 Taylor, *White Knight*, 46–47.

30 Lewis Carroll, *Through the Looking Glass* (London: Macmillan, 1887), 88.

31 Taylor, *White Knight*, 88–89.

32 *Through the Looking Glass*, 36.

33 Ibid., 38–39.

34 Ibid., 114.

35 Lewis Carroll, *Sylvie and Bruno* (London: Macmillan 1899), 352–54.

36 Probably the best discussion of Carroll's relations with little girls (and their subsequent interpretations) is Morten Cohen's article, "When Love was Young," in the *Times Literary Supplement*, September 10, 2004.

37 *Through the Looking Glass*, 103.

38 Carroll knew MacDonald well. They had met in the 1850s through a Dr. James Hunt, who treated Carroll for his stammer (Greville MacDonald, *George MacDonald and his Wife* [London: Allen & Unwin, 1924], 301; hereafter referred to as *GMD and Wife*). MacDonald refers to some of Carroll's mathematical work in his essays, and as before mentioned his children received the honor of having the manuscript of Alice read to them when Carroll was wondering whether to publish it.

39 *Through the Looking Glass*, 74–75.

40 He may well have known also the parallels in Hindu mythology—that we, and all our world, are the dream of Brahma. Something of the same literary technique has been employed to good effect by Jostein Gaarder in *Sophie's World*, trans. Paulette Moller (New York: Farrer, Straus & Giroux, 1994)—where a fictional heroine has to struggle with her own fictionality.

41 *Through the Looking Glass*, 164.

42 Taylor, *White Knight*, 87.

43 Immanuel Kant, *Kant's Inaugural Dissertation and Early Writings on Space*, translated by John Handyside (London, Open Court, 1929), 21–22.

44 *Through the Looking Glass*, 19.

45 For the following interpretations see Robert Phillips, ed., *Aspects of Alice* (London: Gollancz, 1972).

46 See Stephen Prickett, *Romanticism and Religion: The Tradition of Coleridge and Wordsworth in the Victorian Church* (Cambridge: Cambridge University Press, 1976), 176–78, 249–50. See also Stephen Prickett, "Ariosto and the Monstrous Crow," *Proceedings of the Australasian Victorian Studies Association*, 1983, edited by Pat Dobrez and Stephen Prickett (Australian National University-Canberra, 1984): 34–45.

47 John Henry Newman, *Lectures on Anglican Difficulties* (London, 1850), 8.

48 Lewis Carroll, *Sylvie and Bruno Concluded* (London: Macmillan, 1899), 170.

49 Taylor, *White Knight*, 137.

50 *Through the Looking Glass*, 191.

51 Taylor, *White Knight*, 143.

52 Ibid., 144.

53 *Through the Looking Glass*, 57. (L stands for "Love" as well as "Liddell.") Carroll also, no doubt, recalled that Jesus, when asked who would be the greatest in the kingdom of Heaven, "called a little child . . . and set him in the midst of them." (Matthew 18:2) Alice stands here in a tradition of child symbolism that includes Dickens's Tiny Tim and Hood's poem "I remember. . . ."

Notes to Chapter 5

1 Taylor, *White Knight*, 51.

2 *GMD and Wife*, 342.

3 Kingsley, *Charles Kingsley: Life and Letters*, 2:137.

4 Ibid., 2:137–38.

5 Charles Kingsley, *The Water Babies*, illustrated by J. Noël Paton (London: Macmillan, 1863), 310.

6 Kingsley, *Charles Kingsley: Life and Letters*, 1:32–36.

7 See for instance, Harvey Darton, *Children's Books in England*, 2d ed. (Cambridge: Cambridge University Press, 1958), ch. 14; or John Rowe Townsend, *Written for Children* (London: Garnet Miller 1965), 41–42.

8 *Alice's Adventures in Wonderland*, 119.

9   Kingsley, *Charles Kingsley: Life and Letters*, 1:210.

10   Ibid., 211.

11   Kingsley, *Water Babies*, 82–83.

12   Ibid., 176–77.

13   Susan Chitty, *Beast and the Monk: A Life of Charles Kingsley* (London: Hodder & Stoughton, 1974).

14   The basis of Kingsley's real detestation of Roman Catholicism seems to have been that its emphasis on celibacy was a sexual perversion. A good deal of the vehemence in his disastrous clash with Newman came, I suspect, from his hatred of homosexuals.

15   Kingsley, *Water Babies*, 22–24. It is interesting to compare Kingsley's approval of this kind of disorganized natural growth with H. P. Lovecraft's use of it as an image of sinister decay in *The Dunwich Horror* (New York: Lancer, 1963).

16   Kingsley, *Charles Kingsley: Life and Letters*, 1:77.

17   See Prickett, *Romanticism and Religion*, 105–9.

18   C. N. Manlove, *Modern Fantasy: Five Studies* (Cambridge: Cambridge University Press, 1975).

19   Ibid., 26.

20   Ibid., 32.

21   Blake, *Complete Writings*, 783.

22   Charles Kingsley, *Literary and General Lectures and Essays* (London: Macmillan, 1880), 106.

23   See my *Romanticism and Religion*, ch. 3, for a fuller discussion of this problem.

24   Ibid., 85–86.

25   George MacDonald, *A Dish of Orts* (London: Sampson Low, 1893), 245–46.

26   Ibid., 247.

27   Chitty, *Beast and Monk*, 221–22.

28   Kingsley, *Water Babies*, 307.

29   Tom, we notice, had "been in prison once or twice himself." Ibid., 10.

30   *Dublin Tract Repository*, undated. Reprinted in de Vries, *Little Wide Awake*, 30.

31   Anon., undated. Farthing Series No. 8, in de Vries, *Little Wide Awake,* 30.

32   Anon., *True Sketches from Life*, 3. Farthing Series No. 76, in de Vries, *Little Wide Awake*, 67.

33   Geoffrey Rowell, *Hell and the Victorians* (Oxford: Clarendon, 1974), 172.

34   Ibid., 173.

35   Ibid., 112.

36   Frederick Denison Maurice, *The Kingdom of Christ*, 4th ed., 2 vols. (1838; London: Macmillan, 1891), 1:274–75.

37   Stated by F. G. Bettany and S. D. Headlam. Cited by Rowell, *Hell and Victorians*, 2.

38 Robert Lee Wolff, "Some Erring Children in Children's Literature: The World of Victorian Religious Strife in Miniature," in *The Worlds of Victorian Fiction*, ed. Jerome H. Buckley (Cambridge, Mass.: Harvard University Press, 1975), 311.

39 Kingsley, *Charles Kingsley: Life and Letters*, 1:78–79.

40 Ibid., 84.

41 John Frederick Maurice, ed., *Life of Frederick Denison Maurice*, 4th ed., 2 vols. (London: Macmillan, 1885), 2:555.

42 Kingsley, *Water Babies*, 307.

43 Dante, *Paradiso*, canto XXXIII, lines 142–45.

44 Kingsley, *Alton Locke*, 265.

45 Kingsley, *Charles Kingsley: Life and Letters*, 2:66–67.

46 Maureen Duffy, *The Erotic World of Faery* (London: Hodder & Stoughton, 1972).

47 Chitty, *Beast and Monk*, 220.

48 Erich Auerbach, *Mimesis*, trans. Willard Trask (Garden City: Doubleday, 1957), 242.

49 Ibid., 247.

50 Kingsley, *Water Babies*, 45.

51 Chitty, *Beast and Monk*, 218.

52 See, for instance, book 2, ch. 32, where Pantagruel puts out his tongue to shelter his army from the rain. The author climbs on to his tongue, and walks along it "two leagues" into his mouth, and discovers there fields, cities, and mountains.

53 Manlove here is apposite: "on practically every issue, even on those—such as their universalism, or their views of nature as chaos—which apparently unite them, Kingsley and MacDonald form a fascinating contrast, almost a Victorian *summa*" (*Modern Fantasy*, 75). He is, of course, wrong about either regarding nature as "chaos," but the comparison is a central one.

54 *GMD and Wife*, 178.

55 Ibid., 297

56 MacDonald, *Dish of Orts*, 317.

57 Ibid., 316–17.

58 George MacDonald, *Miracles of Our Lord* (London: Strahan, 1870), 153.

59 George MacDonald, *Unspoken Sermons*, second series (London: Longmans, 1885), 49–50.

60 MacDonald, *Dish of Orts*, 5.

61 We recall in this context Wordsworth's lines about his own "visionary power:"
      I deem not profitless those fleeting moods
      Of shadowy exultation: not for this,
      That they are kindred to our purer mind
      And intellectual life; but that the soul,
      Remembering how she felt, but what she felt

Remembering not, retains an obscure sense
Of possible sublimity [. . .] (*The Prelude, Book Two*, 311–18).

62   MacDonald, *Phantastes and Lilith*, 227.

63   *GMD and Wife*, 482.

64   MacDonald, *Phantastes and Lilith*, 81.

65   Charles Kingsley, *Madam How and Lady Why*, 2nd ed. (London: Macmillan, 1889), 113.

66   Ibid., 112–13.

67   MacDonald, "The Fantastic Imagination," in *Dish of Orts*, 314.

68   *GMD and Wife,* 11. In the Introduction to Greville MacDonald's life of his father, Chesterton writes, "I for one can really testify to a book that has made a difference to my whole existence, which helped me to see things in a certain way from the start; a vision of things which even so real a revolution as a change of religious allegiance has substantially only crowned and confirmed. Of all the stories I have read [. . .] it remains the most real, the most realistic, in the exact sense of the phrase the most like life. It is called the *Princess and the Goblin*." (9).

69   MacDonald, *Princess and the Goblin*, 11.

70   Ibid., 8.

71   Ibid., 155.

72   Ibid., 12.

73   Thackeray, "The Rose and the Ring," in *Works of William Makepeace Thackeray* , 396. See also A. D. Nuttall's discussion of the problems of allegory, in *Two Concepts of Allegory: a Study of Shakespeare's* The Tempest *and the* Logic of Allegorical Expression (London: Routledge, 1967).

74   See, for instance, Wolff, *Golden Key.*

75   MacDonald, *Princess and Curdie*, 221.

76   *GMD and Wife*, 156.

77   Ibid., 157.

78   Genesis, ch. 29; see my article, "Dante, Beatrice and M. C. Escher: Disconfirmation as a Metaphor," *Journal of European Studies* 2 (1972): 350–52.

79   J. R. R. Tolkien, *Tree and Leaf* (London: Allen & Unwin, 1964), 59.

80   Such feelings link the youth of Wordsworth, Newman, and Tolstoy in the nineteenth century, and in our own century both Tolkien and Lewis have been drawn to MacDonald by what they describe as very similar intuitions.

81   MacDonald, *Phantastes and Lilith*, 420.

Notes to Chapter 6

1   MacDonald, *Phantastes, and Lilith*. The passage has had a chequered history since two further mistakes were made in the transliteration at the initial printing of the novel. [See Wolff, *Golden Key*, 42–44.] The corrected German text reads as follows:

Es lassen sich Erzählungen ohne Zusammenhang, jedoch mit Association, wie Träume, denken; Gedichte, die bloss wohlklingend und woll schöner Worte sind, aber auch ohne allen Sinn und Zusammenhang, höchstens einzelne Strophen verständlich, wie Bruchstücke aus den verschiedenartigsten Dingen. Diese wahre Poesie kann höchstens einen allegorischen Sinn im Grossen, und eine indirecte Wirkung, wie Musik haben. Darum ist die Natur so rein poetisch, wie die Stube eines Zauberers, eines Physikers, eine Kinderstube, eine Polterund Vorrathskammer. [. . .]

Ein Mährchen ist wie ein Traumbild ohne Zusammenhang. Ein Ensemble wunderbarer Dinge und Begebenheiten, z. B. eine Musikalische Phantasie, die harmonischen Folgen einer Aeolsharfe, die Natur selbst.

In einem echten Mährchen muss alles wunderbar, geheimnissvoll und zusammenhängend sein; alles belebt, jeders auf eine andere Art. Die ganze natur muss wunderlich mit der ganzen Geisterwelt gemischt sein; hier tritt die Zeit der Anarchie, der Gesetzlosigkeit, Freiheit, der Naturstand der Natur, die Zeit vor der Welt ein. [. . .] Die Welt des Mährchens ist die, der Welt der Wahrheit durchaus entgegengesetzte, und eben darum ihr so durchaus ähnlich, wie das Chaos der vollendeten Schöpfung ähnlich ist.

2   See Rosemary Ashton, *The German Idea: Four English Writers and the Reception of German Thought, 1800–1860* (Cambridge: Cambridge University Press, 1980).

3   See ibid; also Andrew Bowie, *Aesthetics and Subjectivity from Kant to Nietzsche* (Manchester: Manchester University Press, 1990), and *From Romanticism to Critical Theory* (London: Routledge, 1997).

4   See, for instance, the opening paragraphs of Mme. De Stael's influential book, *On Germany: On the Appearance of Germany,* in *Selected Writings of Germaine de Stael,* translated and introduction by Vivian Folkenflik (New York: Columbia University Press, 1987):

Many vast forests are the sign of a new civilization: the ancient land of the South has almost no more trees, and the sun falls straight down on earth ravaged by men. Germany still offers some traces of uninhabited nature. From the Alps to the sea, between the Rhine and the Danube, you see a countryside covered with chestnut and fir trees, crisscrossed by impressively beautiful rivers, and cut across by picturesque mountains. [. . .]

The ruined castles one glimpses on mountaintops, the houses built of earth, the narrow window, the snow that buries the plains in winter all give a harsh impression. (292)

5   See John Claiborne Isbell, *The Birth of European Romanticism* (Cambridge: Cambridge University Press, 1994).

6   For a discussion of one aspect of this imbalance, see Hans Frei, *The Eclipse of Biblical Narrative: A Study in Eighteenth- and Nineteenth-Century*

Hermeneutics (New Haven, Yale University Press, 1974), 142; also Stephen Prickett, *Origins of Narrative: The Romantic Appropriation of the Bible* (Cambridge: Cambridge University Press, 1996), ch. 5.

7   Johann Georg Sulzer, *General Theory of the Fine Arts* (Leipzig, 1773–1775), cited by Martin Swales, *Thomas Mann: A Study* (London: Rowman & Littlefield, 1980), 19.

8   See Wolff, *Golden Key,* 43–45.

9   Ibid., ch. 2.

10   Lewis, *Surprised by Joy,* 169.

11   This cupboard is almost certainly the origin of C. S. Lewis's backless wardrobe, in *The Lion, the Witch, and the Wardrobe* (London: Macmillian, 1950).

12   MacDonald, *Phantastes and Lilith,* 63–64.

13   T. S. Eliot, "The Hollow Men," *Complete Poems and Plays* (New York: Harcourt Brace, 1952).

14   See above, 7–8.

15   Gabriel Josopivici, *The Book of God* (New Haven: Yale University Press, 1988), 6–7.

16   Alan Richardson, ed., *A Theological Word Book of the Bible* (London: SCM Press, 1950), 215.

17   Lewis, *Surprised by Joy,* 70–71.

18   C. S. Lewis, *The Pilgrim's Regress* (London: Collins, 1980), 9.

19   MacDonald, *Phantastes and Lilith,* 19–20.

20   An image which could well have come straight out of his friend John Ruskin's *King of the Golden River.*

21   MacDonald, *Phantastes and Lilith,* 192–93.

22   See *GMD and Wife,* 73, 259; Wolff, *Golden Key,* 45; Manlove, *Modern Fantasy,* 274; Rolland Hein, *The Harmony Within: The Spiritual Vision of George MacDonald* (Grand Rapids: Eerdmans, 1982), 7.

23   W. H. Bruford, *The German Tradition of Self-Cultivation: "Bildung" from Humboldt to Thomas Mann* (Cambridge: Cambridge University Press, 1975), 31–32.

24   Johann Wolfgang von Goethe, *Wilhelm Meister's Apprenticeship and Travels,* trans. Thomas Carlyle, 2 vols. (New York : J. D. Williams, 1882), 2:14.

25   For a partial but interesting discussion of some of the religious symbolism of the *Travels,* see Ruth ap Roberts, *The Ancient Dialect: Thomas Carlyle and Comparative Religion* (Berkeley: University of California Press, 1988), ch. 2.

26   Goethe, *Wilhelm Meister,* 2:225.

27   Ibid., 2:230. The link with Mossy and Tangle in MacDonald's *Golden Key* is obvious.

28   Ibid., 1:444.

29   Wilhelm von Humboldt, *On Language,* trans. Peter Heath, introduction by Hans Aarsleff (Cambridge: Cambridge University Press, 1988), xiv.

30 Bruford, *German Tradition*, vii.
31 Martin Swales, *The German Bildungsroman from Wieland to Hesse* (Princeton University Press, 1978), 12.
32 Wilhelm Dilthey, *Leben Schleiermachers*, 2 vols. (Berlin: G. Reimer, 1870), 1:282. Cited by Michael Beddow, *The Fiction of Humanity: Studies in the Bildungsroman from Weildand to Thomas Mann* (Cambridge: Cambridge University Press, 1982), 1.
33 Wilhelm Dilthey, *Das Erlebnis und die Dichtung: Lessing, Goethe, Novalis, Höklerlin* (Leipzig & Berne, 1913), 394. See Swales, *German Bildungsroman*, 3.
34 Swales, *German Bildungsroman*, 12.
35 Walter Hooper, ed., See *They Stand Together: The Letters of C. S. Lewis to Arthur Greeves (1914–1963)* (London: Collins, 1979), 92–93, 94, 96, 106, etc.
36 Beddow, *Fiction of Humanity*, 5.
37 For a fuller discussion of this sense see Kathleen Wheeler, ed., *German Aesthetic and Literary Criticism: The Romantic Ironists and Goethe* (Cambridge: Cambridge University Press, 1984), viii.
38 Ibid. This applies to nearly all the works called by Wheeler in this volume.
39 "On Goethe's Meister" (1798), cited by Wheeler, *German Aesthetic*, 64.
40 "The Old English Theatre" (1811), cited by Wheeler, *German Aesthetic*, 120.
41 For a further discussion of the implication of these two terms and their historical significance, see Stephen Prickett, *Words and the Word: Language, Poetics, and Biblical Interpretation* (Cambridge: Cambridge University Press, 1986), 83.
42 Goethe, *Wilhelm Meister*, 1:7.
43 William Wordsworth, *Preface to the Lyrical Ballads*, ed. R. L. Brett and A. R. Jones (London: Methuen, 1965), 249.
44 For an account of the impact of German literature in Edinburgh in the 1820s, see Ann-Marie Jordens, *The Stenhouse Circle* (Carlton: Melbourne University Press, 1979), ch. 1.
45 G. W. F. Hegel, *Vorlesungen über die Ästhetik*, ed. F. Bassenge (Berlin: Aufbau-Verlag 1955), 557–58. Cited by Swales, *The German Bildungsroman*, 20–21.
46 Swales, *The German Bildungsroman*, 21. As James Heffernan has pointed out, this is, of course, also the ending of Mel Brooks's *Young Frankenstein* ("Looking at the Monster," 142).
47 See Introduction, 2–3.
48 MacDonald, *Phantastes*, 166.
49 Ibid., 2:189.
50 Ibid., 2:415–16.
51 Ibid., 1:345.

52 For an extended discussion of this point without mentioning MacDonald, see Paul Coates, *The Realist Fantasy: Fiction and Reality Since Clarissa* (London; Macmillan, 1983).

53 See, for instance, Jerome Buckley, *Season of Youth: The Bildungsroman from Dickens to Golding* (Cambridge, Mass.: Harvard University Press, 1974).

54 Hein, *Harmony Within*, 111.

55 Manlove, *Modern Fantasy*, 60.

56 Ibid., 62.

57 Hooper, *They Stand Together*, 459–61.

58 Karen Swann, "'Christabel': The Wandering Mother and the Enigma of Form," *Studies in Romanticism* 23.4 (Winter 1984): 533–53.

59 For the relationship between MacDonald and Coleridge see Prickett, *Romanticism and Religion*, 223–48.

60 George MacDonald, *Lilith*, Introduction by Lin Carter (New York: Ballantine Books, 1969), 3.

61 Ibid., 156.

62 Ibid.

63 MacDonald, *Phantastes and Lilith*, 216.

64 Ibid.

65 Ibid., 400–401.

66 Ibid., 405.

67 Ibid., 220.

68 Chesterton, *Victorian Age*, 152.

69 A theme again closely reminiscent of that of *The King of the Golden River*.

70 J. R. R. Tolkien, "On Fairy Stories," in *Tree and Leaf*, 59.

71 Friedrich Schleiermacher, *On Religion: Speeches to its Cultured Despisers*, trans. Richard Crouter (Cambridge: Cambridge University Press, 1988), 134.

72 *GMD and his Wife*, 548.

73 MacDonald, *Lilith*, 274.

74 Roderick McGillis, "*Phantastes and Lilith*: Femininity and Freedom," in *The Gold Thread*, ed. William Raeper (Edinburgh: Edinburgh University Press, 1990), 49–50.

Notes to Chapter 7

1 Letter from Henry James to Miss Grace Norton, Christmas Day 1897, cited in Charles Carrington, *Rudyard Kipling: His Life and Work* (London: Macmillan, 1955), 344–45.

2 See Robert Buchanan, "The Voice of the Hooligan," *Contemporary Review*, 1899, reprinted in *Kipling: The Critical Heritage*, ed. Roger Lancelyn Green (London: Routledge, 1971).

3 C. S. Lewis, "Kipling's World," in *They Asked for a Paper: Papers and Addresses* (London: Geoffrey Bles, 1962), 91.

4 Bonamy Dobrée, *Rudyard Kipling: Realist and Fabulist* (London: Oxford University Press, 1967), 146.

5 Rudyard Kipling, *Something of Myself: For my Friends Known and Unknown* (London: Macmillan, 1964), 190.

6 Ibid., 43.

7 Ibid., 52–53.

8 Lewis, "Kipling's World," 87, 89.

9 Rudyard Kipling, "The Bridge Builders," in *The Day's Work* (London: Macmillan, 1898), 1–2.

10 Rudyard Kipling, "The Finest Story in the World," in *Many Inventions* (London: Macmillan, 1893), 95–96.

11 Ibid., 127.

12 Jeffrey Iverson, *More Lives than One?: The Evidence of the Remarkable Bloxham Tapes* (London: Souvenir Press, 1976).

13 Kipling, *Something of Myself*, 189.

14 J. I. M. Stewart, *Rudyard Kipling* (London: Gollancz, 1966), 173.

15 See Lyall Watson, *Supernature: A Natural History of the Supernatural* (London: Coronet Books, 1974), ch. 2.

16 The reference, of course, is to 1 Samuel 28.

17 Kipling, *Something of Myself*, 215.

18 Carrington, *Rudyard Kipling*, 369.

19 Kipling, *Something of Myself*, 185.

20 Rudyard Kipling, *Puck of Pook's Hill* (London: Macmillan, 1906), 158–59.

21 Ibid., 57.

22 Ibid., 303.

23 Kipling, *Something of Myself*, 190–91.

24 Ibid., 12.

25 Ibid.

26 Ibid., 14.

27 MacDonald, *At The Back of the North Wind*, 115.

28 Kipling, *Puck of Pook's Hill*, 29.

29 On the obvious parallels between Kipling and Nesbit, Julia Briggs writes: "The question of Edith's borrowings is a complex one, because while she drew on other books extensively and usually very openly, she bitterly resented it when she suspected other authors of plagiarising from her. In January 1906, alongside the ninth episode of *The Amulet*, The *Strand* published the first chapter of Kipling's *Puck of Pook's Hill*, "Weyland's Sword" . . . For four months, the two serials ran side by side, and Edith who until then has been an ardent admirer of Kipling, now privately accused him of pinching her ideas and even her treatment of them. She wrote indignantly to H. G. Wells, 'I say—do read Kipling in the January *Strand* and read my *Five Children and It*—will you?'" (*A Woman of Passion: The Life of E. Nesbit 1858-1924* [New York: New Amsterdam Books, 1997], 253).

30 Since Bland was also a near pathological liar, it is difficult to be sure of any facts that depend on his unsubstantiated word. He certainly seems to have deceived Nesbit about his family of "ancient North Country stock," which is referred to by Doris Langley Moore (*E. Nesbit: A Biography*, 88). According to Norman Mackenzie he was born in Cable Street. His business ventures seem equally obscure.

31 Moore, *E. Nesbit: A Biography*, 15.

32 Norman and Jeanne MacKenzie, *The Time Traveller: The Life of H. G. Wells* (London: Weidenfeld & Nicolson, 1973), ch. 14.

33 Moore, *E. Nesbit: A Biography*, 18.

34 Ibid., 221.

35 Ibid., 255.

36 The pen name of Thomas Anstey Guthrie (1856–1934), author of many novels and shorter pieces, mostly of a fantastic nature. He was a great admirer of Nesbit.

37 Moore, *E. Nesbit: A Biography*, 191–93.

38 But without the clash of personalities that always threatened to wreck that brilliant partnership. Millar accepted Nesbit's unpunctuality with calmness and recourse, and never wavered in his admiration for her as a writer. But this did not mean uncritical agreement. On one occasion he pointed out to her that her passionate hatred of the vast new housing developments was quite inconsistent of her, since it was for what she, as a socialist, had been fighting for years.

39 Dobrée, *Rudyard Kipling*, 167.

40 Lewis, *Surprised by Joy*, 17.

41 He is of course based on Dr. Wallis Budge of the British Museum, whom Nesbit met while researching background for *The Story of the Amulet*. It was he who steered her away from ancient Egyptian legends, explaining that they were too full of sex to be useful in a children's book. He became her confidant, and possibly her lover. *The Story of the Amulet* is dedicated to him.

42 Edith Nesbit, *The Story of the Amulet* (London: Puffin, 1959), 183.

43 Ibid., 187.

44 Ibid., 148.

45 Ibid., 223.

46 Ibid., 231–32.

47 Edith Nesbit, *Harding's Luck* (London: Ernest Benn, 1947), 183.

48 Edith Nesbit, *The House of Arden* (London: Ernest Benn, 1958), 240–41.

49 Nesbit, *House of Arden*, 166.

50 In what is, technically, much the most interesting of his fantasies, *Tourmalin's Time Cheques* (London: John Murray, 1891), F. Anstey had already suggested an ingenious way of breaking this seemingly inflexible rule. Peter Tourmalin is irritated by the prospect of gaining hours of boring extra time as he sails westwards on his way back from Australia to England. A mysterious stranger on

the ship suggests that he deposits the *extra* time with him in his "Time Bank," and cashes the cheques as he wants them later. All he has to do is to write a cheque for so many minutes and place it under the nearest clock. He will instantly find himself back on board the SS Boomerang enjoying in sunlit southern seas the time he has so prudently "saved." The following winter Tourmalin does so. To his mingled delight and horror he finds that though on his voyage home he had, to the best of his knowledge, avoided any shipboard romances and remained true to his Sophia, his fiancée who was to meet him at Gibraltar, in the "saved" time he has apparently become romantically entangled with two extremely attractive girls from the ship. Each time he returns it is clear that things are getting more and more out of hand—with passionate scenes and threatened suicides in a style not unworthily anticipating G. Wodehouse. In England, in the "present," he is now married to the earnest and virtuous Sophia, and the hard pressed Tourmalin clearly relishes these "past" romances, in spite of their threatening complexities. When Sophia finds out, she explains that it is his duty to "return" to the ship and clear up these entanglements—which are clearly "real" since they have happened in the past. Protesting, Tourmalin eventually does so, only to plunge deeper and deeper into the toils so that by the time he reaches Gibraltar both girls believe him engaged to them. Sophia, joining the ship at Gibralter, discovers all and breaks off their engagement forthwith. His protest that he is already married to her, and that it is because of her that he is in this mess, is, of course, treated by the Sophia of the past with the contempt it deserves. Unfortunately, having set up this fascinating situation, in which the key events are only happening because of other events in the future which now cannot happen, Anstey hastily breaks off the story by declaring it was a "dream." Nevertheless, the basic paradox is one that deserves further and better treatment in science fiction.

51 Nesbit, *Harding's Luck*, 180.

52 Ibid., 1-3.

53 Edith Nesbit, *Wet Magic* (London: Ernest Benn, 1945), 121-22.

54 The amulet is a good example of how Nesbit can take classic metaphors of literature and give them a visual and concrete form. It grows into an enormous arch for the children to step through into "other worlds"—past or future. We recall Tennyson's *Ulysses*:

> "[A]ll experience is an arch wherethrough
> Gleams that untravelled world whose margin fades
> for ever and for ever when I move. (19-21)

55 Moore, *E. Nesbit: A Biography*, 307.

56 Ibid., 265.

57 Roger Lancelyn Green, Anthea Bell, and Elizabeth Nesbitt, *Three Bodley Head Monographs*, ed. Kathleen Lines, rev. ed. (London: Bodley Head, 1968), 146. The one dissenter from this chorus of disfavor was Noel Coward, who

hoarded his pocket money as a child in order to buy a whole year's worth of the *Strand Magazine* and so read Nesbit's stories right through without a break. There were a few numbers missing of the year that had *The Magic City*, and so, he tells us, "I stole a coral necklace from a visiting friend of Mother's, pawned it for five shillings, and bought the complete book at the Army and Navy Stores. [. . .] In later years I told E. Nesbit of this little incident and I regret to say she was delighted." (146–47).

58 Moore, *E. Nesbit: A Biography*, 324.
59 Nesbit, *Magic City*, 106.
60 Ibid., 84.
61 See for instance T. S. Eliot, "Tradition and the individual Talent" in his *Selected Essays* (London: Faber & Faber, 1951) and W. B. Yeats's poem, "Sailing to Byzantium."
62 See Prickett, *Coleridge and Wordsworth*, 115–20.
63 Plato, *Rep. X.*
64 Nesbit, *Magic City*, 218.
65 Plato, *Phaed.* 72B; *The Last Days of Socrates*, trans. Hugh Tredennick (London: Penguin, 1954), 94–95.
66 Again, see Plato, *Phaed.*
67 Nesbit, *Enchanted Castle*, 346–49. It is interesting to compare this passage with the parallel one at the end of C. S. Lewis's *Perelandra* (London: Pan Books, 1953), which also draws on Dante. Though Lewis had read a great deal of Nesbit, I do not know if he had ever read *The Enchanted Castle*.

Bibliography

Alexander, Boyd. *England's Wealthiest Son*. London: Centaur Press, 1962.

Allderidge, Patricia. *The Late Richard Dadd 1817–1886*. London: Tate Gallery, 1974.

Andersen, Hans Christian. *Wonderful Stories for Children*. New York: Wiley & Putnam, 1847.

Ang, Susan. *The Widening World of Children's Literature*. London: Palgrave, 2000.

Anonymous. *Anecdotes and Adventures of Fifteen Gentlemen*. London: E. Marshall, 1820.

——. "Bob the Cabin Boy." "The Death at School." "The Swearer's Prayer." In *Little Wide Awake: An Anthology from Victorian Children's Books and Periodicals*. Edited by Leonard de Vries. London: Arthur Barker, 1967.

——. *The New Comic Annual*. London: Hurst Chance & Co., 1831.

Anstey, F. (Thomas Anstey Guthrie). *The Brass Bottle*. London: John Murray, 1900.

——. *Tourmalin's Time Cheques*. London: John Murray, 1891.

——. *Vice Versa*. London: John Murray, 1882.

Arabian Nights' Entertainments. Translated by E. W. Lane. London: C. Knight, 1840; Translated by Sir Richard Burton. 1885–1886.

Aristophanes. *Lysistrata*. Illustrated by Aubrey Beardsley. London: Academy Editions, 1973.

Arnold, Matthew. *Poems*. London: Longmans, 1854.

Ashton, Rosemary. *The German Idea: Four English Writers and the Reception of German Thought, 1800–1860.* Cambridge: Cambridge University Press, 1980.

Auden, W. H. "Introduction." In *The Visionary Novels of George MacDonald.* Edited by Anne Fremantle. New York: Noonday Press, 1954.

Auerbach, Erich. *Mimesis.* Translated by Willard Trask. Garden City: Doubleday, 1957.

Austen, Jane. *Sanditon.* Edited by B. C. Southam. Oxford: Oxford University Press, 1976.

Ballantyne, R. M. *The Coral Island: a Tale of the Pacific Ocean.* London: T. Nelson, 1858.

———. *The Gorilla Hunters: a Tale of the Wilds of Africa.* London: T. Nelson, 1861.

Balston, Thomas. *The Life of Jonathan Martin.* London: Macmillan, 1945.

Barfield, Owen. *History in English Words.* London: Faber & Faber, 1962.

Beardsley, Aubrey. *The Best of Beardsley.* Edited by R. A. Walker. London: Bodley Head, 1948.

———. *The Later Work of Aubrey Beardsley.* New York: Dover, 1967.

———. *Under the Hill* (completed by John Glassco). Paris: Olympia, 1959; repr. London: New English Library, 1966.

Beddow, Michael. *The Fiction of Humanity: Studies in the Bildungsroman from Weiland to Thomas Mann.* Cambridge: Cambridge University Press, 1982.

Beckford, William. *Caliph Vathek.* London, 1786.

Bell, Anthea. *E. Nesbit.* See Green, Bell, and Nesbitt.

Bewick, Thomas. *Water Birds.* Newcastle: Edward Walker, 1816.

Blake, William. *Complete Writings.* Edited by Geoffrey Keynes. London: Oxford University Press, 1966.

Blanchard, Jerrold, and Gustave Doré. *London: A Pilgrimage.* London: Grant, 1872.

Bowie, Andrew. *Aesthetics and Subjectivity from Kant to Nietzsche.* Manchester: Manchester University Press, 1990.

———. *Romanticism to Critical Theory.* London: Routledge, 1997.

Bradley, Ian. *The Call to Seriousness: The Evangelical Impact on the Victorians.* London: Cape, 1976.

Briggs, Julia. *A Woman of Passion: The Life of E. Nesbit, 1858–1924.* New York: New Amsterdam Books, 1987.

Bruford, W. H. *The German Tradition of Self-Cultivation: "Bildung" from Humboldt to Thomas Mann.* Cambridge: Cambridge University Press, 1975.

Brockman, H. A. N. *The Caliph of Fonthill.* London: Werner Laurie, 1956.

Buchanan, Robert. "The Voice of the Hooligan." *Contemporary Review* 1899. Reprint in *Kipling: The Critical Heritage.* Edited by Roger Lancelyn Green. London: Routledge, 1971.

Buckland, William. "Notice on the Megalosaurus or Great Fossil Lizard of Stonesfield." *Transactions of the Geological Society London.* Series 2. Vol. 1 (1824): 390–96.

Buckley, Jerome Hamilton. *The Victorian Temper.* New York: Vintage Books, 1951; repr. 1964.

——. *Season of Youth: The Bildungsroman from Dickens to Golding.* Cambridge, Mass.: Harvard University Press, 1974.

Bulwer Lytton, Edward. *The Last Days of Pompeii.* London: Routledge, 1903.

Burnett, Frances Hodgson. *Little Lord Fauntleroy.* London: Frederick Warne, 1886.

Burwick, Frederick. *Poetic Madness and the Romantic Imagination.* University Park: Pennsylvania State University Press, 1996.

Byron, George Gordon, Lord. "The Vision of Judgement." In *Byron.* Edited by Jerome McGann. Oxford: Oxford University Press, 1986.

Carlyle, Thomas. *Collected Works of Thomas Carlyle.* 16 vols. London: Chapman & Hall, 1858.

——. *Sartor Resartus. "Collected Works."* Vol. 1. London: Chapman & Hall, 1870.

——. "Signs of the Times." In *Selected Writings of Thomas Carlyle.* Edited by Alan Shelston. London: Penguin, 1971.

——. "The State of German Literature." *Critical and Miscellaneous Essays.* 4 vols. London: Chapman & Hall, 1869.

Carpenter, Humphrey. *The Inklings.* London: Allen & Unwin, 1978.

——. *Oxford Companion to Children's Literature.* Oxford: Oxford University Press, 1984.

——. *Tolkien: A Biography.* Boston: Houghton Mifflin, 1977.

——. *Secret Gardens: A Study of the Golden Age of Children's Literature.* Boston: Houghton Mifflin, 1985.

Carrington, Charles. *Rudyard Kipling: His Life and Work.* London: Macmillan, 1955.

Carroll, Lewis (Charles Lutwidge Dodgson). *Alice's Adventures in Wonderland* and *Through The Looking Glass*. London: Macmillan, 1887.

——. *The Hunting of the Snark*. London: Macmillan, 1876.

——. *Sylvie and Bruno*. London: Macmillan, 1899.

——. *Sylvie and Bruno Concluded*. London: Macmillan, 1899.

Cavaliero, Glen. *The Supernatural in English Fiction*. Oxford: Oxford University Press, 1995.

Chesterton, G. K. *The Victorian Age in Literature*. London: Williams & Norgate, 1925.

Chitty, Susan. *The Beast and the Monk: A Life of Charles Kingsley*. London: Hodder & Stoughton, 1974.

Clark, Kenneth. *The Gothic Revival*. Harmondsworth: Penguin, 1964.

Clare, John. *Letters*. Edited by J. W. and Anne Tibble. London: Routledge & Paul, 1951.

Clifford, Lucy. "The New Mother." In *Anyhow Stories, Moral and Otherwise*. London: Macmillan, 1882. Reprinted in *Little Wide Awake: An Anthology from Victorian Children's Books and Periodicals*. Edited by Leonard de Vries. London: Arthur Barker, 1967.

Clubbe, John. *Victorian Forerunner: The Later Career of Thomas Hood*. Durham: Duke University Press, 1968.

Coates, Paul. *The Realist Fantasy: Fiction and Reality Since Clarissa*. London: Macmillan, 1983.

Cohen, Morten. *Lewis Carroll: A Biography*. New York: Knopf, 1995.

——. "When Love was Young: Failed Apologists for the Sexuality of Lewis Carroll." *Times Literary Supplement*. September 10, 2004: 12–13.

Coleridge, Samuel Taylor. *Aids to Reflection*. Edited by T. Fenby. Edinburgh: Grant, 1905.

——. *Biographia Literaria*. Edited with his aesthetical essays by J. Shawcross. 2 vols. Oxford: Oxford University Press, 1907.

——. *Collected Letters*. Edited by E. L. Griggs. 6 vols. Oxford: Clarendon, 1956.

——. *Lay Sermons*. Edited by R. J. White. London: Routledge, 1972.

——. *Notebooks*. British Museum Manuscript Room. Add. Mss. 47,537.

——. *The Poems of Samuel Taylor Coleridge*. Edited by E. H. Coleridge. London: Oxford University Press, 1912.

——. *The Rime of the Ancient Mariner*. Illustrated by Gustave Doré. New York: Dover, 1970; *Coleridge's Rime of the Ancient Mariner*. Illustrated by J. Noel Paton. London: Art Union, 1863.

Collins, Robert A. and Howard Pearce, eds. *The Scope of the Fantastic.* Westport, Conn.: Greenwood Press, 1985.

Craven, Elizabeth, Countess of. *Modern Anecdote of the Ancient Family of the Kinkvervankotsdarsprakengotchderns: A Tale for Christmas.* London, 1779.

Croxon, Mary. "The Emancipated Child in the Novels of E. Nesbit." *Signal.* May 1974.

Dante. *The Divine Comedy.* Translated by H. F. Carey. Illustrated by Gustave Doré. London: Cassell 1904.

——. *The Divine Comedy.* Translated by John D. Sinclair. New York: Oxford University Press, 1969.

——. *The Divine Comedy.* Translated by Ichabod Charles Wright. Illustrated by John Flaxman. London: H. G. Bohn, 1854.

Darton, Harvey. *Children's Books in England.* 2d ed. Cambridge: Cambridge University Press, 1958.

Darwin, Charles. *The Origin of Species.* Introduction by John Burrow. Harmondsworth: Penguin, 1968.

Davidson, Angus. *Edward Lear: Landscape Painter and Nonsense Poet.* London: John Murray, 1938.

Day, Thomas. *Sandford and Merton.* London: John Stockdale, 1783–1789.

Defoe, Daniel. *Robinson Crusoe.* London: W. Taylor, 1719.

de Vries, Leonard and Ann and Ferdinand Renier, ed. *Little Wide Awake: An Anthology from Victorian Children's Books and Periodicals.* London: Arthur Barker, 1967.

Delgado, Alan. *Victorian Entertainment.* Newton Abbot: Victorian (and Modern History) Book Club, 1972.

Desmond, A. J. *The Hot-Blooded Dinosaurs.* London: Blond & Briggs, 1975.

Dickens, Charles. *The Battle of Life.* London: Bradbury & Evans, 1846.

——. *Bleak House.* London: Bradbury & Evans, 1853.

——. *The Christmas Books.* Vol. 1. Edited by Michael Slater. Harmondsworth: Penguin, 1971.

——. *Hard Times.* London: Bradbury & Evans 1854.

——. *Sketches by Boz.* Illustrated by George Cruickshank. London: Chapman and Hall, 1869.

Dilthey, Wilhelm. *Leben Schleiermachers.* Vol. 1. Berlin: G. Reimer, 1870.

——. *Das Erlebnis und die Dichtung: Lessing, Goethe, Novalis, Hölderlin.* Leipzig: Teubner, 1913.

Dingley, Robert. "Count Dracula and the Martians." In *The Victorian Fantasists*. Edited by Kath Filmer. London: Macmillan, 1991.

Dobrée, Bonamy. *Rudyard Kipling: Realist and Fabulist.* London: Oxford University Press, 1967.

Docherty, John. *The Literary Products of the Lewis Carroll–George MacDonald Friendship.* Lampeter: Edwin Mellen Press, 1997.

Downes, David A. *The Temper of Victorian Belief: Studies in the Religious Novels of Pater, Kingsley, and Newman.* New York: Twayne, 1972.

Duffy, Maureen. *The Erotic World of Faery.* London: Hodder & Stoughton, 1972.

Dyer, John. "Grongar Hill." In *A New Miscellany: Being a Collection of Poetry from Bath, Tunbridge, Oxford, Epsom, and other Places, in the Year 1725.* London: T. Warner, 1726.

——. *The Fleece: a Poem in Four Books.* London: R. & J. Dodsley, 1757.

Edgeworth, Maria (with Richard Lovell Edgeworth). *Practical Education.* London: J. Johnson, 1798.

——. *Moral Tales.* new ed. London: Simpkin, Marshall, 1856.

Eliot, George. *Middlemarch.* Edinburgh: W. Blackwood, 1871–1872.

Eliot, T. S. "The Hollow Men." In *Complete Poems and Plays.* New York: Harcourt Brace, 1952.

——. "Tradition and the Individual Talent." In *Selected Essays.* London: Faber, 1951.

Empson, William. *Seven Types of Ambiguity.* 2nd ed. Harmondsworth: Penguin, 1961.

Feaver, William. *The Art of John Martin.* Oxford, Clarendon , 1975.

——. *John Martin, 1789–1854.* London: Hazlitt, Gooden & Fox, 1975.

——. *When We Were Very Young.* London: Thames & Hudson, 1977.

Feltham, John. *The Picture of London, for 1806: Being a correct guide to all the curiosities, amusements, exhibitions, public establishments, and remarkable objects, in and near London.* London: W. Lewis, 1806.

Filmer, Kath, ed. *The Victorian Fantasists: Essays on Culture, Society, and Belief in the Mythopoeic Fiction of the Victorians.* Basingstoke: Macmillan, 1991.

Francis, Anne Cranny. "The Education of Desire: Utopian Fiction and Feminist Fantasy." In *The Victorian Fantasists.* Edited by Kath Filmer, Basingstoke: Macmillan, 1991.

Frei, Hans. *The Eclipse of Biblical Narrative: A Study in Eighteenth and Nineteenth-Century Hermeneutics.* New Haven: Yale University Press, 1974.

Gaarder, Jostein. *Sophie's World.* Translated by Paulette Moller. New York: Farrar, Strauss & Giroux, 1994.

Gaunt, William. *Arrows of Desire.* London: Museum Press, 1956.

——. *The Pre Raphaelite Dream.* London: Cape, 1943.

Gerard, Alexander. *Essay on Genius.* London: W. Strahan, 1774.

Goethe, Johann Wolfgang von. *Wilhelm Meister's Apprenticeship and Travels.* Translated by Thomas Carlyle. 2 Vols. New York: J. D. Williams, 1882.

Gombrich, E. H. "Imagery and Art in the Romantic Period." In *Mediations on a Hobby Horse.* London: Phaidon, 1963.

Gosse, Edmund. *Father and Son.* London: Evergreen Books, 1941.

Green, Rober Lancelyn, Anthea Bell, and Elizabeth Nesbitt, *Three Bodley Head Monographs.* Edited by Kathleen Lines. Rev. ed. (London: Bodley Head, 1968).

——. *Tellers of Tales.* Rev. ed. New York: F. Watts, 1965.

Grimm, Jacob Ludwig Carl and Wilhelm Carl. *German Popular Stories.* Illustrated by George Cruikshank. London: C. Baldwyn, 1823.

——. *Grimm's Popular Stories.* Edited by Edgar Taylor. Introduction by John Ruskin. London: Oxford University Press, 1905.

Grossmith, George and Weedon. *The Diary of a Nobody.* London: Dent/Dutton, 1940.

Gunther, Adrian. "The Multiple Realms of George MacDonald's *Phantastes.*" *Studies in Scottish Literature* 29 (1966): 174-90.

Haggard, H. Rider. *Ayesha: the Return of She.* London: Ward Lock, 1905.

——. *King Solomon's Mines.* London: Cassell, 1886.

——. *She: a History of Adventure.* London: Longmans, 1887.

Haines, Sheila. "Thoughts for the Labouring Classes." Master's thesis, University of Sussex, 1975.

Hartley, David. *Observations on Man, his Frame, his Duties, and his Expectations.* 2nd ed. London, 1793.

Harrison, Dorothy. *Kipling's Codes.* Master's thesis, University of Sussex, 1972.

Hawkins, Thomas. *The Book of the Great Sea Dragons: Ichthyosauri and Plesiosauri.* London: W. Pickering, 1840.

Hein, Rolland. *The Harmony Within: The Spiritual Vision of George MacDonald.* Grand Rapids: Eerdmans, 1982.

——. *George MacDonald, Victorian Mythmaker.* Nashville: Star Song Publishing Group, 1993.

Heffernan, James. "Looking at the Monster: 'Frankenstein' and Film." *Critical Inquiry* 24.1 (Autumn 1997): 133–58.

Hegel, Georg Wilhelm Friedrich. *Vorlesungen über die Ästhetik*. Edited by F. Bassenge. Berlin: Aufbau-Verlag, 1955.

Hogg, James. *The Queen's Wake*. Edinburgh: Andrew Balfour, 1813.

Hood, Thomas, ed. *The Gem*. 1828.

——. *The Comic Annual*. London: Hurst, Chance, 1830–1842.

——. *Whims and Oddities*. London: L. Relfe, 1826–1827.

——. *Poems*. Illustrated by Gustave Doré. London, 1872.

——. *Comic Poems of Thomas Hood*. London: Ward Lock, 1876.

——. *Serious Poems of Thomas Hood*. London: Ward Lock, 1876.

Hooper, Walter, ed. *They Stand Together: the Letters of C. S. Lewis to Arthur Greeves (1914–1963)*. London: Collins, 1979.

Houghton, Walter E. *The Victorian Frame of Mind 1830–1870*. New Haven: Yale University Press, 1957.

Hudson, Derek. *Lewis Carroll*. London: Constable, 1954.

Humboldt, Wilhelm von. *On Language*. Translated by Peter Heath. Introduction by Hans Aarsleff. Cambridge; Cambridge University Press, 1988.

Huxley, Francis. *The Raven and the Writing Desk*. London: Thames & Hudson, 1976.

Isbell, John Claiborne. *The Birth of European Romanticism*. Cambridge: Cambridge University Press, 1994.

Iverson, Jeffrey. *More Lives than One?: The Evidence of the Remarkable Bloxham Tapes*. London: Souvenir Press, 1976.

Jackson, Rosemary. *Fantasy: the Literature of Subversion*. London: Methuen, 1981.

James, M. R. "Oh, Whistle and I'll Come to You my Lad." In *The Collected Ghost Stories of M. R. James*. London: Edward Arnold, 1931.

Jerrold, Blanchard. *The Life of George Cruikshank*. London: Ward Lock Reprints, 1970.

Jordens, Ann-Marie. *The Stenhouse Circle*. Carlton: Melbourne University Press, 1979.

Josipovici, Gabriel. *The Book of God*. New Haven: Yale University Press, 1988.

Jung, C. G. *The Archetypes and the Collective Unconscious*. In *Collected Works*. Edited by H. Read, M. Fordham, and G. Adler. Translated by R. F. C. Hull. London: Routledge, 1959.

Kant, Immanuel. *Kant's Inaugural Dissertation and Early Writings on Space*. Translated by John Hanyside. London: Open Court, 1929.

Keats, John. *Poems*. Oxford; Oxford University Press.

Keay, Carolyn. *Henry Fuseli*. London: Academy Editions, 1974.

Keble, John. *The Christian Year*. 43rd ed. Oxford: Parker, 1853.

Kegler, Adelheid. "Silent House: MacDonald, Brontë and Silence within the Soul." In *The Victorian Fantasists*. Edited by Kath Filmer. London: Macmillan, 1991.

Ketton Cremer, R. W. *Horace Walpole: a Biography*. 3d ed. London: Methuen, 1964.

Kingsley, Charles. *Alton Locke, Tailor and Poet: an Autobiography*. London: Macmillan, 1890.

——. *Glaucus*. London: Macmillan, 1854.

——. *Hypatia*. London: Macmillan, 1884.

——. *Literary and General Lectures and Essays*. London: Macmillan, 1880.

——. *Madam How and Lady Why*. London: Macmillan, 1889.

——. *The Water Babies*. New Edition with illustrations by Sir Noël Paton and Percival Skelton. London: Macmillan, 1863.

Kingsley, F. E. *Charles Kingsley: His Letters and Memories of his Life*. 7th ed. 2 vols. London: H. S. King, 1877.

Kipling, Rudyard. "Ba Ba Blacksheep." In *We Willie Winkie*. London: Macmillan, 1892.

——. "The Bridge Builders." In *The Day's Work*. London: Macmillan, 1898.

——. "The Brushwood Boy." In *The Day's Work*. London: Macmillan, 1898.

——. "The Finest Story in the World." In *Many Inventions*. London: Macmillan, 1893.

—— *The First Jungle Book*. London: Macmillan, 1894.

——. *Just So Stories*. London: Macmillan, 1903.

——. *The Light that Failed*. London: Macmillan, 1891.

—— *The Second Jungle Book*. London: Macmillan, 1895.

——. "Proofs of Holy Writ." Sussex edition. Vol. 30. London: Macmillan, 1934.

——. *Puck of Pook's Hill*. Illustrated by H. R. Millar. London: Macmillan, 1906.

——. *Rewards and Fairies*. Illustrated by H. R. Millar. London: Macmillan, 1910.

——. *Something of Myself for my Friends Known and Unknown*. London: Macmillan, 1964.

——. *Stalky and Co*. London: Macmillan, 1899.

——. "They." "Wireless." In *Traffics and Discoveries*. London: Macmillan, 1904.

Kipling, Rudyard. "Unprofessional." In *Limits and Renewals*. London: Macmillan, 1930.

——. "The Wish House." In *Debits and Credits*. London: Macmillan, 1926.

Klingender, F. D. *Art and the Industrial Revolution*. New Edition. London: Cory, Adams, & Mackay, 1968.

Knoepflmacher, U. C. *Ventures into Childhood: Victorians, Fairy Stories, and Femininity*. Chicago: Chicago University Press, 1998.

Lang, Andrew. *The Grey Fairy Book*. London: Longman, 1900.

Larkin, David, ed. *The Fantastic Kingdom*. London: Pan Books, 1974.

Leach, Karoline. *In the Shadow of the Dreamchild: a New Understanding of Lewis Carroll*. London: Peter Owen, 1999.

Lear, Edward. *The Complete Nonsense of Edward Lear*. Edited by Holbrook Jackson. London: Faber, 1947.

L'Engle, Madeleine. "George MacDonald: Nourishment for a Private World." In *The Classics We've Read, the Difference They've Made*. Edited by Philip Yancey. New York: McCracken Press, 1993.

Levine, George. "Review of *Frankenstein*." *The Wordsworth Circle* 6.3 (Summer, 1975).

—— and U. C. Knoepflmacher, eds. *The Endurance of Frankenstein: Essays on Mary Shelley's Novel*. Berkeley: University of California Press, 1979.

Lewis, C. S. "Kipling's World." In *They Asked for a Paper: Papers and Addresses*. London: Geoffrey Bles, 1962.

——. *The Lion, the Witch, and the Wardrobe*. London: Macmillan, 1950.

——. *Out of the Silent Planet*. London: Macmillan, 1952.

——. *Perelandra*. London: Pan Books, 1953.

——. *The Pilgrim's Regress*. London: Collins, 1980.

——. *Surprised by Joy: The Shape of my Early Life*. London: Fontana, 1955; repr. 1959.

Lewis, M. G. *The Monk: a Romance*. London: J. Bell, 1796.

Lewis, W. S. *Horace Walpole*. London: Hart-Davis, 1961.

Locke, John. *Essay Concerning Human Understanding*. Edited by J. W. Yolton. London: Dent, 1961.

Lochhead, Marion. "George MacDonald and the World of Faery." *Seven* 3 (1982): 63–71.

Longinus. *On the Sublime*. Translated with an introduction by A. O. Prickard. Oxford: Clarendon Press, 1906.

——. *On the Sublime*. Translated by W. Rhys Roberts. Cambridge: Cambridge University Press, 1935.

——. *On the Sublime.* Translated by D. A. Russell. Oxford: Clarendon Press, 1964.

Lovecraft, H. P. *The Dunwich Horror* (New York: Lancer, 1963).

Lovejoy, A. O. *The Great Chain of Being.* Cambridge, Mass.: Harvard University Press, 1936.

Lurie, Alison. *Don't Tell the Grown-Ups: Subversive Children's Literature.* Boston: Little Brown, 1990.

Lyell, Sir Charles. *Principles of Geology.* London: J. Murray, 1830-1833.

MacAndrew, Elizabeth. *The Gothic Tradition in Fiction.* New York: Columbia University Press, 1979.

MacDonald, George. *At the Back of the North Wind.* London: Strahan, 1871.

——. *A Dish of Orts.* London: Sampson Low, 1893.

——. "The Light Princess." "The Golden Key." In *Short Stories.* London: Blackie, 1928.

——. *Miracles of Our Lord.* London: Strahan, 1870.

——. *Phantastes and Lilith.* Introduction by C. S. Lewis. Grand Rapids: Eerdmans, 1964.

——. *Phantastes.* Introduction by Derek Brewer. Woodbridge, Suffolk: Boydell Press, 1982.

——. *Phantases and Lilith.* Introduction by Lin Carter (New York: Ballantine Books, 1969).

——. *The Princess and Curdie.* Illustrated by Helen Stratton. Harmondsworth: Puffin, 1966.

——. *The Princess and the Goblin.* Illustrated by Arthur Hughes. Harmondsworth: Puffin, 1964.

——. *Unspoken Sermons: Second Series.* London: Longmans, 1885.

MacDonald, Greville. *George MacDonald and his Wife.* London: Allen & Unwin, 1924. [= *GMD and Wife*]

Machen, Arthur. *Hieroglyphics: a Note upon Ecstasy in Literature.* Rev. ed. London: M. Secker, 1912.

——. *The House of Souls.* London: Grant Richards, 1906.

MacKenzie, Norman and Jeanne. *The Time Traveller: The Life of H. G. Wells.* London: Weidenfeld & Nicolson, 1973.

Magill Frank M., ed. *Survey of Modern Fantasy Literature.* Los Angeles: Salem Press, 1983.

Manlove, C. N. *Christian Fantasy: from 1200 to the Present.* Bloomington: University of Notre Dame Press, 1992.

——. *The Impulse of Fantasy Literature.* Kent, Ohio: Kent State University Press, 1983.

Manlove, C. N. *Modern Fantasy: Five Studies.* Cambridge: Cambridge University Press, 1975.

——. *The Impulse of Fantasy Literature.* London: Macmillan, 1983.

Mantell, Gideon. *Journal.* Edited by Cecil Curwen. London: Oxford University Press, 1940.

——. "Notice on the Iguanodon, a Newly Discovered Fossil Reptile, from the Sandstone of Tilgate Forest, in Sussex." *Philosophical Transactions of the Royal Society* 115 (1825): 179–86.

——. "Notice on the Megalosaurus." *Transactions of the Geological Society*, London, series 2, Vol. i.

——. *Wonders of Geology.* London: Relfe & Fletcher, 1838.

Marcus, Steven. *The Other Victorians: A Study of Sexuality and Pornography in Mid-Nineteenth-Century England.* London: Corgi Books, 1969.

Maurice, F. D. *The Kingdom of Christ.* 4th ed. 2 vols. 1838; London: Macmillan, 1891.

Maurice, John Frederick, ed. *Life of Frederick Denison Maurice.* 4th ed. 2 vols. London: Macmillan, 1885.

McGillis, Roderick, ed. *For the Childlike: George MacDonald's Fantasies for Children.* Metuchen, N. J.: Scarecrow Press, 1992.

——. "George MacDonald–The Lilith Manuscripts." *Scottish Literary Journal* 4.2 (December 1977).

——. "*Phantastes and Lilith*: Femininity and Freedom." In *The Gold Thread.* Edited by William Raeper. Edinburgh: Edinburgh University Press, 1990.

——. *The Nimble Reader: Literary Theory and Children's Literature.* London: Prentice Hall, 1996.

Mellor, Anne K. *Mary Shelley: her Life, her Fiction, her Monsters.* New York: Methuen, 1988.

Michalson, Karen. *Victorian Fantasy Literature.* Lampeter: Edwin Mellen Press, 1990.

Mill, J. S. *Autobiography of John Stuart Mills.* New York: Columbia University Press, 1924.

Mills, Alice. "Happy Endings in Hard Times and Granny's Wonderful Chair." In *The Victorian Fantasists.* Edited by Kath Filmer. London: Macmillan, 1991.

Milton, John. *Paradise Lost.* Illustrated by Gustave Doré. London: Cassell, 1882.

Moore, Doris Langley. *E. Nesbit: A Biography.* Rev. ed. London: Ernest Benn, 1967.

Morris, William. *The Early Romances of William Morris*. London: Dent, 1907.

Nesbit, E. *The Book of Dragons*. Illustrated by H. R. Millar. London: Harper, 1901.

———. *The Enchanted Castle*. Illustrated by H. R. Millar. London: Ernest Benn, 1956.

———. *The Five Children and It*. Illustrated by H. R. Millar. Harmondsworth: Puffin, 1959.

———. *Harding's Luck*. Illustrated by H. R. Millar. 7th impression. London: Ernest Benn, 1947.

———. *The House of Arden*. Illustrated by H. R. Millar. London: Ernest Benn, 1958.

———. *The Magic City*. Illustrated by H. R. Millar. London: Ernest Benn, 1958.

———. *The Phoenix and the Carpet*. Illustrated by H. R. Millar. Harmondsworth: Puffin, 1959.

———. *The Story of the Amulet*. Illustrated by H. R. Millar. Harmondsworth: Puffin, 1959.

———. *The Treasure Seekers*. Illustrated by Cecil Leslie. Harmondsworth: Puffin, 1958.

———. *Wet Magic*. Illustrated by H. R. Millar. 7th impression. London: Ernest Benn, 1945.

Nethercot, Arthur. *The Road to Tyermaine*. New York: Russell & Russell, 1962.

Newman, John Henry. *Callista: A Sketch of the Third Century*. New York/Boston: D & J Sedlier, 1890.

———. "The Dream of Gerontius." In *Verses on Various Occasions*. London: Burns Oates, 1876.

———. *Lectures on Certain Difficulties Felt by Anglicans in Submitting to the Catholic Church*. London: Burns & Lambert, 1850.

Newsome, David. *The Parting of Friends: a Study of the Wilberforces and Henry Manning*. London: John Murray, 1966.

Noakes, Vivien. *Edward Lear: the Life of a Wanderer*. London: Collins, 1968.

Novalis (Friedrich von Hardenberg). *Henry von Ofterdingen: a Novel*. Translated by Palmer Hilty. Prospects Heights, Ill.: Waveland, 1964.

———. *Hymns and Thoughts on Religion*. Translated by W. Hastie. Edinburgh: T & T Clark, 1888.

———. *Philosophical Writings*. Edited and translated by Margaret Stoljar. Albany: State University of New York Press, 1997.

Nuttall, A. D. *A Common Sky*. London: Chatto for Sussex University Press, 1974.

——. *Two Concepts of Allegory: a Study of Shakespeare's* The Tempest *and the* Logic of Allegorical Expression. London: Routledge, 1967.

Opie, Iona and Peter. *The Classic Fairy Tales*. New York: Oxford University Press, 1974.

Packer, Lona Mosk. *Christina Rossetti*. Cambridge: Cambridge University Press, 1963.

Paget, Francis Edward. *The Hope of the Katzekopfs*. London: John Masters, 1847.

Patten, Robert. *George Cruikshank's Life, Times, and Art*. 2 vols. New Brunswick, N.J.: Rutgers University Press, 1992–1996.

Peppin, Brigid. *Fantasy: Book Illustration 1860–1920*. London: Studio Vista, 1975.

Pevsner, Nikolaus. *Cambridgeshire*. Harmondsworth: Penguin, 1954.

——. *The Englishness of English Art*. London: Architectural Press, 1956.

Phillips, Robert, ed. *Aspects of Alice*. London: Gollancz, 1972.

Pinnock, W. H. *An Analysis of Scripture History*. Cambridge, 1848.

Plato. *Phaedo*. (*The Last Days of Socrates*). Translated by Hugh Tredennick. London: Penguin, 1954.

——. *The Republic*. Translated by H. D. P. Lee. London: Penguin, 1955.

——. *The Symposium*. Translated by W. Hamilton. London: Penguin, 1951.

Poe, Edgar Allan. *Tales of Mystery and Imagination*. London: Daily Express Publications, 1933.

——. *The Fall of the House of Usher* (Philadelphia: William E. Burton, 1839).

Pointon, Marcia. *Milton and English Art*. Manchester: Manchester University Press, 1970.

Prickard, A. O. *Longinus on the Sublime* (New York: Oxford University Press, 1906).

Prickett, Stephen. "Ariosto and the Monstrous Crow." *Proceedings of the Australasian Victorian Studies Association*, 1983. Edited by Pat Dobrez and Stephen Prickett. Australian National University-Canberra 1984.

——. *Coleridge and Wordsworth: The Poetry of Growth*. Cambridge: Cambridge University Press, 1970.

——. *Origins of Narrative: The Romantic Appropriation of the Bible*. Cambridge: Cambridge University Press, 1996.

——. *Romanticism and Religion: The Tradition of Coleridge and Wordsworth in the Victorian Church.* Cambridge: Cambridge University Press, 1976.

——. *Words and the Word: Language, Poetics, and Biblical Interpretation.* Cambridge: Cambridge University Press, 1986.

Pugin, A. W. *Contrasts.* London, 1836.

Quennell, Peter. *Byron in Italy.* Harmondsworth: Penguin, 1955.

Rabelais, Francis. *The Works of Mr Francis Rabelais, Doctor in Physik.* Illustrated by Heath Robinson. London: The Navarre Society, 1931.

Radcliffe, Mrs. Anne. *The Mysteries of Udolpho.* London, 1794.

Raeper, William. *George MacDonald.* Tring, Herts England: Lion 1987.

——. ed. *The Gold Thread: Essays on George MacDonald.* Edinburgh: Edinburgh University Press, 1990.

Raverat, Gwen. *Period Piece.* London: Faber, 1952.

Reade, Brian. *Aubrey Beardsley.* Victoria & Albert Museum Series. London: H.M.S.O., 1966.

Reid, J. C. *Thomas Hood.* London: Routledge, 1963.

Reis, Richard H. *George MacDonald.* New York: Twayne, 1972.

Richardson, Alan, ed. *A Theological Word Book of the Bible.* London: SCM Press, 1950.

Richardson, Joanna. *Edward Lear.* London: Longman, 1965.

Riga, Frank P. "From Time to Eternity: MacDonald's Doorway Between." In *Essays on C. S. Lewis and George MacDonald: Truth, Fiction, and the Power of Imagination.* Edited by Cynthia Marshall. Lewiston: Edwin Mellon Press, 1991.

Reader, W. J. *Victorian England.* London: Batsford, 1974.

Robb, David. *George MacDonald.* Edinburgh: Scottish Academic Press, 1987.

Roberts, Ruth ap. *The Ancient Dialect: Thomas Carlyle and Comparative Religion.* Berkeley: University of California Press, 1988.

Roberts, W. Rhys, transl. *Longinus: On the Sublime.* Cambridge: Cambridge University Press, 1935.

Rossetti, Christina. *Poems.* Illustrated by Dante Gabriel Rossetti. London: Macmillan, 1891.

Rowell, Geoffrey. *Hell and the Victorians.* Oxford: Clarendon Press, 1974.

Rudwick, Martin J. S. *Scenes from Deep Time: Early Pictorial Representations of the Prehistoric World.* Chicago: University of Chicago Press, 1992.

Ruskin, John. *The King of the Golden River*. Vol. 1 of *The Works of John Ruskin*. Edited by T. Cook and A. Wedderburn. 39 vols. London: George Allen, 1903.

——. *Unto this Last*. London: George Allen, 1901.

Russell, D. A., trans. *Longinus: On the Sublime*. Oxford: Clarendon Press, 1974.

Ryan, J. S., ed. *The Nameless Wood: Victorian Fantasists—Their Achievements—Their Influence*. Proceedings of the Second Annual Conference of the Mythopoeic Literature Society of Australia, Dept. of English, University of Queensland, 1986.

Schenkel Elmar. "Domesticating the Supernatural: Magic in E. Nesbit's Children's Books." In *The Victorian Fantasists*. Edited by Kath Filmer. London: Macmillan, 1991.

Schleiermacher, Friedrich. *On Religion: Speeches to its Cultured Despisers*. Translated by Richard Crouter. Cambridge: Cambridge University Press, 1988.

Sewell, Elizabeth. *The Field of Nonsense*. London: Chatto, 1952.

Seven: An Anglo-American Literary Review. Published by the Marion E. Wade Centre of Wheaton College, Illinois.

Sinclair, Catherine. *Holiday House*. Reprint. London: Hamish Hamilton, 1972.

Shelley, Mary. *Frankenstein*. Frontispiece by T. Holst. London, 1831.

——. *Frankenstein*. London: Dent, 1912.

Sheridan, Louisa. *Comic Offering or Ladies' Melange of Literary Mirth*. London: Smith & Elder, 1833.

Sky, Jeanette. "From Demons to Angels: Fairies and Religious Creativity in Victorian Children's Literature." Ph.D. diss., University of Oslo, 2003.

Spark, Muriel. *Mary Shelley*. New York: New American Library, 1988.

Stael, Mme. de (Anne-Louise-Germaine). *De l'Allemagne*. Paris, 1810. Reprinted and edited by Henry Weston Eve. Oxford: Clarendon Press, 1906.

——. *On Germany: on the Appearance of Germany, in Selected Writings of Germaine de Stael*. Translated and introduction by Vivian Folkenflik. New York: Columbia University Press, 1987.

Sterne, Laurence. *The Works of Laurence Sterne*. Edited by J. P. Browne. 4 vols. London: Bickers, 1885.

Stevenson, Robert Louis. *Dr. Jekyll and Mr. Hyde*. London: Longman, 1896.

Stewart, J. I. M. *Rudyard Kipling*. London: Gollancz, 1966.

Strugnell, John. "Richard Jeffries' Vision of London." In *The Victorian Fantasists*. Edited by Kath Filmer. London: Macmillan, 1991.

Sulzer, Johann Georg. *General Theory of the Fine Arts*. Leipzig, 1773-1775.

Swales, Martin. *The German Bildungsroman from Wieland to Hesse*. Princeton: Princeton University Press, 1978.

——. *Thomas Mann: A Study*. London: Rowman & Littlefield, 1980.

Swann, Karen. "'Christabel': The Wandering Mother and the Enigma of Form." *Studies in Romanticism* 23.4 (Winter 1984).

Swinburne, Algernon Charles. *"Laus Veneris." Poems and Ballads*. New York: Carlton, 1905.

Taylor, A. L. *The White Knight*. Edinburgh: Oliver & Boyd, 1952.

Tennyson, Alfred, Lord. *In Memoriam*. London: 1850.

Thackeray, William Makepeace. *Mrs Perkins Ball*. London: Chapman & Hall, 1847.

——. *Stray Papers by W. M. Thackeray 1821-1847*. Edited by Lewis Melville. London: Hutchinson, 1901.

——. *The Works of William Makepeace Thackeray*. London: Smith Elder, 1891.

Todorov, Tzvetan. *The Fantastic*. Translated by R. Howard. Cleveland Ohio: Case Western Reserve Press, 1973.

Tolkien, J. R. R. *Tree and Leaf*. London: Allen & Unwin, 1964.

Tolstoy, Count Leo. "Where God is Love is." *Twenty Three Tales*. World's Classics. London: Oxford University Press, 1906.

Tompkins, J. M. S. *The Art of Rudyard Kipling*. London: Methuen, 1965.

Townsend, John Rowe. *Written for Children*. London: Garnet Miller, 1965.

Tucker, Abraham. *The Light of Nature Pursued*. London: 1768.

Twitchell, James B. *The Living Dead: a Study of the Vampire in Romantic Literature*. Durham: Duke University Press, 1981.

Vance, Norman. *The Sinews of the Spirit: the Ideal of Christian Manliness in Victorian Literature and Religious Thought*. Cambridge: Cambridge University Press, 1985.

Vax, Louis. *L'Art et la Literature Fantastiques*. Paris: Presses Universitaires de France, 1974.

Walpole, Horace. *The Castle of Otranto*. 1764.

——. *The Yale Edition of Horace Walpole's Correspondence*. Edited by W. S. Lewis. 43 vols. New Haven: Yale University Press, 1961.

——. *Hieroglyphic Tales*. London: Elkin Mathews, 1926.

Ward, Heather. "Earth's Crammed with Heaven: Fantasy and Sacramental Imagination in George MacDonald." *Chesterton Review* 27 (February–May 2001): 25–37.

Watson, Jeanie. *Risking Enchantment: Coleridge's Symbolic World of Faery.* Lincoln, Nebraska: Nebraska University Press, 1990.

Watson, Lyall. *Supernature: A Natural History of the Supernatural.* London: Coronet Books, 1974.

Wells, H.G. *The Time Machine.* London: H. Heinemann, 1895.

Wheeler, Kathleen, ed. *German Aesthetic and Literary Criticism: the Romantic Ironists and Goethe.* Cambridge: Cambridge University Press, 1984.

Wilde, Oscar. *The Picture of Dorian Gray.* Harmondsworth: Penguin, 1949.

Wilt, Judith. *Ghosts of the Gothic: Austen, Eliot & Lawrence.* Princeton: Princeton University Press, 1980.

Wolff, Robert Lee. *The Golden Key.* New Haven: Yale University Press, 1961.

——. *Gains and Losses: Novels of Faith and Doubt in Victorian England.* New York: Garland, 1977.

——. "Some Erring Children in Children's Literature: The World of Victorian Religious Strife in Miniature." In *The Worlds of Victorian Fiction.* Edited by Jerome H. Buckley. Cambridge, Mass.: Harvard University Press, 1975.

Wordsworth, William. *The Prelude 1805.* Edited by E. De Selincourt. Oxford: Oxford University Press, 1933.

——. *Preface to the Lyrical Ballads.* Edited by R. L. Brett and A. R. Jones. Revised impression. London: Methuen, 1965.

Yeats, W. B. *Collected Poems.* 2d ed. London: Macmillan, 1950.

Index of Names